AMERICAN
STORY

Also by Bob Dotson

. . . In Pursuit of the American Dream
Make It Memorable

AMERICAN STORY

A Lifetime Search
for
Ordinary People
Doing
Extraordinary
Things

Bob Dotson

VIKING

VIKING
Published by the Penguin Group
Penguin Group (USA) Inc., 375 Hudson Street,
New York, New York 10014, U.S.A.
Penguin Group (Canada), 90 Eglinton Avenue East, Suite 700,
Toronto, Ontario, Canada M4P 2Y3
(a division of Pearson Penguin Canada Inc.)
Penguin Books Ltd, 80 Strand, London WC2R 0RL, England
Penguin Ireland, 25 St. Stephen's Green, Dublin 2, Ireland
(a division of Penguin Books Ltd)
Penguin Group (Australia), 707 Collins Street, Melbourne,
Victoria 3008, Australia (a division of Pearson Australia Group Pty Ltd)
Penguin Books India Pvt Ltd, 11 Community Centre,
Panchsheel Park, New Delhi–110 017, India
Penguin Group (NZ), 67 Apollo Drive, Rosedale, Auckland 0632,
New Zealand (a division of Pearson New Zealand Ltd)
Penguin Books (South Africa), Rosebank Office Park, 181 Jan Smuts Avenue,
Parktown North 2193, South Africa
Penguin China, B7 Jiaming Center, 27 East Third Ring Road North,
Chaoyang District, Beijing 100020, China

Penguin Books Ltd, Registered Offices: 80 Strand, London WC2R 0RL, England

First published in 2013 by Viking Penguin, a member of Penguin Group (USA) Inc.

3 5 7 9 10 8 6 4 2

Excerpt from "Stopping by Woods on a Snowy Evening" from the book *The Poetry
of Robert Frost*, edited by Edward Connery Lathem. Copyright © 1923, 1969 by
Henry Holt and Company, copyright © 1951 by Robert Frost. Reprinted
by arrangement with Henry Holt and Company, LLC.

LIBRARY OF CONGRESS CATALOGING-IN-PUBLICATION DATA
Dotson, Bob.
American story : a lifetime search for ordinary people doing
extraordinary things / Bob Dotson.
pages cm
ISBN 978-0-670-02605-0
1. United States—Social life and customs—Anecdotes. 2. United States—Biography—
Anecdotes. 3. National characteristics, American—Anecdotes. I. Title.
E169.12.D68 2013
973—dc23
2012037847

Printed in the United States of America
Set in New Caledonia LT Std
Designed by Francesca Belanger

ALWAYS LEARNING   PEARSON

To

Aden Robert Wogan

Our first grandchild,

the next chapter

I do not claim that I can tell a story as it ought to be told. I only claim to know how a story ought to be told.

Mark Twain, How to Tell a Story (1897)

Contents

Preface

I've been in more motel rooms than the Gideon Bible, crisscrossing this country, covering over four million miles, just about nonstop, in the course of forty years, searching for people who are practically invisible, the ones who change our lives but don't take time to tweet and tell us about it. They may not run for president or go on talk shows, but without their contributions, the kind of country we love would not exist. These are people with thoughtful solutions to problems we all face, incredible ideas that work, blueprints for our own dreams and ways to make America better. The country survives and thrives because of all those names we don't know, the ordinary people who live life with passion, who succeed not just on talent and hard work but on curiosity and imagination.

This book is for everyone who yearns to feel better about America again. It focuses on the incredible things of which we are capable:

- The truck driver who taught microsurgery
- The fourteen-year-old who invented television
- The brothers who searched for sixty years until they found what the navy could not—their father's lost submarine

Most of what we read today tells us about our frustrations—the widening gap between the haves and the have-nots, middle-class jobs moving to China and India, hate-filled politics that prefers gridlock to compromise. What we know about America comes mostly from journalists who travel in herds, trailing politicians or camped out on big stories, pouncing on problems they repeat over and over. They offer up celebrity experts for solutions, people who spend their busy days spouting opinions to cameras, while others unnoticed quietly make America work. Here you will discover people who live the values our country cherishes:

- The boss who came out of retirement to start a new company for his former employees who could not find work
- The band director who turned his back on celebrity to save lives
- The man who used his lottery winnings to send all the kids in his neighborhood to college

In this time of rapid change, rediscovering the enduring values that built what's best about America helps us find our own way. I have spent my life seeking solutions from people who are seldom asked, shining a light in neglected corners, revealing answers that others rush past. Here, then, is their collective wisdom. Wisdom doesn't always wear a suit.

This book grew out of a television news series, *The American Story with Bob Dotson,* which began on the *Today Show* back when the earth was cooling. Well, sometimes it felt that way, especially mornings when I was up before dawn shivering in the cold with only a camera light for comfort. One recent frosty sunrise, shifting from foot to foot, I tallied up all the truly amazing folks I'd found in my long career, few of whom had become household names. Telling tales on television is a bit like writing on smoke: After a brief mention, the men and women I profiled drifted away. The lessons they left with me, though, lingered in my memory, and their importance was undiminished. So, night after night, when my day job was done, I scribbled down details of my encounters with them that couldn't be accommodated by the blink of TV.

Each of these people was as hard to find as a gold nugget. When I started this quest in 1979, I kissed my wife and daughter good-bye and searched for 252 days, popping home on weekends, a pattern that has persisted for more than four decades of marriage. Happily, my wife,

Linda, supports this pursuit. She has sacrificed much, but we're still together, and our daughter, Amy, is now raising a curious little traveler of her own, our first grandbaby, Aden Robert Wogan. I decided to dedicate this book to him after he turned two and asked a woman from Turkey, "What is your country like? Is it a lot like chicken?"

The camera crews who travel with me are family, too. In the days before cell phones and satellite radios, we sometimes linked our caravan of cars with a wireless microphone and speakers so I could read them "naptime" stories while the producer drove. Fortunately, no one fell asleep as we bounced down all those back roads. Shunning superhighways, chain restaurants, and crowds of reporters, we chatted with the locals and listened carefully. We found our gold.

Quite often when we knocked on someone's door, he or she was disappointed. Secretly, they had been hoping to meet one of the *Today Show* hosts, but instead got a guy who acted like he worked in their local hardware store. We talked about everyday life as my crew's electrical cords snaked across their living rooms and TV lights circled our chairs. By the time a camera was focused on their faces, they had grown comfortable enough to tell me things they'd never expected to reveal.

I noticed that people nearly always answered my questions in three parts. First, they told me what they thought I wanted to hear and then they explained in more detail. If I didn't interrupt—if I let the silence between us build—their answers got more precise and passionate, because they figured I hadn't yet understood what they were trying to convey. They soon began to tell me things I didn't know them well enough to ask. For instance, an eight-year-old once filled the silence with the reason why children in her neighborhood on a small island off the coast of South Carolina wrote wonderful poetry.

"It's so far away," she said, "the mind can be your best friend."

She showed us what our cameras could not see. All the people in this book do that, but the days of simply wandering around, hoping to find someone special, are over. Television has become too expensive to make that feasible, so we must rely on suggestions from viewers. Four to five hundred tips arrive every month. About a dozen look promising, but our executive producer picks only one, so we spend many days researching to make sure it is the right one. As a rule, we shun press-release storytelling. Constant deadlines make that difficult for most reporters, who are often forced to trust televised news conferences, publicists, and the Internet—the same sources of information everyone else has. Today's storytellers scamper from tweet to tweet, failing to give much context. It's a lot like working in a circus. The writer who can get a story out instantly is applauded for putting up the tent in a hurry. Trouble is, no one tunes in just to look at the tent. We crave perspective. We all know what is and what ought to be. We need to know what *was*. That's what you're holding in your hands.

Bob Dotson
New York City

AMERICAN STORY

Chapter One

Out Beyond the Limits
of Settled Lives

Juan Delgadillo looked like a Shriner who had lost his parade. He cruised by my car window on a dusty day west of the Grand Canyon driving an ancient convertible painted the colors of a dripping ice-cream cone. It was a griddle-hot morning in July, but a decorated Christmas tree stood tall in his backseat. At the top a sign read: "Follow me to dead chicken sandwiches."

"Hey, buddy!" I shouted. "What's with the dead chicken sandwiches?"

"Don't you hope all of them are?" Juan yelled back.

My cup holder held the only water for miles, but the little man in the clown car sported a yachtsman's cap. He pulled it off and waved toward a freeway exit, motioning me to follow. Of course I did, and other drivers pulled off, too. Who could resist a desert Pied Piper blowing a kid's wolf whistle?

Juan led us away from Interstate 40 toward Seligman, Arizona. He stopped at the Snow Cap Drive-in, a sandwich shop where customers are confronted with two front doorknobs. I turned the one on the right, next to the latch. Nothing happened. I spun the one on the left. The door popped open and swung backward on hidden hinges, revealing Juan laughing inside.

"Would you like catsup with fries?" he called from behind the counter.

"Sure."

He grabbed a catsup bottle and squeezed it at me.

"Here you go!"

Red yarn exploded out of the nozzle and all over me. I scanned the parking lot for Alice and the Queen of Hearts; clearly I had landed in Wonderland.

"I dreamed all my life of opening this place," Juan told me, as I cleaned myself off. "Built it out of scrap lumber collected over many years."

The tables were cobbled together at odd angles, and brightly colored. They could have been borrowed from the Mad Hatter's tea party.

"I worked evenings after finishing my job as a laborer on the Santa Fe Railroad," Juan said.

Took him nearly a quarter of a century. He opened the Snow Cap Drive-in with the Fates aligned against him: He began business on the same day that Interstate 40 was completed, bypassing Seligman, Arizona. Cars started roaring down the interstate without stopping.

Juan's brother, Angel, ran a barbershop next door.

"There was no one here. I look one way. Look the other. Stand out in the road, old Route 66. Empty."

Juan's father and mother came to Seligman from Mexico. Built a pool hall and raised nine children. The business flourished, then faded in the 1930s during the Great Depression. The family packed its things and prepared to follow the great flood of people who passed by its door, heading west, looking for work. On the morning they were to leave, Juan found a job playing in a dance band. Eventually he got positions for all his brothers in the group, but for a time he went hungry so that his youngest brother, Angel, could eat.

"Juan put food on the table and saved the family," Angel said quietly. That's why Juan hopped in his old car and headed out to the interstate, looking for customers twelve hours a day, seven days a week, with the "dead chicken sandwiches" sign. Before Juan died in 2004, a parade of tour buses would follow him to his little sandwich shop in the desert—sixty-four each week—filled with friends who told friends they must search for the silly man in Seligman.

"You want catsup with those fries?"

Nothing overcomes human apathy quicker than a laugh.

That day in the desert I asked Juan what was so special about his place. He ducked his head and glanced up through bushy black eyebrows.

"Me!"

That kind of attitude helped build America, which has always attracted pioneers with intensity and drive—people who inspire the novels that get made into movies, whose stars, rather than the individuals they portray, are then interviewed by the media. Our country is a forge whose citizens have spirits of hammered steel. You pass by them every day. The real American story is tucked away in people who believe their lives hold something of value regardless of whether their dreams soar or shatter.

No one had time for the old man squatting over a box of vegetable peelers on a New York City street corner. The crowds swirled around him on their way to work, but he didn't seem to notice. The solitary street vendor flicked a slice of potato off his thousand-dollar suit, smiled to himself, and asked, "Why would you buy four peelers, if they last a lifetime? Well, you have four friends. That's why."

He pulled out a carrot and began to peel it. Finally a woman stopped to watch him, and then another, and another. He ignored them until a circle of onlookers had gathered around and then looked up, holding out the long carrot.

"Here," he said quietly to the woman who had been the first to stop, "try for yourself. Just pull the peeler along the carrot. Easy."

His cultivated British accent made her grin. He continued his demonstration. People at the back of the crowd stood on tiptoes to see.

"Come closer," he said softly. "I'm not going to ask for money," he assured her, smiling warmly. "You can keep your watch."

Even the people in front had to lean in to hear.

"This peeler is the finest ever made," he said. "Comes from Switzerland. Costs only five dollars. You can't buy anything from Switzerland for five dollars these days."

Joe Ades could talk a starving dog off a meat truck. A woman rummaged through her purse, pulled out some bills, and dangled them in front of him. He ignored the money until others brought out their dollars, too. That's when he finally made eye contact with his crowd, selling the peelers as fast as he could pull them from a box. In the garden of life, big things can grow from small beginnings, provided you use enough fertilizer.

That man in the thousand-dollar suit sold his five-dollar potato peelers on New York City street corners six days a week, ten hours a day—a work ethic that helped pay for an apartment on Park Avenue, one of the priciest streets in America. When I visited him there, Joe led me down a beautiful hallway filled with art to show me his warehouse. Boxes and boxes of vegetable peelers—nine thousand of them—were stacked in what once was a maid's room. He lived on what he could sell every day. He had no savings, no credit cards, and no checking account.

"Never underestimate a small amount of money, gathered by hand for sixty years," Joe explained.

His business made him something of a mystery man in his posh neighborhood.

"Some people suspected he might be Sean Connery," said Kathleen Landis, a pianist at the nearby Pierre Hotel.

Joe would show up every evening to hear her play, and he'd buy an expensive bottle of champagne. Most folks figured he probably owned the place. The gawkers who watched Joe at work out on the street, however, had another idea: "He's got an English accent, but he's probably from Mobile, Alabama," Frank Rosado suggested.

His accent was, in fact, as real as the bombs in his boyhood backyard.

Joe grew up in Manchester, England, during World War II, learning from pitchmen who set up in the rubble. "Joe Squinters. Black Dougie. Heckle and Peckle . . ." He remembered their lyrical names as if they were lines from a cherished song. "They were brilliant," he recalled.

The poor kid from Manchester started attracting his own crowds, first in postwar England, then in Australia and Ireland, before moving to New York City in the 1980s.

What's the most unusual thing he ever sold? Joe savored the question as he would a sip of wine.

"Unusual? Ah, Christmas trees in February." He smiled. "Sold them for Chinese New Year!"

He taught his daughter, Ruth, how to hawk children's books on the street so she could put herself through Columbia University. Why did she think her dad was so successful? "Tenacity and patience," Ruth replied. Joe chimed in, "I think that's the secret of happiness. Not doing what you like, but liking what you do."

The dapper Mr. Ades had the kind of life most of us only see in movies, but he wanted to share it with someone. So he took out an ad, looking for a new wife—his fourth. He got six hundred proposals and picked three "maybes."

The next evening he met the woman he would marry. She had not seen the ad.

"Ah, that was the happiest time of my life," Joe said, looking at a photo of his wife, Estelle, who had died two years earlier. After she passed away he began working for the other women in his life, his three granddaughters. The man who had no savings wanted to pay for their college education. That's why Joe got up before dawn every day to push vegetable peelers.

"Do you ever take a vacation?" I asked.

"Life is a vacation!" Joe laughed. "Every day is a vacation."

When Joe died in 2009 he left his daughter "forty boxes of peelers and a bag of carrots," Ruth recalled with a laugh, as well as instructions on how to gather a crowd. If she sold all those peelers, she'd have ninety-six thousand dollars for her daughters' college funds.

"The inheritance wasn't just the peelers, really," Ruth admitted. "It was the lessons on how to earn a living."

Joe taught her to savor the glorious uncertainty of starting every day—with nothing.

The day I turned two my own opportunities seemed limited when I tried to pop out of bed to wake my parents, but discovered I could not stand.

Our family doctor diagnosed polio.

"Bobby's left leg will be shorter than his right," Dr. Liedig told my folks, "but with therapy, he may walk again."

Mom was so determined that I would that she drove me to the rehab center at Barnes Hospital in St. Louis three days a week for years.

I had plenty of playmates there, victims of the polio epidemic that struck the United States after World War II. Twenty thousand children contracted the disease in 1948, the same year that two doctors, Jonas Salk and Albert Sabin, started looking for a vaccine that eventually would save millions.

Mom, however, could not wait. The disease had already shriveled the tendon in my left ankle, and I couldn't put down my heel. Dr. Liedig tried a cast designed to stretch the muscle, but it tore into my ankle instead, leaving me with scars as a memento sixty years later. After patching up the cuts, Dr. Liedig gave me a book, *The Little Engine That Could*.

"Don't give up hope," he urged me. "If you try real hard, you'll not only walk again. You'll lead a normal life."

That evening my mother read aloud the lines of what was to become my favorite childhood book, the tale of the little switch engine that pulled a heavy load to the top of a mountain, bravely puffing faster and faster, "I think I can, I think I can, I think I can. I know I can, I KNOW I CAN . . ."

Thirty years later, that kid who suffered polio was climbing up the outside of the Statue of Liberty.

Gulls pumped past me into the rising sun as boats grumbled below. My feet shifted on the aluminum ladder, it shook, and a face peered down.

"You okay?" the man ascending above me asked.

Clutching tightly to the rung, I closed my eyes. "Sure," I lied.

I had pursued many American dreams for the *Today Show*, but this was a nightmare. We were eighteen stories above New York Harbor, clinging to a thin metal ladder tilted between the pedestal and the big toe of the Statue of Liberty. Behind us the sun began to burn through an ashen sky as we inched on.

"Give me your hand," my guide said.

I looked up at the rust riddling the statue's moss-colored gown. My partner in this craziness steadied me while I threw my leg over a broken chain at the base of the statue.

"Careful," he said. "She gives underfoot."

I took a tentative step. Her copper skin was as dry as old canoes.

"Easy . . ."

I lurched around the ladder and grabbed the statue's big toe. It was the size of a couch.

"Oh, wow! Look at the national park rangers down there," my companion shouted, but I was too busy hugging the statue's toe.

"Listen," he said, and I heard a sound like crickets.

We peeked over the toenail. Down below, dozens of people were taking pictures.

"Help me with the pole."

My fellow adventurer twirled a camera onto the end of a small rod and telescoped it seventeen feet out over the edge. A fine thread ran from the shutter button to an assistant below.

"Fire!" he ordered, and *click* went the shutter.

"Oh, that's nice," he said approvingly.

Peter B. Kaplan was well known for these daredevil shots. He had taken photos from atop the TV tower of the Empire State Building and while suspended beneath the Brooklyn Bridge. Now the National Park Service was letting him go where no photographer had gone before. He had hung from Liberty's torch; shot from the tablet tucked under her arm; crawled over her crown. Kaplan's pictures of Lady Liberty's many moods, taken from these remarkable positions, would help raise money for the statue's restoration.

"I've been injured only once," he said with a smile, scuttling back from the edge. "In a fall from a folding chair, taking wedding pictures."

This assignment, however, would be his most difficult.

"When I go into the torch," he explained, settling onto the toe, "sometimes it can be cruel as hell. The arm sways seven feet in the wind. As you go up, hand over hand, the wind can shift and the whole arm goes 'bong!' I've almost lost my fingers from the cold up there," he added, bringing his camera to his eye. "But the view—oh, that view is beautiful."

You could fill an ocean liner with the people who take the statue's picture each day. They see the hope of America in her face. Kaplan was looking for what has not yet been seen.

"We're sitting here on her toe," he said, stroking the surface. "Who would ever dream we'd be sitting on the statue's toes? I feel I'm a part of her, almost.

"Most people call this place a jungle," he said softly, as our eyes lingered on the New York skyline. "I call it a jungle gym."

After a while Kaplan rose and stepped over a fold in Liberty's dress. It had a hole large enough to take pictures through, so he did. The statue's rivets were clearly crumbling away—wind and salt and time had taken their toll.

"I don't know how she's survived," he sighed.

Lady Liberty still stands because a young French engineer, Gustave Eiffel, figured a way to hang each of its copper sections independently, so that none would weigh on its neighbor. The young man was so successful, he was asked to build a tower in Paris. Eiffel said he would. Liberty was a gift to America from Frédéric Auguste Bartholdi. He fashioned the statue's face in the image of his mother and modeled its arms after his wife's. The soul he found in all of us.

Liberty raised her torch just as America opened wide its shores. Today eight out of ten of us have ancestors who first saw America from beneath that torch. They journeyed a troubled road, dreading the darkness they might find at its end, but found there a gentle mother who held up hope. Not all the immigrants found success, but the wilderness beyond that torch was part of their geography of hope.

More than forty-five thousand sunsets have colored New York Harbor in the years since the statue was built, yet she still stands—a kind of national conscience—welcoming, sheltering. The Statue of Liberty has become an enduring monument to what can be.

"I think the broken chains attracted me to the statue more than anything else," Kaplan said, stepping over the shattered shackles at Lady Liberty's feet. "Liberty triumphing over tyranny." He started down the ladder. "I thought I might get bored. She's so familiar, but I just watch the people. They never stop coming." Much like the man with the bad leg who climbed with him.

Storytelling often takes me out beyond the limits of my settled life. I've been to Yellowstone in winter, where it's so cold, spit bounces. I've been to Alaska chasing sled dogs as they scramble eleven hundred miles along the Iditarod trail. I've marveled at a mountain climber scaling Yosemite's El Capitan—with a broken back. But none of that compares to the life Will Steger has carved out for himself. He searches for land that hasn't felt footsteps—the coldest parts of our earth, where the north wind bullies and temperatures drop to seventy below. In the vast wildernesses near the North and South poles he seems oddly out of place, plodding carefully through the massive ice, alone. Steger believes, "You have to go where there's resistance. That's where the adventure lies."

His parents insisted he pay for his adventures. "I used to cut lawns, caddy, babysit my brother and sisters"—all eight of them, he recalled. "With one bathroom." They grew up in the Minneapolis suburbs. "My parents never camped out a day in their lives," he said, but they did give him the freedom to work for his dream. He put himself through college, and then taught himself to survive on the trail.

Will Steger had explored the unknown—one step at a time—for more than forty years, living his life in swirling snow, beneath mean skies and low clouds. Stitching back and forth between the poles, however, Will began to notice the warming of our world. "It's only by walking on it and skiing on it, day after day, month after month, that you can get a sense, really the planetary sense, of what's happening here. Every ice shelf I've ever been on is collapsing into the ocean. It shows you how fast the climate's changing."

When Will first set out on his adventures in 1963, the country faced many of the same problems it faces today—an unpopular war, and conflicts over both civil rights and women's issues. Will Steger's generation banded together and built a broad-based coalition to make life better. He thinks a similar response today can help save our planet.

"One by one the small pegs underpinning our environment are

being pulled out," he observed. Some ice fields are now so thin, his sled dogs fall through. While science alone might not be able to fix this, Will believes that people coming together and working for the common good might. So at age sixty-two he gave up his life of grand adventures to chart a course on crowded freeways, searching for schools, churches, and civic clubs—speaking to any group willing to help.

However many blisters we may get on our hands, and calluses on our dreams, the ally he seeks is the part in all of us that knows what is right. Many preach about saving the planet; Will just puts his boots on and does so.

The most remote place I've ever been is a forest the size of Maryland with only four miles of road, which circles the town of Aniak, Alaska. Aniak is home to fewer than six hundred people. The youngest among them have set a standard for community service unmatched anywhere in America. That's why I wedged myself into a narrow-bodied plane the locals called "the flying culvert" and endured three hours bent like a pretzel to make a trip there. We soared west from Anchorage to the far side of the Russian Mountains, seeking that little town in ten thousand miles of wilderness. My companions were mostly moose hunters. The pilot told us we were free to move about the cabin; that is, if we could crawl over the rifles that lined the aisle. We were a lighthearted group, perhaps because this was the first flight in forever without a security checkpoint before boarding.

My knees were turning numb when the plane finally made a tight circle beneath the towering mountains and we skimmed over the treetops looking for a landing strip. The forest verged on a mighty river that thundered past the homes of the six hundred souls who chose to live out here. As we touched down on the banks of that wet highway, Aniak shimmered in the afternoon sun.

Our group didn't take long to freshen up. We tottered over to the Diamond Willow Café for a welcoming meal—salmon and moose jerky, moose curry and rice, pickled salmon, and Eskimo ice cream (blackberries and lard mixed with flaked white fish and sugar). Mel, the owner, told me that in winter people drive up from Bethel on the frozen Kuskokwim River for a taste of his fabulous food. "It's just one hundred and thirty miles," he said wistfully, looking out the window. "In spring, when the ice begins to break up, I stick a sign on the shore that says 'Road Under Construction.'"

The man at the next table, Pete Brown, smiled. He'd heard the story many times. Pete was dining with the eight teenage girls I had come to meet. They were the only emergency medical team serving three thousand people in fourteen villages.

Aniak had no full-time medical service when a car hit one of Pete's sons and knocked him into a snowdrift, breaking the boy's legs and crushing his hands. He lay in the snow for forty-five minutes before help arrived. The next day Pete, a former army medic, started teaching teenagers how to save lives. No adults could spare the time. "We went from approximately twenty calls a year up to four hundred and fifty," Pete said, "an average of more than one a day, too many for parents with families and jobs." So it was up to the kids to assume the responsibility.

High school teacher Dave LeMaster wasn't too happy about letting his students cut class for all those emergency calls, until one day the rescue pager sounded, and Pete's daughter, Mariah, screamed, "Oh my God, the principal just fell!"

Today, LeMaster shook his head in disbelief. "By the time the ambulance got here, they already had him stabilized."

And now?

"It's like *Ghostbusters*." LeMaster grinned. "Who you gonna call?" The kids decided to call themselves the Dragon Slayers, and within three years they were chosen the best ambulance service in Alaska— even though they didn't have an ambulance.

"We'd grab the first pickup truck we could find," Patty Yaska recalled, "or first float plane or boat or snowmobile."

They've saved hundreds of lives, including those of some of their own members.

Dragon Slayer April Kameroff once swallowed two handfuls of Tylenol. "It was a cry for help," she told me. Patty found her and quickly gathered other team members. April would soon realize that "people really do care about me." Not only did the Dragon Slayers save her life, they helped her turn it around. The day I visited she was starting a new job at the town clinic, studying to be Aniak's first nurse.

Behind America's success story are untold tales of endurance. The people who succeed in this country come from sturdy stock, the ones who have always carried on when the going got tough. Their ancestors thought America's streets would be paved with gold. What they found instead was the opportunity to build, discover, create, achieve, survive, and grow.

For many that chance started in wilderness. They carved out lives, planted dreams, and worked hard. In wilderness, time does not drift back into the past, but renews itself. The same is true of people, or so I had heard, which is why I went searching for another place few ever find.

A moose munched his lunch by the side of a bubbling stream as my four-wheel drive waddled across the creek and continued up a mountain a few hundred miles southeast of Anchorage. At the top was a remote Alaskan village where the rhythm of life still resembled that in 1650.

The story of how people came to this distant corner of Alaska reads like a chapter in a "Choose Your Own Adventure" book. The settlement of the mountaintop dates back to a great split in the Russian Orthodox Church. When reformers in the seventeenth century changed the holy texts and the method of worship, Old Believers vowed to remain true to the traditional ways. Tsar Peter the Great ordered them to pay double taxes and a separate tax for wearing beards. They weren't allowed to hold government jobs, and many were beaten and burned.

The Old Believers fled to remote parts of the vast Russian Empire, searching for places so isolated they would go unnoticed. After the Russian Revolution in 1917, a considerable number escaped to Manchuria in China, where they stayed until the Communist takeover in 1949 forced them even farther from home. Some settled two hundred miles southwest of São Paulo, Brazil. In 1963, after they had spent three centuries wandering the world, Attorney General Robert F. Kennedy helped them come to America.

A few stayed in Oregon; others pushed on to Alaska. In 1968 six families punched through a thick forest and hacked out a new, one-mile-square town, Nikolaevsk, in a high mountain valley on the Kenai Peninsula, north of Homer, Alaska.

Four hundred people were living in town the day I arrived. Their houses were modern, but custom dictated that women wear long skirts and cover their heads with scarves. Men wore colorful linen shirts without collars, similar to those worn by eighteenth-century Siberian peasants.

In the 1990s village elders had asked Nicholas Yakunin to give up his commercial fishing business and begin studying Christianity's oldest texts. Now he was their priest.

"You're a fisherman for God?" I asked Father Nicholas.

"I try to be," he said with a smile. "But I have better luck catching real fish than being a priest."

He paused to listen to a teenager's question, asked in archaic Russian. Like their lifestyle and customs, the Old Believers' language is frozen in time, unchanged since their grandparents fled Peter the Great in 1650. Father Nicholas and I sat in front of the village's onion-domed church, its entryway covered with ancient icons.

I asked him how he could balance the need for change with the things that need to be kept constant.

He leaned in, as if to whisper a secret, and said, "I live in a remote area!"

But these vast mountain ranges could never keep their kids corralled, even if Father Nicholas ruled with an iron hand. Instead, he encourages them to start businesses they can run from Nikolaevsk. Father Nicholas spoke with pride about the villagers' small fleet of ultra-modern fishing vessels, equipped with the latest electronic equipment. Fishing is their main source of income.

His oldest son, Nick Jr., captains a fifty-six-foot commercial fishing boat. There is nothing seventeenth century on board, except Nick Jr.'s clothes. We found him installing a new computer monitor. "It's not the same anymore," he insisted, touching the design of his tunic. "I believe in the advancement of man."

His mom, Masha, likewise believes in the advancement of women. She put her first four babies in orange crates aboard her husband's boat so she could fish alongside him. Now she watches over thirty-eight children in a day care center she opened in Homer, Alaska, a forty-minute drive from Nikolaevsk. That was a tough decision, she acknowledged. Traditionally, women who were Old Believers did not run businesses outside the community, but her husband approves.

"What's tradition?" he pondered. "There's always been progress going on."

Even in a church that never changes. the Old Believers' brightly colored chapel was decorated with faces of saints that stared out at the world with vivid eyes. Bells above them called the faithful to a wedding. My producer, Amanda Marshall, and I hoped to be among them. She was dressed in an ankle-length skirt and a headscarf similar to the ones worn by the Old Believers, some of whom smiled approvingly when they saw her.

"Orthodox Jews wear those," a woman said, pointing at the scarf.

"I bought it in New York City," Amanda admitted. "Close as I could find."

"Good try," Father Nicholas said.

He had never before allowed television cameras inside his church, and there we stood with our crew, wondering if we had come forty-five hundred miles for nothing. We needn't have worried—I married well. My wife, Linda, walked around the side of the church with her new friend, Father Nicholas's wife, Masha. They were discussing the pie recipe Linda had brought as a gift. It wasn't as old as the Old Believers, but it had been passed down through Linda's family for generations. We outsiders were insiders before the ceremony began.

Katalia, the bride, was also an outsider. She grew up in Anchorage and had to study church customs before Father Nicholas would approve the marriage.

"It was the right decision," Katalia asserted.

She and her husband-to-be, Anecta, fell in love at a gas station ninety miles from the village. A cousin had persuaded him to give

Katalia a call. Eight months before the wedding they decided to meet at those gas pumps halfway from her home.

"I liked his eyes!" she giggled.

Anecta rolled his but admitted, "I got lucky. Really, *really* lucky!"

Custom requires that the bride and her friends sew wedding outfits for the groom's extended family, which is a large one. Men and boys sport richly decorated shirts and handwoven belts. Women and girls wear colorful ankle-length dresses and kerchiefs, which they exchange for a cap covered with a scarf after they get married and take the title "house hostess."

There's a reason these large families stay so tightly bound together: Before the honeymoon, couples endure a sort of newlywed boot camp. They move in with the groom's parents to learn what the community expects of them in married life. On their wedding day, the bride and groom must hold tight to a scarf, a reminder of their lifelong obligation to family and community.

The wedding celebration itself would last a week, but now the groom's family—all dressed in green—and the bride's—wearing gold—gathered for pictures. Digital cameras popped out of all those seventeenth-century pockets as everyone crowded together. The outside world may be creeping closer, threatening to change all this, but the community keeps attracting new people with its commitment to helping one another. Survival requires change, but tradition illuminates what matters most.

As a young reporter I began to wonder why we didn't go looking for stories like these. People who signed my paychecks typically only sent me to interview ordinary Americans after something had shattered their lives. But what did people do between tragedies? I was pondering this question while picking my way through the aftermath of a tornado in Enid, Oklahoma. There had been no deaths or injuries, but several homes had been smashed.

The other reporters on the story went looking for the mayor, who announced, predictably, "These people will need our help," but my attention had been caught by a guy in bib overalls who was rummaging through the rubble, searching for something. I followed him, watching as he stopped at every mound of trash and poked through the mess.

Was he looking for a lost photo album? I asked.

"No," he grunted.

A keepsake?

"No," he repeated, as he began scanning the contents of what had been his attic, now scattered across the block. The winds around his house had been so powerful that they'd sucked grass out of the lawn. He pointed to his bowling trophy, which was now stuck in a telephone pole at the end of his driveway.

After a few minutes more of surveying the ground he pulled a big hunk of pink goo from the muck and, turning to me, put it next to his face, smiling a toothless grin.

"Well," he said, "the tornado got my teeth, but it didn't get me!"

That ordinary person added the perspective that is so often missing in the story of our lives. If we hear only bad news, tragedy begins to seem normal. It is not. Nothing is more American than optimism that overcomes hardship.

"Are you ready for the rock?" Mike Corbett turned and asked the man he carried on his back. Mark Wellman was paralyzed from the waist down, but together they were about to climb El Capitan, the tallest unbroken cliff on earth. Two men, one with good legs, another with powerful arms, would share their strength to pull themselves three-quarters of a mile, practically straight up.

It had been seven years since Wellman made his last climb. He was on his way down when he slipped on some loose rocks and tumbled at thirteen thousand feet. He lay alone on the mountain for thirty hours, longing to be rescued.

"The darkness was so cold," Wellman recalled. "I couldn't wait until the sun would warm me."

While his legs were paralyzed in the accident, his spirit was not. Wellman bounced back, took a job as a ranger in Yosemite National Park, and began to dream of climbing again.

"I'm right below you," Wellman called to Corbett, who was scampering up the cliff to anchor their ropes. Corbett was wearing hand-stitched canvas chaps to keep his legs from rubbing against the cliff. He had also designed a special ratchet that would allow Wellman to rise but not slip back, holding him in place until he could pull again.

"Everything looks good!" Corbett yelled.

No one knows El Capitan better than Mike Corbett. By age thirty-four he had scaled it a record forty-one times.

To improve his grip Wellman hung from a device built to resemble a mountain ledge. "Nice and easy. Don't strain," Corbett reminded him.

Wellman had trained every day for six months, staring his fear and physical limitations squarely in the face. "You have one life to live," he told me. "You better enjoy that life you have. If you don't, you're wasting it."

He had just his two hands and two arms to pull him up those ropes, six inches at a time. On the first day of training he did two thousand pull-ups.

"I couldn't do that," laughed Corbett. "I could do seven."

Wellman's powerful arms would have to catch Corbett if he fell.

"My life was in Wellman's hands, and vice versa," Corbett said. "I trust him."

Wellman held the lines while Corbett ranged far above, lifting himself on nubbins of rock the size of bottle caps. Together they studied the cliff as if it were a puzzle, trying to exploit its weaknesses—cracks in the surface where Corbett could set supports so that Wellman could hoist himself up.

Before the two could crest the summit, Corbett would have to climb the mountain three times, scrambling up the rock wall to tap in a pin and thread Wellman's rope through a pulley, down to help his friend, and then back up again to retrieve the peg. The ascent took place during July.

"God, it was hot today!" Corbett sighed, gulping water.

Temperatures reflecting off El Capitan reached 120 degrees during their climb.

"I'm beat, man," Wellman admitted after the first day. That evening, they hunched on a portable ledge thousands of feet above the valley floor, sleeping one fitful turn from the abyss.

The two were an unlikely pair to hurl themselves at a mountain: Wellman with his broken back and withered legs, Corbett weighing less than the two hundred pounds of supplies he pulled up with them. But they pressed on, helping each other. The mountain had made them equals. On El Capitan, everyone is limited physically.

On the fourth day, they inched their way over a massive ledge that stretched like a roof above them. It was the most dangerous part of their ascent.

"We'll be hanging until we set the ledge," said Corbett.

Wellman had to swing twenty-five feet away from the cliff. He grunted, "It's like a hundred thirty feet up there, huh?"

"No, more like a hundred and fifty," said Corbett.

"Okay, keep holding me!" Wellman called, as he began to dangle like a spider building a web.

Twenty climbers with good legs had died on El Capitan. Wellman and Corbett knew gravity's unforgiving nature.

"It's okay to be afraid," said Corbett. "It's okay to be scared, because I think that keeps you alive."

They were no longer pulling with muscles alone, but with their hearts.

"If you have a dream," Wellman said, "that dream's only going to happen if you do it."

It wasn't just the mountain Mark Wellman was trying to conquer: He was trying to overcome his fear. He was not just pulling up, but away from the memory of that tragic moment that changed his life forever.

For a week they lived in this harsh, tilted world.

"I've got five cigarettes left," Corbett joked. "I figure we'll have to make it to the top pretty soon."

Somewhere above them, swallowed in shadow, lay the summit. They could all but feel the peak.

"After you've been up there five or six days," Corbett explained, "you get what's called summit fever. And all you can think about is the top."

The heat had put them behind schedule. Now the wind hammered them, but they were careful not to rush: Tired climbers tend to get sloppy. When the sky is under your feet, the essence of good sense is to be aware of your limitations and keep within them.

"I'm cautious," Corbett said. "I'm not a daredevil."

After a week of news coverage, the whole world was pulling for the paralyzed park ranger to make it to the top. Wellman thought the world should remember who had pulled for him first.

"Corbett's a real good pal. He's my legs."

They were united by a bond far stronger than either had in the world below. For 168 hours they had hung together, on tiny pins pounded into a vast granite wall. El Capitan had been more than a proving ground of strength and skill. Wellman discovered he had not lost his courage.

On the last morning, the two rose slowly, like men with boulders on their shoulders. Wellman had done seven thousand pull-ups in seven days.

"I can smell the summit!" he shouted, his grim determination cracking with a smile.

"Almost there!" Corbett shouted back, swirling gusts making it difficult for him to look up.

"Yeah! I feel it!" Wellman said and picked up the pace, pumping to the top.

Their adventure ended as it began, with Mike Corbett carrying his friend the last few yards to the summit. Only sky was left to climb.

After eight days, Mark Wellman, the park ranger with the fractured spine, had scaled the largest single piece of granite in the world.

Wellman's amazing feat changed forever the way Americans perceived disability. The following year, on the anniversary of that historic climb, President George H. W. Bush signed the first comprehensive civil rights law for people with disabilities. Wellman had proved to the world that the disabled, like the rest of us, have few limits.

Stories like that remind all Americans that they are not adrift in a sea of circumstances without any control. They might start on the sidelines, but they believe that no one has to stay there. Americans favor hope. Their dreams are not just dust awaiting the broom. While they know they have to attend to the small print in their lives—the effort and sacrifice it takes to succeed—their brains give up less easily than their bodies. They will find a way.

Chapter Two

See What We All See, but Think What No One Else Has Thought

America is a sly dog most of the time, hiding wisdom in plain sight. People just like us connect the seemingly unconnected every day and find commonsense solutions to any number of problems, which they implement with little fanfare. These individuals appear so ordinary that we seldom seek their knowledge, but what they have learned about life could send a committee to lunch.

Photographer Rex Ziak (pronounced *zeek*) spent almost a decade trying to get a new national park established at the point where American explorers Lewis and Clark ended their westward journey. He tramped along the last bit of trail they blazed near his home in southwestern Washington, studied their journals, and discovered that no one had accurately pinpointed that place on the Pacific coast. So Ziak spent years searching their path until he found it. That work led directly to the creation of the Lewis and Clark National Historical Park, but Ziak didn't attend the opening ceremony. He planned it that way.

"You take a big project to a certain point, and then other people who live and die to get their names in the paper are going to say, 'Aha! Here is something I can attach my name to!' If you step up beside them to take credit, money and power back away."

People who ache to have their faces on television want the world to believe they are the reason things get accomplished.

"So if you want their help," Ziak said, "approach the problem like a parent teaching a child how to ride a bike. When the kid finally wobbles away, you don't run alongside and shout, 'Boy, Dad did a good job!' You step back and applaud."

That's why Rex Ziak stood back. He believes there's no limit to what a person can do, as long as you don't mind who gets the credit.

He shared this insight with me while the two of us were hiking past trees so old, they moaned, creaking with the slightest breeze. The grove was filled with ancient cedars born during the Dark Ages, before all the kings of England or France. We were standing a few feet from busy Highway 101 near his home in Teal Slough, Washington.

"I watched the forest disappear," Ziak said as we climbed over a root the size of his leg. "Thousands of acres became hundreds of acres. Most clear-cut for lumber."

These few, towering above us, were next. This son of a logger wanted to save them. "I realized, 'This is it!' So I'll try to do something."

But Bill Gordon, the man who would decide the fate of this last little patch, lived in Boston—three thousand miles away.

"I couldn't get him to come out and see the trees," Rex said. "What I could do was take the trees to Boston."

The professional photographer lugged his camera down a logging road that had already been punched in to start the cutting. He was determined to take a photo that would persuade Gordon to halt the chainsaws. But how would he get his attention? Ziak agonized over the image he would send. Finally, he asked a friend to circle one of the giant cedars with a cord while he held the other end. It took several minutes to plod through the dense underbrush, pulling thirty-eight feet of rope around its girth, but in the end, Ziak snapped what he hoped would be a persuasive picture, showing the ancient tree sporting a measuring tape. He mailed that picture and the cord—all thirty-eight feet of it—to Gordon.

"It was almost like showing him the trousers of a very large person," Ziak said. "You hold 'em up and you won't need to see the person; you go, WOW THIS WAS A BIG MAN!"

What did Gordon think when he got a thirty-eight-foot rope in a brown paper box?

"Well, I was very suspicious," Gordon told me later. "I was concerned that it could be a bomb."

But he could tell the tree was huge, so his company, John Hancock, agreed to sell the towering cedar and its neighbors to the Nature Conservancy. Now they would never be logged. When Bill Gordon retired, he left all of his company awards behind, but took Ziak's rope and his photograph of the tree as a reminder of what one person can accomplish.

Wisdom is often found in unexpected places. Tools for some of the first microsurgeries, for example, were invented in a garage where an out-of-work truck driver tinkered with and perfected them until they changed our world. It all seemed as easy to Jimmy Crudup as rewiring his old car.

I met him one pretty spring day outside Forest, Mississippi, when I paused to admire his beautiful '46 Ford. The coupe and I were the same age, and Crudup smiled when I observed, "Looks like it's in better shape than me."

"You can't always tell about a car—by its polish," he replied.

The same is true of people. The former truck driver with that beautiful Ford taught surgery for thirty years with only a high school education, even though he could not stand the sight of blood and didn't like needles.

Crudup started driving trucks after he got out of the army. When his business hit hard times, he took a job cleaning medical tools at a research lab at the University of Michigan. One evening he borrowed a doctor's books and began teaching himself surgery.

Dr. Sherman Silber heard some of the older surgeons talking about this amazing guy, Jimmy. "He just watched what they were doing, and he did it better than them."

Dr. Silber was a struggling med student in the 1960s. "I had no manual ability whatsoever!"

Crudup had explained that surgery is mostly in the mind rather than in the hands, and then showed him how to think the process through, easing the med student's frustration. Dr. Silber became one of the pioneers of microsurgery and a leading fertility specialist, using techniques he perfected with tools Crudup made for him.

"We practiced on rats," he recalled. "Once a surgeon can do a heart transplant on a rat, it's not a big deal to do a testicle transplant on a human."

Of course, Crudup was not allowed to work on people, but because the professors did not know how to use those microsurgery tools, they sent students to learn what only he could teach.

I asked Crudup: "How did the young doctors react when they were told to learn from a guy who cleaned their tools?"

"They didn't know that I was black," he chuckled. "They would come over and say, 'Well, where's Jimmy?' I'd just say, 'You're looking at him!'"

Crudup had a way of making it pretty obvious by the end of one or two operations that he knew a lot more about surgery than they did, and then their relationship would change accordingly. Still, the gentle man with the ready smile never became a doctor himself. He started working at the hospital in his late thirties with four kids to raise—and all those students. Crudup helped many doctors to greater fortune than his own.

"What did you get out of all this?" I asked.

A rueful smile crossed his face. "One day I knew I'd be on an operating table with one of my students holding a knife over me. I could rest assured they were well taught."

Each year the best surgical student at the University of Michigan is awarded a plaque that bears a likeness of Jimmy Crudup's face. The head of vascular surgery, Dr. Thomas Wakefield, told me it was his department's most important distinction, "and it's named after our most important teacher." To his neighbors Jimmy Crudup was just that quiet old guy who could fix anything. Crudup seldom mentioned what he'd achieved. His accomplishments spoke for themselves.

Great ideas seldom start in high-rise buildings. People in corner offices may buy them, but most begin in places where folks feel comfortable enough to fail. I have spent my life working in a business that popped up in an Idaho potato field.

Television did not begin in New York or Los Angeles. It was the brainchild of a fourteen-year-old farm boy, the vision of a fellow with a funny name: Philo T. Farnsworth. A kid named Corbin McMurtrey told me about him, explaining, "He invented the first picture tube and the first TV."

Farnsworth was plowing a field on the family farm near Rigby, Idaho, daydreaming about sending pictures through the sky, when he noticed the sun glinting off the parallel lines he had made in the dirt. In a single, blazing moment of inspiration, it occurred to him that a picture could be broken down into lines, too, beamed into space, and then put back together, line by line, on a television screen. The teenager drew a sketch of his camera tube for chemistry teacher Justin Tolman, who was impressed enough to keep it. That's all Farnsworth needed. By his twenty-first birthday, with no formal training, he had successfully built a TV camera that could do what he had envisioned in that potato field. His son Skee told me, "The first human image on TV was my mother. My dad was getting some kind of funny glaze on her picture in the monitor and he couldn't figure out what it was coming from."

Was there a fire? Farnsworth ran into the other room and saw that his cameraman had lit a cigarette. Its smoke, drifting in front of the lens, was one of the first moving images on television.

You'd think such deeds would have made Philo famous, but when TV was introduced at the 1939 World's Fair, he saw it on a set in a department store window. David Sarnoff, head of NBC, was announcing the discovery. He had bought Philo's ideas after years of battling him for his patents, but he never mentioned the father of television in that famous World's Fair broadcast. I asked Skee how that affected his dad.

"He had a physical collapse."

World War II delayed the development of television. By the time most of us had sets in our homes, Farnsworth's patents had largely expired, but he kept inventing—an incubator for infants, an electronic microscope, and some of the designs that made possible the first air traffic control system. Two years before his death in 1971, Farnsworth watched a man walk on the moon through the electronic eyes he had invented for all of us. The pictures were sent back by miniature versions of his cameras.

What does it say about us as a people that something that has changed the lives of so many was thought up by a kid in a potato field? Skee, the inventor's son, thought for a moment.

"Well," he said, "it's kind of a clue. Think about all the creative power that goes unnoticed out in the country, just waiting to be discovered"—discovered by someone willing to move down roads the world has ruled impassable.

In Farnsworth's hometown, kids celebrated what would have been his one hundredth birthday with an Invention Convention. A nine-year-old decided her partially blind teacher needed Braille socks. Another rigged a doorbell ringer to help handicapped people—and then there was a blinking pacifier.

"It won't get lost in the dark," Emily Thomas proudly announced, pointing to her baby brother sucking on a twinkling light.

Tristen Sorenson invented something he called the Snotty Sleeve Saver.

"You just hook a pack of Kleenex on your coat and you can wipe your nose."

He was not much younger than Farnsworth was when he invented TV. Nice to know the kids in Rigby, Farnsworth's hometown, still have his rare gift—to see what we all see, but think what no one else has thought.

Most of us are lucky if we have one good idea. Thomas Edison had 1,093—more moneymaking patents than anyone else in American history. The most successful inventors today have about half that many. John Spirk and his best buddy, John Nottingham, were perfecting their 465th patent when I dropped by their office in Cleveland, Ohio. They worked in an old cathedral that they bought when it was down to a congregation of termites.

"It's inspirational," John Spirk chuckled, waving his hand over the sanctuary, which had been transformed into office space where dozens of people tested the partners' ideas. "Sixty thousand square feet filled with ideas, an innovation factory."

Most of us have never heard of Nottingham, Spirk, or their colleagues who helped design such commercial inspirations as Dirt Devil vacuum sweepers, SpinBrush electric toothbrushes, and Scotts fertilizer spreaders, but their products are all around us. These inventors work differently. Instead of dreaming up something they hope we will buy, they look for what we need.

"Haven't you ever been in the kitchen," asked Nottingham, "picked up something, and said, 'They should do something?' Well, we're the 'They.' "

Their products earn billions.

Spirk pointed out that "most inventors feel they have to create something revolutionary, brand new, never been done before. That's wrong! Everything is a variation on something that existed in the past."

Their partnership started in a little café. The two men designed their company logo while walking home, and sealed the deal with a handshake. They went into business with six hundred bucks and countless ideas.

"Everybody thought we were nuts," Nottingham admitted, "including us."

But their partnership has lasted as long as their marriages—many years. All their kids have worked in the company. Daughter Rachel Nottingham Colosimo has been testing toys since she was two.

"I just thought I was playing back then," she recalled.

"Remember those times when your dad came to school?" Spirk smiled. "We were always superstars!"

"We were always mobbed," Nottingham agreed.

"Because, 'Oh my GAWD!' " Spirk exclaimed, speaking in a child's voice. "'Your dad makes candy things? And toy things!' Who could be better than that?"

The two still shared an office in that huge cathedral.

"We always work together," Nottingham said. "Whatever it is, it's been a fifty-fifty partnership from the very beginning."

How did they keep their egos in check?

"You really can't have an ego in the inventing business," Nottingham answered. "They block good ideas."

Nottingham and Spirk looked at things we already use and then dreamed up ways to make them simpler to operate. That day they were working on a water-powered broom. A hose ran down the handle, funneling high pressure through the bristles.

Spirk washed off a driveway in a matter of minutes, then propped an arm on the broom handle and motioned me over. He had something to tell me but didn't want to shout. We put our heads together and he spoke softly.

"Inventions that make money," Spirk confided, "must be mindlessly simple to use."

The genius of these two inventors is in their ability to find the simplest solutions. A contractor wanted to charge them $26,000 to paint the vaulted ceiling of their cathedral. He would have to erect scaffolding. The job would keep them from working, and would take weeks to complete. Instead, they did it themselves.

"We had a fishing pole and a sponge," Spirk explained. "One of our guys dunked the sponge in the paint. Lifted the pole to the ceiling.

THUNK, THUNK, THUNK!

"Finished in one afternoon. It looks pretty good, doesn't it?"

Cost them a six-pack of beer.

America has always been a beacon for people with unusual ideas, offering them the freedom to try them out. We all know what happened when two lights blinked bright in the bell tower of Boston's Old North Church: Paul Revere rode away, and the American Revolution began. Twenty-five years before that fateful night, though, John Childs had jumped from the same belfry three times, holding on to a big umbrella with wings, thus surviving one of the world's first parachute jumps.

Nearly three centuries later, Army Ranger Monty Reed wasn't so fortunate. He broke his back when a parachute failed to open.

"It was a night jump, and we were jumping low," Reed recalled. "We were training. Somebody got too close to my parachute." That jumper came in underneath Reed, blocking the air.

Reed's chute closed, and he crashed a hundred feet to the ground, breaking his back in five places.

"It hurt to breathe. It was difficult to move, but the Army Rangers train us to just keep going."

Reed did not realize how badly he was injured. The worst pain was in his ankle, which was also broken.

"I wrapped some tape around it. Tightened the straps on my gear and walked. We had to hike eight miles to the helicopter."

The next morning, Reed could not move.

"Doctors said that it was likely I would never walk again. It was permanent damage and would only get worse."

That night Reed stared out of his hospital window, wondering what the future would hold. He hadn't been much of a student; his grades in high school had been terrible. He sighed, recalling: "I couldn't do math and couldn't spell because of a learning disability." His guidance counselor told him to forget about going to college. It was the saddest moment of his life.

"The experts told me my brain doesn't work. And now the experts are telling me my body doesn't work! What am I supposed to do?"

He picked up a book to distract himself—Robert Heinlein's *Starship Troopers*. The science fiction classic imagines a set of man-made "muscles" that would enable people to carry as much as two thousand pounds.

"And I thought, if I could build a lightweight version of that, it might lift me out of the wheelchair."

Turns out, Reed never needed the invention. After decades of rehabilitation, he made an amazing recovery—even jumping out of an airplane again to celebrate. But he wanted to do something for others with the second chance life had given him. He would perfect a working model of a robot people could "wear," one that would get the injured, the elderly, and the paralyzed walking again. Reed didn't wait for financing; he fashioned his first artificial skeleton out of carpenter levels connected at the joints with old CDs, ones he'd been using as coffee coasters. For more advanced prototypes, he borrowed his son's car seat and hockey shin guards.

"Twenty years ago, when I was first talking about robot suits, a lot of people thought I must have hit my head when I broke my back," Reed laughed, "but the design needed to be simple to operate so that anybody who could drive a powered wheelchair would be able to drive one of these robot suits."

The version I saw looked like something Frankenstein's monster might date, a man-size Erector set filled with clicking parts. It hung in the rented basement of a ninety-nine-cent store near Seattle. Reed was hunched over a cluttered workbench making last-minute adjustments.

"Ready?" he asked, lowering himself into a harness and strapping his legs to computerized muscles.

"Clear," I said, after ducking behind a counter crammed with toys, tools, and a tiny model of his old wheelchair. "Crank that monster up."

He flicked a switch and a chorus of cricket chirps filled the room as man-made muscles, tiny pistons, lifted a beaming Monty from his chair.

"Watch this," he said, plodding across the workshop. The device was not perfect, but it worked. He had programmed the robot's computer to record the way a person normally moves and then replicate those actions using tiny motors to control his man-made muscles. The contraption took top honors two years running at the International RoboGames.

"Those wins make sense," said Dr. Steven Stiens, an associate professor at the University of Washington Medical School, who, along with forty other volunteers, gathered in Monty's workshop twice a week, helping him do the things he could not. "I think we're on the right track because we have a unique solution to the problem."

With a few improvements, Dr. Stiens believed that the wearable robots might be able to help people like himself. He has been in a wheelchair most of his life. Reed watched as the doctor made an adjustment and then said: "I think it would be the best gift I could give Dr. Stiens."

He was a daily reminder of the way Reed's life could have gone.

"I envision a quadriplegic putting on a future life suit and being able to play the piano again," Reed said. "It would react to their thoughts. They wouldn't need a controller. They'd just think about it. They'd be able to compete in marathons and go swimming and ice skating and dancing and mountain climbing."

"What if you don't live long enough to see such success?" I asked.

"It means nothing," Reed answered. "I've already seen what the thing looks like twenty years from now."

He's envisioned it in his marvelous mind, which means that ultimately we may see it, too.

"It's totally sci-fi," Dr. Dan Ivankovich agreed. "Totally! If they can
make this work for my pal Mike Williams, it will work for everybody."

Williams was massive, nearly seven feet tall, and weighed more
than 250 pounds. None of the models that Reed or other scientists
had built so far were big enough to support him, but he had offered to
test the limits of the robotic legs. When the big man straps one on, he
will serve as a symbol of what old friends and teammates can accomplish.

They roared up one morning in a black muscle car, its engine
growling. A tiny silver skull wired to the brake lights blinked with red
eyes, the same color as the cross painted on the car's roof. Two words
decorated its side: "Bone Mobile."

Anyone looking for wonder among the world's ordinariness would,
as they say in old movies, "follow that car."

Its driver, Dr. Dan, wore clothes that echoed his auto's color
scheme: long black coat, black cowboy hat, black boots with a touch of
silver trim on the toe. He was as tall as his friend Mike, who was riding
shotgun, dressed like a jock. They were talking basketball.

"You give me the ball, I'm going to the hole, baby!" Willams
pretend-dunked the dashboard. "Referee calls a timeout; wait for the
backboard to stop shaking." Just as Williams was shaking, and belly-
laughing as loud as a jet breaking the sound barrier.

"You ever break a backboard?" Ivankovich asked.

"I broke three, man."

They were driving down Memory Lane on Chicago's South Side.
Williams pressed his face to the window, staring at a snow-covered
basketball court.

"Wow, remember, man?"

"Dude, I got a ball in the back," Ivankovich grinned.

"We should get a shovel, get out there, and play right now," Williams said wistfully. But he didn't move. He couldn't.

• • •

Thirty years ago, Mike and Dan were teammates, high school all-stars. Williams went on to play at Bradley University, Ivankovich at Northwestern. Both were good enough to turn pro, and Williams did, becoming an intimidating forward for Sacramento and the Atlanta Hawks.

But Ivankovich blew out his knee, so the kid who was born in Croatia became a blues musician. "A flame-throwing guitar player," he said with a grin.

Eight bullets brought the old teammates back together. On Thanksgiving weekend of 2009, Williams tried to break up a fight in an Atlanta nightclub. "I started hearing shots," he recalled. "I felt one hit my back, and my legs went numb. I'm thinking, Aw, man. Not me!

"I hit my mom's number on speed dial so she could at least hear the commotion and know something was wrong," Williams continued. "I was lying on a floor with beer bottles and trash and I'm thinking, I can't go out like this. No way.

"So I just started fighting." Heartbeats clocked the time. "I told myself, Stay conscious. Stay awake until the paramedics get here."

When they arrived, they rushed Williams out into the night, and he overheard one of them saying the hospital was eighteen minutes away. "'Dude, hurry up, man!' Williams urged him. 'I haven't got eighteen minutes. Hurry up!'"

Williams's voice dropped to a whisper. "The last thing I remember saying was: 'Give me something for the pain. Give me something for the pain.'"

Williams slipped into a coma for two months, and when he woke up he was partially paralyzed. He figured he'd be in a wheelchair for the rest of his life.

Then, while watching television, he saw a face he had not seen for thirty years. "That's Dan. Big Dan!" he cried.

Ivankovich was featured in a newscast for his work saving children in Haiti. The blues musician had become a top-notch orthopedic surgeon. Maybe his old pal could get him walking again, Williams thought. But those eight bullets had dusted bone shrapnel all over his nerve endings.

"It pounds," Williams groaned. "Then it needles. It pounds and needles, and alternates back and forth all day long. Every day."

The man who went one-on-one with the best in the NBA now battled his own disability. The day I visited him at Glencrest Nursing & Rehabilitation Centre in Chicago, Williams could only shuffle thirty steps with a walker. Watching him make his way down the hall, Ivankovich was filled with emotion: "I feel every step, when the pain is shooting through his legs."

A series of operations had eased Williams's agony, but Ivankovich was aiming for something more: He wanted to play basketball with his old teammate again.

"There are some old scores we have to settle," he said with a sly smile.

The odds are long, but "friendship is a powerful medicinal force," Ivankovich insisted, especially when it's teamed with the cutting-edge science that began in the basement of a ninety-nine-cent store.

My daughter's fourth-grade teacher, Mrs. Boehme, used to tell the kids, "Stop whining about what you can't do and figure out what you can. Life is unfair; otherwise, my husband would have hair."

Bill Peters would have been her best student.

"Hey, Boss," Peters greeted Albuquerque sheriff Darren White, as he did each morning.

"Hi, Bill," White replied, looking up from his papers. "What do you know?"

"Nothing," Peters said, "and I can prove it." The big bear of a man waved and shambled away to his cluttered office, crammed with dusty boxes and an ancient microfilm-viewing machine. Peters handled the cold cases, cases that were slowly fading away on film.

"To say he's old school is an understatement," Sheriff White explained.

Peters was one of the FBI's first profilers. He studied physics in the air force during the Korean War and planned to be a scientist, until one morning, while listening to a college lecture, he caught himself daydreaming about his part-time job as a cop.

"He's up there lecturing up a storm, and I'm thinking, How am I gonna get Jimmy McBride? He just got us for another safe last night!"

For fifty years since then, Peters has chased criminals all around the globe.

"There are times when age helps," Peters asserted. In his seventies he solved three murders no one else could. "I just don't like the idea of walking away from 'em until I got the guy in the slammer!"

That's why White coaxed Peters into postponing retirement. The sheriff knew a victim's pain firsthand.

"My grandfather was murdered many, many years ago," he said, "and my father, until the day he died, could not talk about it" because the murder remained a mystery.

In the next room, Bill Peters rummaged through a pile of files tilting on his desk.

"Here it is. I knew I had it!" Peters pulled out an aging mug shot that had helped him crack his first cold case in just seven months, one that had puzzled investigators for thirteen years.

Kathryn Dockweiller's body was found in a shallow grave in a remote location—bound, gagged, strangled, and raped. Thunderstorms had washed away all clues. Peters solved the mystery with old-fashioned police work, traveling to Texas to talk to someone whom other investigators had dismissed, a suspect's former wife. She provided what he needed: She'd found a day planner in her husband's van with Dockweiller's name on it.

"We got enough 'probable cause' to get the suspect's DNA," Peters explained. It matched DNA recovered from Kathyrn's body and put a drifter, John Green, behind bars.

Kathryn's husband sat staring at their wedding photo.

"Your wife's case was just gathering dust for thirteen years," I said, "until the right set of eyes looked at it."

"A caring set of eyes!" Chris Dockweiller said intensely.

Kathryn disappeared two days before their fifth wedding anniversary. That year would have been their twenty-fifth.

"It's just like yesterday to me," Dockweiller said, unable to take his eyes from her picture.

"Did you ever remarry?"

"No. She's all I can think of."

Kathryn was a lawyer who loved the outdoors. She was only twenty-nine on the last day he saw her. "I bent over the bed and kissed her. And I got her right here," Dockweiller said, pointing to his chin. "My last kiss was in a hurry. I had never missed her lips before."

Bill Peters and I walked with him to Kathryn's grave, and Dockweiller leaned close to read the inscription.

"Nineteen eighty-eight—a lifetime ago." But now he knew the end of the story. Bill Peters spent his seventies writing final chapters to real-life mysteries. In seven years, he not only solved three murders but also found five missing women. TV would have us believe that high-tech methods are what ultimately catch criminals, but only about a third of the cases get solved with DNA evidence. The rest rely on people whose minds never retire.

Like Bill Peters, many storytellers never stop working, either. When we stare out the window, we're working. When we daydream, we're working. When we're curious, we're working. Our job is to look beyond the normal. It's fascinating work, but not as interesting as the people we discover.

In this age of celebrity journalism, that sentiment could easily be considered career suicide. To survive, your name and your face must be seen as often as possible. That's why a lot of people in media spend more time commenting on the news than covering it, which leaves only a few moments available for original reporting. We end up spouting the two or three facts everyone else is broadcasting. Appearing to know, we build our careers.

Longtime network cameraman Darrell Barton tells the story of a journalist who showed up late for a governor's news conference. He asked the governor to stay and answer just one more question. The governor, up for reelection, obliged. The journalist turned on his camera and said, "Go ahead, Governor, answer a question."

"What question?"

"Well, I don't know. Didn't you just have a news conference?"

"Yes."

"Did reporters ask a lot of questions?"

"Of course."

"Well, pick one out and give me eight seconds!"

And, you know—he did.

Our country would be better served if we listened more to people who don't have titles in front of their names. Ordinary Americans of all ages and in all walks of life have good ideas. These days, almost anyone anywhere has access to information, but the facts and rumors fly so fast, keeping up is often like trying to read a book whose pages are being flipped by a four-year-old. We must all start digging for what's significant and refusing to settle for clichés. We must learn to identify the people who can offer genuine perspective. Social media can tell us what is and what ought to be, but those individuals can tell us what *was*—and that is the key to understanding.

Charles Banks Wilson asserts that "America was built by 'just folks.'" As he stared out the window of his art studio, behind him hung huge images of cowboys and Indians, trappers and pioneers—four paint-spattered murals, twenty-seven feet tall. Propped around them were the relics of their creation—pencil sketches and clay figures. Dozens of history books were stacked on tables. Five years earlier Wilson had set out to paint the world's largest textbook—a heritage for ordinary people.

"I felt I owed it to that guy who dug the water well, or that surveyor with the interesting story," he explained, pointing to the figures in the paintings, "to show them just as well as I could."

Wilson turned and walked through the shaft of light that came through his east window. He crossed the room, which was big and dark, then pulled himself up onto a wooden scaffold and climbed forty feet above the concrete floor.

"In most written history, they tell you who, what, when, where, and how," he said as he picked up a palette and began working with a fine brush. "They almost never tell you what things looked like."

He dabbed paint on a small cabin.

"If you notice," said Wilson, "in that little shack is a blacksmith. A blacksmith is a black man, which very few people realize. Over in Europe the man who did that kind of work was called a 'smithy' or 'smitty.' But when folks came over here, black men prepared the metal products in many trading posts, so naturally they were called black-smiths."

Wilson shifted his brush to the figure of a massive Indian wrapped in fur pelts.

"The Osage Indians were lovers of dogs," he continued after a stroke or two. "In my research I found that the Osage Indians wore buffalo robes around their waists and their legs, even in the summer-time. I asked, why? Well, they wore these buffalo robes not to protect them from the weather, but to protect them from the dogs that didn't have enough to eat. The dogs would eat their leggings off! I found accounts where overnight the dogs would eat up a whole teepee."

"Why'd they keep the dogs?" I asked.

Wilson touched his mustache. "Well," he said matter-of-factly, "they liked dogs."

The Oklahoma legislature commissioned Wilson to paint his visual textbook—a work that would hang under the dome at the state capitol. For two years he did not place a stroke on canvas, as he searched dusty archives and drifted back roads looking for inspiration for what he would paint.

"I wanted people who stood before my murals to say, 'Those folks looked just like that,'" he explained.

There are few monuments to common people, but traces remain in the weeds of time. Later that day we took a small boat and went searching.

"When you cross the bridge and look to the right, you'll see the falls of the Verdigris River," Wilson said as we floated through shad-ows and sun. "To the left, on that high knoll, is the location of Chou-teau's fort. He was an old French trader.

"There were nine thousand Indians at his fort. Three thousand trappers and something like five thousand traders. Every spring they built flatboats to carry their pelts down to New Orleans. There weren't any pensions or that sort of thing in those days. So, the benefit—the fringe benefit—was so much whiskey a week. And I understand that Sam Houston, who would later become the first president of the Republic of Texas, was probably the biggest whiskey dealer that ever came up the Verdigris. I'm not taking anything away from the man's fame, but he was criticized by other traders because he had more whiskey and could get more flatboat builders."

We nosed our boat ashore and stepped into the forest.

"Those flatboats," said Wilson, "were built out of exotic woods— walnut, pecan, anything that was available. They were filled with buffalo robes and deer hides for shipment to New Orleans and then on to Europe. Of course, once they got the stuff to New Orleans, they had an empty flatboat and they couldn't bring it back upriver. So they'd sell the wood right there. This wood would be sold to a French woodcarver in New Orleans, and he would turn it into a fine piece of furniture. It would stay around New Orleans for a couple of hundred years, and then someone from out west, who was down there visiting the Mardi Gras, would see this beautiful piece and bring it back up the Verdigris as an antique."

The wind blew the tall grass between the trees, and the waterbirds rose toward the bridge, screaming at passing cars. We shoved our boat back into the river.

"I was afraid of this job," Wilson admitted, "because I knew what was going to happen, and I doubted that I was really capable of doing what was expected. I went through hell," he recalled, watching the birds for a moment. "I couldn't sleep at night. I had nightmares. I knew what was coming! I knew I was going to have to give up everything else I was doing."

Perhaps it would have been easier simply to paint pictures of well-known people. Perhaps there was no need for years of research and late-night wandering. But Charles Banks Wilson was working for the people who never had time to own a dream. And he was signing it for them.

Several months later Wilson called to tell me that the job was finished. When I dropped by to see him, the streetlights had just come on outside his studio window. As we approached the huge figures through the shadows, Wilson said, "Late one evening, a few weeks before the murals were completed, I sensed that something was wrong."

He got dressed and went to his workshop and discovered that the door to his office was open.

Wilson bounded up the stairs and there stood a man staring up at the painting. Fumbling for a light, Wilson recognized him—Joe Noel, a roofer who had posed for the mural, and one of the last of the pure-blood Choctaws.

"You know, Charlie," said Noel, turning to face him, "I just had to come back and take a look."

The man turned back to look at his massive image.

"Choctaws are really happy that I'm up there," Noel said finally, before straightening his hat, walking to the stairs, and bidding Charlie good night.

The next morning Wilson was up on his scaffold again, touching up that painting of Joe Noel's figure.

Think what it must have been like when only people who could afford to have their pictures painted were able to see representations of themselves in color. The rest were frozen in black-and-white photographs until 1935.

That year saw the appearance of the first successful color film—a game changer as revolutionary as the Internet or the iPhone. The pundits said God and man invented it: Leo Godowsky Jr. and Leopold Mannes met as teenagers. Both were fascinated by the little box cameras that the Eastman Kodak Company made and wondered why they weren't capable of capturing more than shades of gray. Both men became notable musicians. Mannes won a Pulitzer Prize for composition, but they continued their quest for color, experimenting in darkrooms, measuring film development times by whistling the last movement of Brahms's Symphony no. 1 in C Minor. Kodak backed their efforts, hiring the two and assigning them a team of researchers. In 1936 the boyhood friends created the first practical film for color photography. Its exceptional quality appealed to both professionals and amateurs.

"Their idea became known as Kodachrome, an amazing film because the color was so vibrant," said Leon Crooks, looking up from the lens he was adjusting. He'd been a photographer for most of his ninety years, recording what he called the three stages of life: "Childhood, middle age, and 'how good you look.'"

The Kodachrome slides had an effect not unlike makeup: They gave you color, but the play of shadow and light they captured could also make you look better. They masked what we didn't like and brightened what we did.

At the height of its use, Kodachrome was processed in lots of places. In the fall of 2009 I went looking for the only one left, Dwayne's Photo in tiny Parsons, Kansas. The little shop sat in a quiet neighborhood of old homes. It had a rambling one-story warehouse out back, where Dwayne's son Grant watched over our final Kodachrome images.

"It's kind of pride mixed with sadness," he said, explaining why he continued to develop the film. "Kodak picked us to process the last roll."

After seventy-four years the company had discontinued a product once so iconic that Utah named a state park after it, the only one in the country that commemorated a brand of film.

The day I drove up to Dwayne's Photo, customers from around the world were scrambling to develop their rolls. That morning a thousand boxes tumbled into the tiny town of ten thousand on the Kansas prairie. They were sorted, sent to the processor, and the closing batch of beautiful color blossomed in the darkroom.

A passing is always a bit sad, but ultimately, it's not the film but the eye behind the camera that takes the pictures we remember. If you could leave only a handful of images behind, what pictures would you take? Tough question in a world where digital cameras let us snap all we want. Students in the Parsons, Kansas, high school photography class that year had shot forty thousand, but sixteen-year-old Lauren Llanes (pronounced *YAW-ness*) was pondering what she would pass on to her grandkids if she had only a few shots left. She took me to a place most people in Parsons pass by—an abandoned train yard where boxcars rust in the sun. Lauren climbed to the top of one and helped me up.

"Railroads," she pointed out, "built our little town." Not many, she said, knew that this was where most people worked before the depot burned and the trains moved on, taking two thousand jobs with them. Yet Parsons, Kansas, survived, creating new work in a color film company that outlasted all the other Kodachrome processors in the world.

Lauren swung out from the side of a rusting boxcar, framing the modern downtown with the fading railroad for her final photo.

Click.

That's a lasting image.

Railroads still thrive in New York City. Grand Central Terminal sees as many trains today as it did in the golden age of steam and steel. Picture the combined populations of Atlanta and Buffalo pouring out of trains and subways every day—seven hundred thousand travelers. Ten thousand pause to grab a meal, a thousand stop to ask directions. Some lose more than their way. In a single month train crews sent Grand Central's lost and found department 300 cell phones, 150 pairs of eyeglasses, and an engagement ring.

The world's largest terminal, like an iceberg, reveals only the tip of its bulk above the surface. Beneath the crowds, ten stories down, is a place so secret that it doesn't appear on any blueprints. During World War II, troops had orders to kill any outsider who came there. The area housed Grand Central's rotary converters, which supplied electrical power to trains all over the Northeast. They operated until the 1990s, when solid-state machines replaced them. All that energy in New York City's deepest basement, but Grand Central has no heating system. The eight hundred trains that pull in each day produce more than enough.

Few arrive in style now, but when the terminal was built, boarding a train in Grand Central was an event. Redcaps rolled out the red carpet, and forty-six people helped you on your way: twelve porters for as many sleeping cars, two dining-car stewards, five chefs, ten waiters, a barber, a train secretary, and a bartender. All that is a distant memory now.

We almost lost Grand Central itself, when in the 1960s developers wanted to tear it down. It was Jacqueline Kennedy Onassis who led the fight to save it.

"If we don't care about our past," Mrs. Onassis argued, "we can't have very much hope for our future. We've all heard that it's too late or that it has to happen or that it's inevitable, but I don't think that's true."

Instead, the terminal was renovated from top to bottom at the cost of a quarter billion dollars, one million spent just to clean the accumulated dirt off its ceiling. It turned out not to be soot from the trains or from the city but tar and nicotine from cigarette smoke. Poking around one afternoon, workers found a priceless tomb. Hidden behind a brick wall was a boxcar designed to hide the fact that President Franklin Roosevelt had polio and could not walk. Instead of arriving in Grand Central, where the public could see their president being carried from the train, the boxcar was pushed to a siding beneath the Waldorf Astoria Hotel on Park Avenue. FDR's car was kept inside it. He could drive himself off the railroad car and into a custom-built elevator that would lift his automobile, all eight thousand pounds of it, directly to his hotel suite. The boxcar was supposed to be kept secret, but somebody saved it when the New York Central started selling off railroad cars. FDR's unusual means of transportation was walled away, waiting for someone with curiosity to wonder what lay behind a brick wall that shouldn't have been there.

Not all of Grand Central's treasures are so hidden. The timepiece above the information booth in the central concourse has been estimated to be worth ten million dollars—all four faces are made of opal. All those travelers are scurrying past one of the most valuable art objects in the city. Sometimes, like Grand Central itself, a treasure can hide in plain sight. Our heritage has become practically invisible, and so we take it for granted. Perhaps it's time to look more carefully at what we encounter every day and learn to appreciate what matters most. We've been so busy racing toward the future that we've let some important things go, focusing instead on the superficial, the meaningless, and the momentary. So much of what we Americans held precious has perished, but now, facing hard times, we are forced to listen more closely to the simple truths that our distracted minds otherwise fail to hear. Our leaders may rule with a playground sense of justice, but the rest of us are beginning to rediscover the fundamental lesson of survival—cooperation and compromise—while maintaining integrity.

Chapter Three

Fanfare for the Common Good

Show me a self-made person, and I'll show you a liar. Yes, America does thrive on rugged individualism, but gaze closely and you'll see other hands that contribute to our success.

"No one succeeds alone," an old man with a faraway look once told me. He was pointing to a picture taken when he was a boy. "I was a lonesome little fellow," he observed. The photograph showed him clutching a suitcase, waiting for a train. "I remember being concerned, frightened because I could see where we could have been lost."

Ed Panzer's father had died. Because his mother couldn't care for them, Panzer and his four brothers were bundled into a train car filled with orphans, all of whom were searching for families who would take them in. Five little boys, looking for a home.

Panzer's older brother, Harold, remembered: "I didn't think that anybody liked me." He scrunched up his face and added, "I didn't give a damn."

The five boys rattling across America in the fall of 1922 were part of a remarkable odyssey. One hundred thousand such children were plucked from the streets of New York City and sent west to a new life. Most were the sons and daughters of immigrants, some found starving and alone. The Children's Aid Society swept them up and shipped them to villages all across the country. At each stop their arrival was advertised. Kids trooped off the trains and lined up, and couples simply picked the one they wanted.

"They went around us and felt our muscles," Harold Panzer said with a bitterness the years had not diluted. "I didn't like that at all. That was just like making a slave out of you." If a child acted up, he could be taken back to the station and put on the next orphan train passing through.

Orphans were often separated from their brothers and sisters, with the result that families were scattered all across the West. Some were adopted and took new last names. Years later, when their brothers and sisters came looking for them, they couldn't be found.

Four of the Panzer boys were chosen when their train stopped in Tekamah, Nebraska. Harold was not. Desperate to be noticed, he sang to get the crowd's attention, holding his little brother.

"They wanted to take George," Harold recalled as his eyes misted with the recollection. "He was an attractive little boy. He had brown eyes and curly brown hair. He hung on to me and wouldn't let go." Harold swallowed hard. "That brings back memories that emotionally I have problems with." Tears began to slide down his cheek. "A dentist took us both because George wouldn't let go."

The other Panzer boys were sent to separate farms. Some found couples who loved them. Ed Panzer ended up with a man who wanted cheap labor.

"He just gave me the god-awfullest beating I have ever had," Panzer sighed. "I didn't cry."

The boys made a pact to keep their last name so that they would never lose track of one another, and they didn't.

Harold Panzer took odd jobs, saved, and helped all of his brothers go to college. They were determined to have more than life had given them.

In the midst of the Great Depression, both Ed and Harold became doctors. Each had worked to put himself and his brother through medical school. Brother Jack built the hospital where Harold opened his practice. Bob Panzer became pastor of one of the largest Methodist churches in California. And George, the baby who kept the brothers together? They all pitched in to start him in the bee business. He retired a millionaire.

The Panzer boys were still at one another's side when Harold Panzer decided to get married—at eighty.

"Where have you been all my life?" the bridegroom laughed, hugging his little brother.

"Oh," George chuckled, "hiding from you."

The Reverend Bob Panzer called them into his church, and the service began.

"Dearly beloved, we are gathered together here in the sight of God and"—he paused—"these brothers."

The congregation roared with laughter.

All four of his brothers stood close to Harold as he slipped a ring on his bride's finger.

"Now, if you can find a person named Panzer," brother Bob said, grinning at Harold, "you may kiss her."

Harold jokingly started to smooch each of his brothers before embracing the newest member of their family. It had been a long time since their ride on the orphan train, but the brothers still had what they had then—one another. They had made a deal with their hearts instead of their heads, and it lasted a lifetime.

In every family there is a history of hardship and endurance, but I never asked about ours. Growing up, my father seemed like every other dad I knew—educated and successful. I assumed he had gone to college, but the night I graduated from the University of Kansas, he told me, "I never went. Your old man dropped out of school in the fifth grade."

"What?" I asked, taken aback by his admission.

"Yes," he said, "I had to. My dad disappeared. Joined the army and left when I was five. I had to go to work and help my mother put food on the table for my little brother, my sister, and me."

I wanted to know more, but sometimes the best question is none at all. People will tell you things to fill the silence. Dad shifted in his chair. Lit a cigarette. Started to speak and then watched the smoke. This moment seemed to be crushing him, as if time had weight, until finally he picked up his story again.

"My mother was a short-order cook, a single mom who couldn't take care of three kids, so she turned me over to a farmer as an indentured servant. He gave me room and board in return for work. I was just ten years old." He told me this with an expression that made him appear as if he'd been squinting too long while looking into a sunset.

"My aunt sent me a letter every week with a dollar inside," Dad said. He cleared his throat and then muttered, "I never saw the money."

The farmer had been steaming open the notes and pocketing Dad's dollars. Eventually, however, his aunt showed up with her brother Lorne, a cop. "She buggy-whipped the farmer," Dad said, shaking his head, "and took me to live with them in St. Louis."

There my father got another job, this time in a factory that made wooden car bodies. He swept up the sawdust that fell from the assembly line.

"Most of the workers were immigrants, German and Italian," he recalled. "They spoke little English." Dad paused. "It was a lonely place to be an eleven-year-old kid."

A few years later, he found better work in an optical store. Dad was still a janitor, but his boss encouraged him to go to night school. "I took classes for twenty-three years!" he said, his pride pushing aside the haunted look in his eyes.

By the time I turned two, my father had earned an honorary master's degree in opthalmics. He bought a cheap lens grinder in Kansas City and rode a night train home with the machine on his lap. The next morning he opened Dotson Optical Company. His business partner stole most of the profit that first year and disappeared, the same month that polio paralyzed his youngest son. Undaunted, Dad saved and struggled until he could open a new business that eventually bankrolled the first Dotson to graduate from college—me.

Dad had three children, like his mother, but we were able to live in a nice home. I assumed he always had, too, until that night I listened to him fill the silence between us. Ever since then, I've made an effort to look behind the media mirror that reflects celebrity and power to search for compelling tales about people who, like my dad, are standing outside the spotlight.

Jack McConnell began to notice them when he stopped to pick up a man who was walking down a dirt road without an umbrella on a drizzly day.

"Where you headed?" McConnell called out the window.

"To look for a job," the man answered. "Any one I can get."

"What's your name?"

"James."

"You married?"

"Yes. I've got two kids and my wife is pregnant with our third."

"What do you do for medical care?" McConnell wondered. He was a retired doctor.

"We have to take care of ourselves," James said. "No one else is going to help us."

His answer would change thousands of lives across the country.

That man on a muddy road started Jack McConnell thinking about all the other people he'd seen trudging by him on the road—waitresses, maids, and the army of workers who preened his retirement paradise on Hilton Head Island, South Carolina. Six thousand working poor could rarely afford to see a doctor.

Jack McConnell decided to treat them for free, and soon began recruiting other retired physicians. At first, they resisted; few of them were licensed to practice in South Carolina, and some were worried they'd be sued and perhaps lose their life savings. McConnell persuaded lawmakers to waive the licensing fees and got cheap insurance that would cover everyone working in his clinic. The day I visited, he had 330 volunteers, doctors and nurses of all kinds, enough to help take pressure off the local emergency room, where many of the poor previously went for all their medical needs.

ER doctor Rob Clodfelter did the math. "If it saved us just four or five thousand visits a year, that's a significant economic impact."

But how "safe" were these older doctors?

"Two thirds of our physicians were medical school faculty," Dr. Frank Bowen said. He was responsible for making sure that those retired doctors could still do the work. "They not only keep current, but they teach younger doctors, as well."

The clinic does more than patch up poor people. Volunteers take the time to get to know patients as friends. McConnell's wife, Mary Ellen, explained, "The clinic brought the two communities together." The haves and the have-nots have been able to communicate in a way they hadn't been able to before.

Every patient has a story, but many people tell their stories only when asked. Cecilia Benitez mentioned she was having some hard times, even though she worked six jobs. The medical volunteers helped her out. In turn, her entire family showed up to clean the clinic every day after work.

"It's my second home," Cecilia laughed.

This country has a quarter of a million doctors who no longer practice medicine and two million nurses who have stopped taking care of the sick, even though many are still young enough to do so. McConnell cited these statistics as he gazed upon his own packed waiting room with an eye not blind to need. What he'd achieved in Hilton Head inspired others to open more than eighty volunteer clinics all around the nation. Those clinics are also always crowded.

"It's not where you come from or where you're going," he said, "but who you help along the way that makes the difference in your life. I learned that lesson around my childhood dinner table. Every night, after my father would say the blessing, he would ask us, 'What have you done for someone today?' If you had nothing to say, pass the gravy and get on eating, but if you did, you were the hero of the night."

Jack McConnell lost a lot of retirement time helping others, but found deep within himself the person he wanted to be.

I spend most of my time telling tales on television. That's a little like writing with smoke: Stories tend to simply drift away. But not always. Those that reveal our better selves seem to linger, becoming signposts pointing us to the capabilities of the human spirit.

I often revisit the subjects of the stories I've reported, curious about how their lives have turned out. Over the years I've called on Jim and Marty Dwyer many times. The Fort Collins, Colorado, couple thought it might be nice to have a little girl in their family. After giving birth to five boys, however, Marty figured that wasn't going to happen, so they agreed to raise someone else's. But she wasn't a baby. And she brought her brother. And those two brought four more.

"What is this?" one of the young Vietnamese sitting at the supper table asked.

"Spaghetti," said the towheaded boy next to him. "It's just like long rice."

The two began to laugh and that laughter spread from place to place as the spaghetti bowl was passed. When it reached Jim Dwyer, he added this observation: "Never sit near the baby." It was spoken with the sure knowledge of a man who'd been married twenty-two years. He tucked in his napkin and repeated, "Never sit next to the baby. You got to feed him."

The accent was Long Island, New York, where Jim and Marty Dwyer met and lived before they moved west. They wanted to own a horse ranch, but they ended up running a muffler shop instead. Their dream changed when the Dwyers agreed to look after an entire additional family. There were fourteen of them around that supper table. The new faces had come two at a time from Vietnam, drifting in from the calm surface of an endless sea.

"After the Communists took over at the end of the Vietnam War, my dad lost his job," Thu-Nga explained. She was the youngest Vietnamese, a slight girl with a cherub's face, just sixteen at the time. She looked much younger, doll-like. "The whole family tried to escape together many times," she explained. "We couldn't make it. By law back then, if you left your home without permission, the Communists would take your house. My mom and dad decided that we had to split up."

Two by two, her father, Tran Van Be, sent his children to freedom. They slipped away in the night down to the ocean.

"Our boat was just a tiny wooden one," Thu-Nga recalled, "about sixteen feet long by seven feet wide. It was built for three people, and could carry cargo. We had three hundred twenty-three people on it. The first day we went out, the engine broke, so we couldn't go anywhere. We found out that we didn't have a pilot. We didn't have any food. Water was in every direction, but you couldn't drink it."

Thu-Nga and her sister, Thu-Van, almost gave up. Their ark was going nowhere.

"We were just waiting to die, but we didn't know if death would come soon or whether the next wave would send us to the bottom. We saw many ships pass by, but none would stop for us. By the seventh evening, we spotted an American ship." Thu-Nga's face began to brighten. "It stopped and picked us up."

Marty Dwyer pulled some spaghetti sauce from the stove and continued the story.

"I remember Thu-Nga's older sister, Thu-Hong, was standing right here when she got the telegram that her sisters had escaped. I almost had to peel her off the ceiling, she jumped so high. Just one incredible leap!"

When we first met in 1984, the parents of those Vietnamese children still lived in Ho Chi Minh City with their youngest son and a daughter who had tried to escape but had been turned back. She and her sixteen-month-old baby made it into a boat. Her husband, Xuong, was forced into another. Xuong was rescued and found a home near the Dwyers. He had not seen his wife and child in three years.

"You can't erase his fears," Marty pointed out. "You can't make him miss his family less. All you can do is offer a hug and understanding."

The day after our dinner the Vietnamese family went horseback riding in the Rocky Mountain foothills. Xuong was holding on to a big chestnut stallion, his stirrups flopping freely beneath his sneakers.

"Here comes Hopalong Xuong!" Jim shouted.

"How do I stop him?" cried Xuong.

"Pull back on the reins!" Jim shouted.

"Eeeek! Wait a minute! Help! Wait!" Thu-Van screamed, as her own horse ambled off the path to munch some grass, lowering its head. Thu-Van was frantically grasping the pommel to keep from sliding down the horse's neck.

"Come on, you rode elephants," Jim said playfully. "You can ride a horse."

He reached for the reins, settled Thu-Van back into the saddle, and prodded the horse on its way.

"See you next week."

"Oh, noooo, Dad . . ."

A Saturday afternoon in the saddle was as close as Jim Dwyer had gotten to his dream of owning a ranch. He tipped back his cowboy hat and pondered that a bit. Finally, he said quietly, "If five more [Vietnamese] came tomorrow, well, we'd just postpone that ranch again."

As he watched his children romping across the meadow, he said, "I don't think that was much of a decision, to tell you the truth."

Jim worked thirteen-hour days, six days a week, at a muffler shop, surrounded by his boys.

"We try to give our children everything they need," he said later that day, taking a break behind the cash register. He looked through the glass divider that separated his office from the garage area. Two sons were changing a tire; another was welding. Shards of blue light broke upon his face.

"We give them everything they need," Jim repeated softly, as if he had just thought of it, "but they have to earn what they want."

His son Brian worked two jobs, leaving the shop on Friday nights and delivering newspapers until dawn. Son Chris tossed them through the week. He first took the job when the Vietnamese arrived, to raise money for college. He had just turned ten.

"When I get mad," said Chris, flipping a newspaper from the back of his mother's station wagon, "sometimes you feel like, 'Oh, it's their fault.'"

Another house. Another flick of the wrist. The paper plopped on a porch.

"But that's just because you're mad." He laughed to himself. "When you stop to think it over, it's not their fault."

Marty Dwyer was enrolled in nursing school when the Vietnamese came into their lives. She dropped out. That evening in the kitchen, I asked if she had ever regretted that decision to take in the new members of their family.

"Of course, of course, we've all said, 'What, am I crazy? I'm broke! Get out, everybody. I'm going to go wild at the Fashion Bar!'"

Two kids looked around the corner. She winked at them and said, "We just can't do that."

The older children were going to college at the time. Thu-Nga, a straight-A student, planned to study medicine at Johns Hopkins.

"Every time we see them accomplish something, we think of what their Vietnamese parents are missing," said Jim, waiting in the living room for dinner. His youngest son was setting the table. As we watched the boy, I realized that I couldn't imagine having to send my own daughter out on the ocean to search for a better life.

"I don't think I could love enough to give them up like that," Marty agreed. "You must love your kids an incredible amount to let them risk their lives."

Jim thought about that for a long moment.

"Their folks passed on their own personal happiness to better their children. I guess that's the ultimate in parenthood."

They had sold everything they had to put the kids on those boats. There was no money left for an escape of their own, so their children worked odd jobs for ten years to pay for their parents' passage to America.

"Is that them?" Thu-Nga cried, straining to spot familiar faces somewhere in a sea of travelers.

She was blocked by security at the Denver airport from going in search of them. The strain of the twelve-year separation from her parents showed on her face. Thu-Nga's brothers and sisters were there, too.

They were children no more, and so much had happened since those dark nights when the family split up. Thu-Nga tearfully recalled the final meal she had shared with her family before leaving Vietnam.

"We had dinner together for the last time," she remembered. "My mother had kept me home from school that day because those were our last hours together. And, so . . ." She halted, stifling her sadness with a courageous smile. "We had dinner together and we prayed together. And . . ." Again she glanced away and forced herself to recall that night. "She said that if we ever make it to America, just do our best."

Tears rolled down her cheeks as she told me, "Well, they just said they had high hopes for us. That we should try to reach it."

All six of the Tran children graduated from college. (All five of the Dwyers' kids attended college, too.) Thu-Nga was second in her class at Johns Hopkins Medical School. She became a doctor and is a highly regarded research physician. The last time I saw Thu-Nga, all four of her parents had gathered for Christmas. Her natural mom and dad had a new home in Colorado, near the American couple who had matched their love.

Thu-Nga was now a mother herself. She watched her children playing with their grandparents and marveled that the entire family was under one roof at last.

"We are really blessed to be loved by them all," she said.

I am always drawn to happy families who are strong enough to take in others who need help, whether they are kids facing chaos in their own homes, the sick, or the sad. That's why I lingered one afternoon in an asphalt meadow to watch the Romaner family cheering on a small boy with a back bent like a pretzel, who was in the process of dancing back and forth, dodging defenders, kicking a soccer ball.

"That's it, Mekonnen!" they shouted. "Run. Run!"

The boy with the twisted spine juked past some of the best players in the league and pounded toward the net, blazing down the field, and scored. His teammates swirled around the little player and lifted him up. They had beaten the best soccer team in Dallas. Mekonnen caught sight of the Romaners, slapping and hugging one another along the sidelines. He raised his hands and beamed at them. They were a great team, too. His coach, Ozzie Denson, observed, "If I had a hundred like him, I could win it all!"

But Mekonnen's moment, naturally, had come with some drama. His twisted back was collapsing like a badly built house. Surgeon Dan Sucato explained, "We've got to take some of the 'house' away first in order to reconstruct the house. It is probably the most dangerous spine deformity surgery that we do."

Mekonnen suffered from congenital kyphosis and was born with an S-shaped spine. Without surgery, the "S" would eventually tighten until he was paralyzed, but his family could not afford such an expensive operation.

"His father makes less than a dollar a day in Ethiopia," Dr. Rick Hodes told me. "He's a day laborer."

Neighbors had brought Mekonnen to Hodes, an American doctor living in Addis Ababa. He called around and found that the Scottish Rite

Hospital in Dallas offered Mekonnen the best opportunity for a normal life. More important, the hospital and its doctors would do the operations for free. Dr. Hodes had linked forty other kids who needed major surgery with hospitals around the world. Ten of those children had come back to live with him in Ethiopia. How did he keep from being overwhelmed?

"Well," he chuckled, "I am overwhelmed, but I'm just trying to help a few people along the way."

He recruited the Romaner family in Dallas to look after Mekonnen while he recovered from his surgeries, a process that would take half a year. Jaynie Romaner slapped her forehead as she remembered, "My husband and I said, 'Okay, what were we thinking!'"

When Mekonnen arrived, he spoke no English. Fortunately, he had a knack for making friends.

"When his face lights up, it's open to the whole world," Jaynie said, "and all you want to do is be there with him."

The thirteen-year-old who loved games faced the biggest contest of his life. He'd already had one surgery to stretch his spine and faced another fourteen-hour operation to rebuild his back. Dr. Hodes flew from Ethiopia to be at Mekonnen's side, bringing along the boy's stepbrother, Dejene, who had undergone a similar operation two years earlier. At the hospital Dejene leaned in close to Mekonnen and promised him, "It will hurt for the first couple of days, but then it will be fine. The Romaners will let me stay with you until you have recovered."

Mekonnen looked pleased as they took him into the operating room. Many hands had worked together to bring the little boy with the bad back to that moment, shaping the world as they wished it would be, one that is filled with happy endings, like Mekonnen's last soccer game before the surgery. Sometimes—even on playgrounds—life becomes a Hollywood version of what a life should be.

Families in this country often help others end nightmares and find dreams. It is the very core of our American story, because most of us also have ancestors who risked everything for a better life. The communities they built prospered because people took care of one another. Some still do.

In Westport, Massachusetts, neighbors donated a million dollars to save a small family farm from developers. They pooled their money, bought the farm, then sold it to an eighteen-year-old farmer for thirty-two thousand dollars. In Brownsville, Texas, the president of Mexico awarded Frank Ferree and his friends five gold medals for feeding poor children along the border. They melted down the medals and bought more beans.

In Philadelphia, Hal Taussig commuted to work on a secondhand bike, pumping the pedals with his only pair of shoes. His company, Un-Tours, made a lot of money taking tourists on trips to Europe, but Hal and his wife, Norma, raised three kids on as little as they could because they'd donated five million dollars, nearly all of their fortune, to projects that help the poor or work for the environment.

Time and again I find entire towns confronting problems with patience, love, and a leveling sense of humor. One of them nestles in a high mountain valley where people survive—even in hard times—without federal aid or giant corporations.

Philipsburg, Montana, is a working-class town that gets things done the pioneer way—together. Jim Jenner paused on Main Street to explain.

"They're tough people," he said. "This is tough country. Tough jobs, like mining and cattle, but they believed in the future."

Philipsburg has always attracted people with intensity and drive. Its pioneers beat everyone to Montana's first silver mine and then built thirty houses in thirty days. They clung to their town, even when the mines boomed and busted, jobs came and went, dreams soared and shattered.

How else could a city of nine hundred build its own opera house or produce two original plays each year? Performers pick up costumes from the local thrift shop where neighbors sell hand-me-down clothing and housewares.

The money they make in the store—more than a million dollars—helps run the town's hospital. People in Phillipsburg guard the things that make it a community. The post office is the one place where folks can check on one another every day, so when the federal government tried to move it, Judy Paige led a successful fight to keep it downtown.

"We were afraid that this place was going to become another ghost town," she said, "like the twenty-nine towns nearby that have already disappeared."

Fewer than two people per square mile live in the valley. Only about one hundred kids go to Philipsburg's elementary school, yet Superintendent Mike Cutler points out that local residents taxed themselves to restore it, at an average of twenty-five hundred dollars a person. Students are learning how to pay that back. The high school shop class built a bathroom for the volunteer fire department—a project that was paid for by local hunters.

"This is what we do," Cutler said, "and if it's not good enough, we'll make it good enough."

We watched the kids work through a haze of sawdust. The sun was slanting behind high purple mountains. It was one of those moments that make you homesick for a place you've just seen. Granite County, Montana, is bedrock America. "It's the last best place," Cutler said. "It truly is. It has to survive."

In 2003, Mike Cutler was diagnosed with leukemia and needed a costly stem cell transplant.

"One day I came back from a golf tournament, and here's this great big tent," Mike recalled. "You know? Like you see at the circus. I could not believe the amount of people."

They handed him a check.

"Close to forty thousand dollars," Cutler said.

There are fewer than one thousand people living in or around Philipsburg.

"It was overwhelming for me. Still is."

"The folks who helped," I asked, "were they all just rich?"

"Oh no," he chuckled. "No, no, no."

They simply valued the town's survival more than personal gain.

People all over the valley donated meals, and nearly everybody showed up to buy them. All the money for Mike Cutler was raised in a single day, an amazing achievement that he pondered until a soft smile warmed his face.

"It takes a community to keep the community."

A few years later, in the depths of a recession, the neighbors rallied again to save the Cutler family, raising $100,000 through auction sales when Mike's nine-year-old daughter, Sydney, needed surgery for brain cancer.

"It's way easier being the patient than the parent of a little girl that's fighting for her life," Cutler said, his voice choking with emotion. After an operation in Seattle, she had to learn how to walk again.

"I had to learn how to see again, too," Sydney added.

Fortunately, she lived in a place that nourished hope.

"People helped me so much. If I couldn't do stuff, my friends didn't care. They just stuck right with me. They didn't go away and do things I couldn't do."

The Cutlers live on a ranch on a hilltop just outside of town. Neighbors took care of their animals for months at a time while Sydney was undergoing cancer treatments far from home. After each trip, Mike's wife, Jody, found new groceries in their fridge.

"Not just food, but casseroles that I would just have to warm up."

How could a county with more cows than people come up with a hundred grand in the midst of a recession? Ranch manager Phil Shields explained: "They gave from their hearts and they gave from their souls."

There was a practical aspect to their giving: Neighbors donated things others needed to buy. Shields, for example, put a cattle chute up for auction. "Most of us figured if there was no town, there'd be no people. So we saved ourselves, is what we did."

Philipsburg reminds us of America as it used to be, where comfort comes with a whiff of river water and the bite of a trout. I stood on a hillside overlooking the town, watching Mike and Sydney herd horses in the frozen pasture below. Her hair had grown back; his was prematurely gray. But both had won their battles with cancer.

Lights winked on in the town as shadows began to blanket the beautiful Victorian buildings that lined Main Street. A single shaft of sunlight remained, illuminating words on an old brick wall, a fading advertisement for "The Golden Rule."

There are still places in this country that call us together, where we feel connected to shared landscape and experience, but it's not just that legacy that draws people close in Philipsburg.

"What you see when you drive downtown isn't what you get," Mike explained. "The candy store is great, and all the buildings are beautiful, but spend a day and visit with some of the people—that's what it's all about."

In places like Philipsburg, the past is not past, but keeps circling back around. Many towns in America share that reverence for their history. Petaluma, California, continues to celebrate a magical summer when kids showed up to shoot a low-budget movie called *American Graffiti*. It launched some big-name careers and boosted an unknown director, George Lucas, into an orbit that would lead to his epic *Star Wars*. History in Petaluma is never far, far away.

Sadly, this town, so tied to movie history, lost its last picture show. Kids had to hop into a car and have their moms drive them to the movies in another town.

"Oh no!" Taylor Norman recalled, looking stricken. "You're not supposed to go with your parents! You're supposed to go with your friends to the movies."

That's when Taylor, Madison Webb, and their pals began daydreaming about opening another theater.

"We were naïve enough, I think," Madison said, "to have enough confidence."

Never mind that they were just twelve at the time. Taylor invited six kids over to find a way to make a Petaluma movie theater profitable. "We had unique ideas," she recalled, "like a souvenir shop and babysitting on-site and an Internet café."

They had so many ideas that they met two hours a week for an entire year until they were finally ready to draft a business plan.

"Their ideas were sound," recalled Taylor's mom, Patty. "Their logic was unflappable. But getting people to actually listen? They were blond and thirteen, so . . ."

They ultimately wrote a letter to the one man who might remember what it means to be young with a dream in Petaluma.

"Dear Mr. Lucas . . ."

The girls got a letter back, inviting them to present their ideas to George Lucas's vice president of marketing, Jim Ward. He told them, "This business plan was better than ninety percent of the business plans that pass through here on a daily basis, and I'm being very serious about that."

He was so serious that Lucas gave the girls permission to show *American Graffiti* on an old brick wall near the site of their proposed theater.

That got them noticed, but when some potential developers still wouldn't return their calls, they sent Girl Scout cookies—a tactic that got callbacks the following day. One developer wanted to include their theater plan in his new shopping mall on the edge of town. The teens turned him down; it was too far to ride their bikes. They continued searching for someone who would build downtown. It took four years, but those seven teenage girls made movie history when a new theater opened on Petaluma Street in the center of the city, and the owner put the girls' names on stars out front.

A lot of kids have big dreams. Perseverance made this one a reality.

"Age doesn't matter," Taylor Norman told me. "Size doesn't matter . . ."

Or, as George Lucas's Jedi Master Yoda would say: "There is no *try*. Just do!"

The girls got lifetime passes for all their hard work, and jobs at the new theater. "Minimum wage," Taylor admitted with a giggle, while cleaning a bathroom. "Our best friends are the broom and the dust pan."

Her pal Ashley Ditmer was on her knees scrubbing those stars with their names in front of the box office, an invaluable lesson for anyone in business: The boss may make you a star, but you have to polish it.

Traditional values like caring and hard work are still guiding our lives in overlooked places, not all of them remote. It was those values that restored Harlem in New York City. The first time I visited there, in the 1980s, parts of it looked like a cattle chute for drugs, funneling users in to buy. Back then, a little boy turned on his pillow in the dreamlike haze of dawn. A little girl looked for a teddy bear lost in the night. The sun slanted to a stack of toys tossed in the corner and came to rest on a doll whose face was smudged with play. The boy woke up, rubbed his eyes, and watched a sliver of dust soar past wallpaper balloons. An abandoned baby bottle lay among the covers. Others in the room began to stir until, one by one, little heads rose up from a dozen cribs and cried.

Childhood should be a season of dreams, but these children awoke each morning from an American nightmare: They were all born addicted to drugs. Raphael Frazier's mother passed on her four-hundred-dollar-a-day heroin and cocaine habit. Emerald Alexander ate paint and added lead poisoning to her tragedy.

Clara Hale saved hundreds of them.

The tiny woman shuffled between the beds, touching and greeting each child in passing, holding her own tattered bathrobe tightly at the neck. She was bone thin, elderly, but unbowed, a woman who faced life with formidable courage.

"Hello, angel," Mother Hale said to one little girl. She was seventy-nine that day, but still stood straight, like a teacher ignoring a busload of grief.

"Hello, precious. What's the matter with you?" she asked, bending to help Raphael, searching for the heel in his sock, which was hiding on top of his foot. He reached for the discarded baby bottle in his crib and stuck it in his mouth, which stopped his crying.

"All of them, they don't have to die," Mother Hale said, stroking the boy's hair. "Because some of them have the determination to live."

The old woman crossed to Emerald Alexander, pulled her up, and patted her gently.

"Come on, children, get dressed. We're going to the park."

Clara Hale lived in a Harlem neighborhood of burned-out homes. Some had gaping black holes where windows had been smashed many times. They seemed to stare down at Mother Hale's little band of toddlers skipping along the sidewalk.

"Look where you're walking, so you won't fall down," she cautioned them, lifting Emerald over an old mattress and kicking aside a rusty can. A large dog snarled. The children grabbed one another's hands and moved on.

"Oh, look at the building," she said, surveying the street. "Isn't it a shame how they let that go?"

A woman swayed drunkenly at the street corner while a black cat sat on a windowsill, blinking silently in the sun. Two people huddled together in a nearby doorway. A crumpled wad of bills passed between them, and a small plastic bag of white powder was pressed into a jacket pocket. Clara Hale's neighborhood was all selling and consuming.

The children of those streets learned early that life is unfair. Clara Hale showed them that it could be lovely, too.

"We're going over here," said Mother Hale, shepherding her small flock through a chain-link fence into the park. The children broke formation and ran for the slide. Hale stood guard near the bottom.

She had not set out to do saintly things, but was in fact on the point of retiring when a drug-addicted mother left her baby by Hale's door. Hale took him in, and word of her charity quickly got around. Soon her tiny apartment was jammed with cribs. She had already spent a lifetime caring for other people's children. Her husband had died young, and she had supported her family by raising forty neighborhood kids. She had three of her own. All forty-three went to college, and all graduated.

She agreed to take care of these new babies on one condition: that their mothers enter drug rehabilitation programs. She did not want to send those children back to mean streets. Before I met her, 497 drug-afflicted babies had passed through her home and all but 11 had been returned to their mothers. Raphael's mom, Nancy Frazier, didn't think people like Mrs. Hale existed anymore.

"She used to talk to me all the time and she said, 'Nancy, you can be anything that you want to be.'" Because of Mother Hale, Nancy was trying to kick her habit.

"Mother Hale! Catch me!" screamed Raphael, making his way down the crowded slide.

Nancy's eyes flicked to her son, held, and then focused somewhere beyond. "She helped me grow, too."

That afternoon, as the children prepared for their nap, I asked Mother Hale if she thought she would ever run out of love. A baby in her arms cooed softly as she leaned back in her old rocker.

"I think if I ran out of love, I'd be out of life."

She kissed the baby's thumb, placed the child in a crib, and drew the shutters closed. The room darkened.

"Here's your teddy bear," said Mother Hale, tucking the cover around another child.

"That ain't no teddy bear," said the small voice beneath the blanket, "that's an elephant."

"Oh, I'm sorry," said Mother Hale, tucking in the elephant. "Good night, sweetie, I'll see you after a while."

She moved from child to child.

"You want to be big like your daddy?"

"Yes . . ."

"Then go to sleep . . ."

Hale could not recall a night without babies by her bed. She had been taking care of them since she was fourteen, her voice a soft whisper against the wind outside. There was no magic to what she did, just love, and that was the best magic of all.

America is made up of many Mother Hales. Unnamed and unsung, they work their wonders, tirelessly helping kids survive the tightrope of childhood. They teach children to understand the differences between people and show them what we all hold in common. Much of what we learn reinforces our separateness and confirms our distrust. The Mother Hales believe that gentleness needs to be nurtured.

"Money will buy a fine dog," she once said, "but only kindness will make him wag his tail." That woman was no mere pundit. She was important for what she did, not for what she said. Neighbors fondly called her "the only living heart donor."

Chapter Four

Thinking More of Others Than They Do Themselves

At twenty-five I married my best friend, a woman who thinks more of me than she does of herself. More important, she thinks more of us than she does of me. We've been a team since "I do." For marriage to succeed, you need to count on more than your fingers. Families thrive when their members invest in one another and spend time together. I'm away from home a lot, but our marriage has lasted four decades for one simple reason: Linda makes sure I remember that work and life are not the same words.

Should I come upon an interesting news story, I'd think nothing of staying up all night to cover it. Linda taught me—by example—to do the same for our only child, Amy. They planned "girl-and-dad days" while I was traveling. Many a lonely night on the road, when I found myself sitting in a motel room, they'd call and tell me about the adventure that was waiting for me—a trip to our "secret park" to sail a fallen leaf in the stream or a ride on the rocking horse in front of our favorite bookstore. When I got home, I didn't rush out and play golf with the guys. Instead I'd give my family the same passion and love I brought to the written word. Work won't hug you when you're old.

My parents' friends were mostly people Dad met at his office. Eye doctors came to dinner at our house. The same was true of our neighbors: Teachers partied with teachers; cops hung out with cops. They all talked shop. Linda fills our table with good storytellers who come as much for her caring personality as for her legendary southern cooking. She is everybody's best friend.

"That's my job," she insists, surprising them with homemade recipes that she knows they will like, even if she herself doesn't. She learned this from her mother, Doris Puckett, who raised six kids and lived on a ranch in southeastern Oklahoma.

At her dinner table Mom Puckett served up a love of the world. She read two or three books a week and always knew something interesting about the places I'd traveled to, even though she'd only been there in her imagination. We started taking her with us on vacations because she was able to show us things we'd otherwise miss, even standing next to her.

One time in Rome, the pope's dresser gave us a "backstage" tour of the Vatican. Mom Puckett so admired all the beautiful robes in the pope's closet that the dresser plucked one out, draped it over her head, and took a picture, causing that tiny Baptist to blush fiercely. Six months later, shortly before Easter, I got a call from her. "Quick, turn on CNN!" she shouted. "The pope's wearing my robe!"

I fell in love with Linda and her mom at the same time.

They taught me their recipe for a happy life: Seek out the good in people, mix in genuine concern for them, and stir with a dash of humor. That's Bud Kolbrener's, too. It helped him make candy. He sold his St. Louis company for a sweet profit, taking early retirement at fifty-four. Bud looked forward to a life of travel, but then he got a call from a couple of longtime employees, Debbie and Marley Otto.

"They needed some help," Bud said. "They needed a place to work."

Marley's unemployment insurance had run out.

"I think I had knocked on everybody's door in St. Louis," Marley recalled.

So Kolbrener bought a little store and staffed it with all those former employees who couldn't find jobs. He gave up his own retirement so they would have paychecks until they reached theirs.

Debbie Otto was boxing chocolate at a conveyor belt when I asked her, "If you could create the perfect candy for Bud, what would it be?"

She thought for a moment, her hands still busy, then simply said, "A heart."

Her boss was pecking at a computer in his tiny office, working his eightieth hour that week.

I asked him why he had taken on his former employees' problems.

"Without their hard work, I would've never been the success that I am," Kolbrener answered. "I wanted to give back."

The Ottos had worked side by side, making chocolates, since they were teenagers. After they retired, Kolbrener began training their son-in-law Bryan.

"On a bad day," Bryan said, "he didn't even yell."

Is that the recipe for a successful boss? Kay Woods thought so. She'd been creating candy with Kolbrener for twenty-eight years.

"He listens to your ideas," she said, adjusting her hair net. "Works with you. Laughs and jokes and cuts up, but is still there to pass along what should be done."

After the new company was up and running, Kolbrener set forth an unexpected plan. "I didn't just start the business to give you jobs," he told his staff. "I want you to learn how to run the company."

Five years later, they were ready to take on that responsibility. The candy company was doing well—even in a recession, profits had dropped only 2 percent—so Bud made his workers a stunning offer: They could have Lake Forest Confections, for free. He was offering them his own version of a golden parachute.

"I hope they get rich," Kolbrener said. "One of the big, sad things about our society today is, we're only interested in short-term profits." He turned to watch Bryan mixing a batch of chocolate. "We need to invest in people."

Kolbrener never married, has no children of his own, but he was about to learn a tough "family" lesson.

Bryan knew he was capable of running the company. He had worked hard, under Kolbrener's guidance, to learn the business, but he agonized about the windfall. After days of discussions with his wife and two kids, he turned down his boss's gift. He came to him with tears in his eyes, saying he wanted his weekends back.

"Life is too short to just worry about money," Bryan told him. "You gotta worry about your happiness."

Kay Woods wouldn't take the company, either.

"I value my family life," she explained. She wanted more time with her six grandkids. The boss understood.

"It isn't just money," Kolbrener said. "If you get up in the morning with a smile on your face and look forward to going to do whatever you do, then that's what you should be doing."

Knowing how the story would end, would he do it again?

"In a second!" Kolbrener said. "If I thought I could help any of these people who helped me over the years, I would do that."

He later sold the business to a family who agreed to keep *his* family working—with the same pay. Bryan, the man who didn't want to be boss, began training his new boss, Dan Abel.

"I'm doing better," Abel admitted, "but I still eat too many mistakes." His dad and Bud Kolbrener had been friendly competitors since both men were in their twenties. Dan Sr. was a happy man that day.

"We picked up incredible employees and we hope they stay on for years and years with us."

What guarantee do they have that they won't be back in the same position they were the last time?

"We've been in business thirty years," Abel explained. "I've never had to lay anyone off."

Kolbrener overheard the conversation and afterward confided, "I'm there in the background if there are any problems."

He'd already built ten successful companies. At fifty-nine, he was willing to start another one to keep his former employees working.

Bud Kolbrener did not find his fairy-tale ending, but Bryan and Kay discovered something they thought was better: their own vision of happiness.

The beat cop's big grin made the little girl giggle. He placed his cap on her head and cocked it sideways.

"Where's Minnie?" he playfully asked.

Flipping through the pages in her storybook, she exclaimed, "There's Minnie!"

"Oh, you're a good little girl," said the heavyset cop. "Take my hand now." He led her to a circle of kids. For nine years, Patrolman Bill Sample had been stationed at Philadelphia Children's Hospital, a beat that took him among children who were very sick. They would talk, and he would listen as they told him of dreams they would not live to see fulfilled. Sample decided to buy some of those dreams. He and his wife, Helene, and a few of their friends sent one child on a trip to touch the snow, and another to see the redwood trees. The Samples' lives soon filled with thank-you letters, grateful for wishes that had come true.

"'Jody had never seen the ocean,'" Helene read from one of the notes. "'What a joy to see her eyes light up with awe and wonder.'" Helene's eyes welled over.

"Those letters always make me cry."

Sample wrapped his arms around his wife's shoulder.

"That little girl will keep a thousand memories in her head," he said. "She does more for our lives than we could possibly do for hers."

The patrolman was nearly always surrounded by kids. Doctors at Philadelphia Children's Hospital always referred their very sick patients to him.

"I guess that's the only fairy tale in the book," said Sample, turning the page for a tiny girl with deep brown eyes. Christina Wilson had leukemia. She sat in his lap that day, dreaming of a mouse named Minnie.

"I wanna kiss her," said Christina, leaning her face toward the page.

"You will," said Sample.

He asked eight friends to help. None of them had much money, so they sold raffle tickets, cookbooks, and cakes; ran bingo games, flea markets, and fashion shows. Soon they had enough to send the little girl to a land beyond her storybooks—to a land where Minnie Mouse actually lives. Christina and her entire family went to Disney World.

"I haven't ridden Dumbo for hours and hours and hours," said Christina, pointing to an amusement ride with gray elephants circling overhead. "Let's go again."

Her small hand was the only concession she offered her parents, who struggled to keep up.

"There's Donald!" she squealed. "Hi, Donald. Have you seen Minnie?"

Her question was lost in the babble of fifty kids surrounding the Disney characters. They all felt compelled to tell their life stories at once.

At first Christina did not notice the big round foot in high-heeled shoes that stepped behind her. Then she caught a glimpse of a thin black tail and whirled, shouting, "Minnie!"

Some moments in life develop slowly, like a sunrise. After all the anticipation and longing, after all the nights filled with dreams, Christina touched Minnie's cheek. Minnie didn't move; Christina said nothing. The little girl lifted her small, see-through purse to look at the picture of Minnie Mouse she had tucked inside.

The real Minnie, the one who stood before her, held out her arms. Christina did not hesitate. She jumped up and fell into the big white hands stretched to greet her.

They held each other for almost a full minute; then Christina leaned back to look at Minnie's face.

"Hi, Minnie," she said, her voice barely a whisper.

The mouse said nothing, but nudged Christina's cheek.

"Minnie, I love you."

Christina's parents glanced at each other. The crowd grew quiet. The little girl bent at the waist, as if bowing to the queen. Minnie knelt down. Her shiny black nose came close and, in a twinkling, Christina kissed it.

Bill Sample was back in Philadelphia, sitting alone at his dining-room table. Outside, the season's first snow fell silently. It was getting dark. He was still in uniform, just home from work. A stack of thank-you notes was piled next to a plate of leftover casserole on the table. The food grew colder as Sample read. To the parents, many of whose life savings had been drained by their children's illnesses, Bill Sample was a miracle worker.

"I just like helping kids," he murmured.

Christina Wilson got more than she dreamed. A couple of years after that meeting with Minnie, her leukemia vanished. In 1980, only one child in five survived cancer, but Christina grew up to be a healthy adult.

"I believe that trip changed everything," Christina told me the day she brought her own baby to show Bill. By then he and his friends had fulfilled more than thirty-five thousand dreams. Caring for others may be the closest we come to the face of God.

The heart is the ultimate muscle, the one that lifts the heaviest burdens. Those who meet Amy Wall notice her heart first. She was born deaf, the nerves in her ears incurably damaged.

"You can't rebuild the inner ear," her doctor, Matthew Bucko, explained. "That is like trying to put a new brain into someone."

Amy's brother and sister asked their mom if they could pray for a miracle. She was skeptical.

"Well, wouldn't *you* be?" asked Connie Wall. "I didn't want them to be disappointed, because this doesn't happen to people like us."

Connie suggested that, rather than asking God directly, her kids pray to a former neighborhood nun, Sister Katharine Drexel, who had spent her life taking care of children.

"We knew her as Katie," Amy confided. "I named my Barbie doll after her."

Shortly after praying to Sister Katharine, Amy's hearing suddenly became normal. The two-year-old began talking as if she'd never been deaf.

"The language came clear and straight through when she started talking," Dr. Bucko said, still amazed. "It was just like turning on a faucet."

A miracle?

Maybe. Thousands of people tell the Catholic Church they experience one every year, but only fifteen have been considered "miraculous" enough to be stored in the Vatican archives for further study. The church has been reviewing some of these cases for more than four hundred years, and most have yet to be named official miracles. Pope John Paul II took less than a decade to decide that what had happened to Amy had no earthly explanation.

Monsignor Alexander Palmieri told me that "two experts totally independent of the case—and they happened to both be Jewish—examined the medical records, and the initial testimony of her mother, and determined that they could find no scientific explanation."

Neither could five other top doctors—two were Hindu, one Muslim—who tested Amy and reviewed more than nine hundred pages of medical testimony.

Cardinal Anthony Bevilaqua was incredulous. "When you see such a complex and rigorous examination, the fact that the miracle goes through is a miracle in itself!"

Amy's miracle was not the first linked to the neighborhood nun from Bensalem Township, Pennsylvania. Rob Gutherman could not hear either until his parents prayed to Sister Katharine.

"They believed that she was in favor with God," he said, "and that she'd be able to help out."

Katharine Drexel did lead a life that reads like a Bible story. She was born shortly before the Civil War in Philadelphia and raised in mansions, but took a vow of poverty. She used to sew shoelaces back together rather than buy new ones, wore pencils down to the nub, gave away all of her twenty-million-dollar inheritance, and then gave herself away, too. At thirty-three she turned down a number of suitors to become a nun. Drexel spent the rest of her ninety-six years traveling to Indian reservations and poor neighborhoods, building missions and schools. She became the first American who was born a Catholic to be named a saint. You would think all those good deeds she did in life were what led to that historic moment, but Saint Katharine was in fact canonized for the cures of Amy Wall and Rob Gutherman long after her death.

The Catholic Church states that only those individuals to whom two officially sanctioned miracles can be attributed may be considered for sainthood.

Katharine's friend, Sister Louis Nestler, confided, "I wouldn't have picked her out as a saint, to tell the truth. She seemed very ordinary to me."

Sister Louis was 103 when I spoke with her. Back when she was born, people were rarely canonized as saints. Pope John Paul II named over four hundred, more than all the other popes combined. I asked Monsignor Palmieri why the pope was so diligent.

He chuckled when he replied, "So that you don't have to look far to find a saint. The saints are in our very midst."

History appoints its messengers in strange, secret places (like a Bethlehem stable) and only rarely do such messengers reveal themselves to us. Katharine Drexel told friends that we all are called to be saints, saying simply, "We all have to try."

I asked Connie Wall why she supposed the two miracles attributed to Saint Katharine were linked to hearing.

"We have to learn to listen," Connie replied. We were walking with Amy. "I hear a bird off in the distance, do you hear that?" Connie asked her. Amy cocked her head. "I hear it."

She was too young to recall the quicksilver moment she regained her hearing, but Amy could tell us the best thing she heard. Connie leaned down and, touching her daughter's face, asked, "What is your favorite sound in the whole wide world?" The little girl stopped twirling long enough to listen. Buses grumbled. A plane roared overhead. Children screamed with laughter on a nearby playground. Amy looked delighted.

"I like the sound of everything."

When we listen closely, we can hear the need around us. A baby's cry came across Dr. Leila Denmark's backyard. She stepped out onto her porch to listen, then dropped down into the mist that draped her vegetable garden. Dr. Denmark was a wisp of a woman, short and slight, who seemed to float when she walked, a ghostly illusion heightened by the white lab coat she wore. She stopped to watch some bees already at work on her flowers, framed in dappled light filtering through the pine trees. The child's cry got her moving again. Dr. Denmark walked to an old cabin at the edge of a clearing. She stepped onto its sagging porch, the floorboards worn smooth from a century of sliding shoes. It had once been a one-room schoolhouse tucked down a quiet country road near Lake Lanier, Georgia. On this day, it was filled with children again.

The physician poked her head through the doorway, glanced at the babies inside, and asked, "Who's the next little angel in my waiting room?"

Leila Denmark had opened her practice in 1928. Atlanta's first female pediatrician had been healing sick babies for seventy years.

"When I started out," she recalled, "we had no immunization."

She treated a set of triplets who eventually died of whooping cough. Their deaths so touched her that she went home and developed a vaccine to help prevent the disease, the same vaccine that now protects millions of youngsters worldwide. At one hundred, Leila Denmark was still giving lectures at medical conferences.

"I took an oath one time to look after sick people," she said earnestly. "They didn't tell me when to quit."

Most days the sun set before Dr. Denmark quit for the day—she often worked ten hours. Some of her patients' mothers drove to the clinic before dawn because Denmark took no appointments. They passed the time swapping medical advice the doctor had given their mothers and their mothers' mothers. No one complained about the wait.

"Not when you get advice that's going to cut down all the time that you'd waste at other doctors' offices," one new mom explained.

To save her patients money, Denmark worked without a nurse for all those years, did her own filing, and answered her own phone. Still, her time was not sliced too thin for thought. Each child received careful diagnosis and all the attention he needed to restore him to health.

"I used to spend a long hour with every new patient," Denmark recalled, her eyes twinkling. "I'd find out why he was sick and then I'd tell the mother how to keep him well. She didn't come back often. It messed up my practice."

That, she explained, was the reason she finally retired—at 103. Her life of leisure lasted more than a decade. Dr. Leila Denmark was 114 when she died, the oldest doctor who ever lived.

Growing up with a bad leg, I spent a lot of time with physicians like that. All of their medical offices had the same Norman Rockwell painting of a kindly country doctor taking the time to treat a little girl's doll. The medical miracles that helped me walk again after polio also took their toll on doctors' time, made them more remote, put them in high-rise offices where they could be close to their life-giving machines. We've got better medicine now, but perhaps something personal has been lost along the way. I found it again the day I stopped in Rushville, Illinois.

Rushville, built on government land and given to veterans, was a bonus for the boys who marched back from the War of 1812. Those who did not come back were memorialized with a statue on the courthouse square. Over the years, sixty-one names had been added to its nearby plaque. Those heroes seemed far away, yet in Rushville there was another sort of hero, one whom local citizens have learned to treasure.

"It's pain!" came the cry from an open window as I approached the town's medical clinic.

"Yeah, but where?" asked a calm voice.

"In my back!"

"Right here?"

"Ouch!"

Dr. Russell Dohner had been taking care of his neighbors for fifty-five years. In all that time, he had not had a vacation, or even a full day off. Dohner had suffered a heart attack a few years earlier, but got out of his hospital bed to make his rounds.

"Did your doctor scold you?" I asked him.

"I needed rest," he said wryly, "and I did get the rest. Instead of walking back and forth, I rode a cart."

Doc Dohner had two hobbies. He planted trees—thousands of them around Rushville—and he sometimes slipped away to go fishing on Thursday afternoons, although he was always near a phone and rarely took off his tie.

"People want a doctor who looks like a doctor," he said, casting his fishing line.

The morning we first shook hands, he had worked all night, performed two surgeries, prepped a broken arm, handled two emergency cases, checked on fifty patients, and had just delivered a baby. It was not yet ten-thirty.

Dohner was born on a nearby farm and was one of seven children. He worked to pay his own way through Northwestern University Medical School. His sister Clarice, who ran his office for many years, bought Dohner his first car so that he could make house calls. Five decades later he still did, seeing sixty patients a week in their homes, sixty more in senior citizen centers. Before the sun rose above the water tower that morning, people were waiting on park benches outside Dohner's office.

Of course, his fee had gone up since he came to town. Back in the 1950s he charged two bucks for a visit. Fifty years later it had risen to five dollars.

"In a mercenary world," a waiting patient told me, "this place is an oasis."

Five dollars was actually Doc's basic fee. He did charge for additional procedures.

"He gave me a shot, right there in the kitchen, and sent me the bill . . ."

"How much was the bill?" I asked.

"I think it was an extra three dollars. Shot and all."

Dohner never believed in tossing things away, which helped keep costs down. The only thing modern in his office was his medicine. Most of his nurses had been with him for nearly as long as his furniture. They'd received raises all along because Doc kept seeing more patients.

"In the beginning, the two dollars covered pretty well," he explained. "And now even the five-dollar fee really doesn't. I know this, so the income isn't as great as it was, but we at least are still getting by."

Not just getting by, though: Russell Dohner had won dozens of awards for the quality of his practice. When other area doctors went on vacation, he took care of their patients, too. Dohner looked after almost everyone. After five decades, he'd delivered more babies than there were people in Rushville. The first baby he brought into the world drove up with her granddaughter. They had traveled thirty miles for an office visit. The old woman chuckled as Doc nuzzled her grand-baby's nose.

"When your little girl gets carried to surgery by the doctor instead of one of the nurses," she said, "that girl will learn to trust him, too."

There are no statues and no plaques to Dohner's devotion, just the testimony of the health and well-being of his patients. He remembers them all, knows who needs help and who is sick, who has died and where they are buried.

While no one in Rushville is overlooked, a short time later I found myself in a forest filled with forgotten lives. Their final resting places were marked, not with names but with numbered stakes, unnoticed until Bud Merritt stumbled upon them. He found the first of six lost graveyards at what was once the largest mental hospital in America: Central State Hospital, Milledgeville, Georgia.

"These people were devalued all through their lives," Merritt said, scraping dirt from one of the stakes, "so it's really no surprise they were not afforded dignity after they died."

Merritt showed me the metal stakes on a lovely spring morning as we hiked through the pines. There were more bodies in those forgot-ten graves than the entire population of Milledgeville, at least twenty-five thousand. Across the nation there were many more—about one hundred thousand—who were hidden away in life, and who in death lost even their names.

"Why didn't families take the bodies of their loved ones home?" I asked.

"In many cases," Merritt said, "families had exhausted every resource they had just to care for the person in life."

After their loved one died, they left it up to the Central State staff to bury them. Numbers were used to mark the graves instead of names to preserve patient confidentiality, but lists of the dead are incomplete. Some of the 167 ledgers that identified the deceased are missing.

Merritt looked up from a crumbling accounting book in the mental hospital's museum. "I think that part of the irony is that there are doc-uments here that will tell you how many mules were bought in 1905, but when it comes to these thousands of human beings, it's almost impossible to find out where they were buried."

In the early 1900s Herbert Williams lost his wife, two kids, and his business—all at once. Depressed, he checked into Central State Hospital and died of heart disease six weeks later. His family had been searching for his grave ever since. One of them, Casey McClain, took a job at the mental hospital so she could look. "The groundskeepers pulled up the stakes," she said, "because it was too inconvenient to mow around them!"

Thousands of stakes were tossed aside. Grave locations were lost.

"Did you have any misgivings coming to work at Central State Hospital?" I asked.

"No," she replied.

"But this was the place that lost your great-grandfather."

"And this would be the place where I found him."

Merritt, who worked there, too, helped.

"Central State, at one time, had ten thousand acres," he said as we climbed to the next graveyard. It also had a population of thirteen thousand patients. Merritt couldn't explore such a large area, but figured the graves would not be on prime land. "If you could put a building on it," he reasoned, "or if you could raise a crop on it, it wouldn't have a cemetery."

That narrowed his search. Six months later Merritt found Papa Williams and opened a map to show Casey.

"Right under this dot is the exact location of your ancestor's grave."

That afternoon Merritt took me to a clearing in the forest. Up ahead Casey McClain was bent over a new headstone, tending her great-grandfather's final resting place. She touched his name and quietly said, "You'll never be forgotten." A field of iron stakes surrounded her.

"This is a battleground," McClain reflected. "Like the Tomb of the Unknowns in Arlington, there are hundreds of thousands of tombs of unknown men and women who didn't survive and didn't have a name, but now my great-granddad does."

·   ·   ·

Buried mysteries have a powerful hold on our lives. Stephen White tried for decades to save a small island for someone he'd never met.

Waves were slowly whittling it away. He told me the tale as we chopped through the water in a tiny boat on Maryland's Chesapeake Bay.

"Holland Island once held sixty houses," White pointed out as we approached what had once been a neighborhood that stretched two miles down the shore. "It was a bustling community that had sixty-eight kids in school until rising tides forced them to abandon the building. My home, built in 1888, is all that remains above water."

Working alone, he hauled hundred-pound stones across Chesapeake Bay to shore up the place. As we hopped across the rocks, I asked: "How much of your savings have you spent on this island?"

"All of it."

A spider was repairing his web in a broken window of White's old house, oblivious to the fact that some people would see this as a losing battle.

"Maybe they think I'm just a dreamer," White said, "but the world is built of dreams."

For a time he seemed to be holding his own against the wind and the tides, even though they sliced his island into three parts. Then a hurricane punched through, destroying nearly all he had done.

"Swept everything out!" White jabbed his hand at the bay. "It was like someone had come in with a big broom."

His house was blown open to the sea, one side was more window than wood, but the island still held him—powerfully.

Why? He showed me the one place that—for him—held an answer. Ospreys circled above a stand of trees. Hidden in the island's last bit of forest lay an overgrown cemetery. A broken gravestone marked the remains of thirteen-year-old Effie Wilson. White knelt to read the faded words chiseled in stone.

"She died in 1893." He wiped the inscription with his hand and read, "'Forget me not is all I ask. I could not ask for more.'"

White looked up. "I knew, when I read that, why I needed to save the island."

White never wavered, and week after week left his other home on the mainland to keep a promise to a little girl he'd never met.

"I vowed that I'd fight till I die to save this island." He paused to watch waves pounding the rocks he'd put down. "If I live long enough, I'll do it"—one rock at a time. He was seventy-five that day.

"Why did you start again after the hurricane?" I asked.

"You succeed when you get up one more time than you've fallen," he replied.

Two ospreys watched him from the nest they had built atop his backhoe. He lifted a heavy stone and plodded on, like a modern-day Job—persistent and patient—alone but not lonely.

"My word, no!" White pointed at the birds. "They're like my family! Look at that! Look at their grace!"

"Why don't you become discouraged?"

"I guess I can't," White said. "I still believe that what I'm doing is going to work."

Holland Island was now less than half the size it had been when White first went there as a boy. I asked him, "Do you think you can beat Mother Nature?"

"Yes," he replied confidently. "With me the island has a chance of surviving. Without me, it doesn't."

White dropped another stone to hold back the water and then squinted into the setting sun.

"'Forget me not' was all she asked."

The rising waters of Chesapeake Bay toppled his house in October 2010. Most of the remaining land on Holland Island is now marsh and at high tide is under water.

Perhaps the past is more precious to those who have more of it. I've collected a lot of memories, gathered from story to story over the course of forty years, but none is more indelible than the one I got from Fred Benson, the richest man on Block Island, Rhode Island, who lived his life in an unheated room in a home he didn't even own.

Benson was eight when a farmer named Gurd Milliken took him in, and eight decades later he still lived in that little space that Gurd had given him. Five generations of Millikens had grown up around him, and though they'd repeatedly asked Fred to move into a bedroom downstairs, where it was warm, he always refused.

A few years back Benson won $500,000 in the Rhode Island state lottery. He threw the biggest birthday party anyone can remember and invited all the children on the island. After the hot dogs and soda pop, Benson announced he'd pay the tuition of any child there who wanted to go to college. Benson always thought of his community first. He had been its police chief, fire chief, head of the rescue squad, baseball coach, teacher, and five-time president of the chamber of commerce. At fifty-four Benson went to college, got a degree in education, and taught high school shop when there was a housing shortage. The island's four builders all got their start with Fred.

He never married, never had children, but for eighty-two years, he dedicated himself to the people who lived on a sliver of land off the coast of Rhode Island. We were sitting together at sunset, watching waves crash against the rocky cliffs, waiting for the Block Island ferry to take me back to the mainland. Benson looked past the lighthouse lulled by the waves. At last he turned and told me a story.

"When I was a little boy, the farmers used to meet for dinner on Saturday night. Each one would boast about his kids. Gurd Milliken had eight sons and me. I sat way down at the end of a long table." Benson paused to look at a pelican on a pole.

"Gurd rose from his chair one night and pointed a long finger past all of his boys. He pointed right at me. 'You fellas wait and see what Fred Benson does. He'll be the best of 'em all.'"

Benson stopped talking for a long moment to stare at the sunset.

"I hope he knows how I turned out," he said quietly. Then, more intensely, he repeated, "I hope he knows how I turned out."

Fred Benson found a safe harbor and then showed others the way.

He left no record of what he accomplished, but it survives in the lives of others. Such devotion rarely gets noticed because its intention is not to attract headlines, but Benson's gentle kindness rippled out into the world and made it better. That eagerness to help others, especially in times of great need, is at the core of our American character. Go to any natural disaster, and you'll find an American working to rebuild. In Joplin, Missouri, a songbird sitting in a broken tree watched volunteers clearing debris beneath a bloodred sky. It began trilling at the dawn, flapping its wings above a half-smashed car that seemed to float on a sea of rubble. The worst tornado in sixty years had raced through its home, shattering nearly everything for thirteen miles, but the songbird didn't seem to notice. It was looking up, not down. The day's first sunbeams lit the car's interior, haloing a picture of the Madonna tilting against the dashboard. Her face was turned toward the window, looking out at what was left of eight thousand homes.

That robin in Joplin, Missouri, was a beautiful reminder of the promise of spring—rebirth, the victory of life over death. We've had so many weather disasters in this century that we tend to forget that promise, but it's always there, rising from the rubble. A walk through Kyle Maddy's house, not far from the songbird, reaffirmed that. The tornado had taken everything from him, except a water-stained wedding dress. Two months later, his fiancée, Kelsi Gulliford, finally had a place to wear it, when diners at the restaurant where Kyle worked helped make their wedding day possible.

His boss, Donnie Bennett, explained, "Some people would come in and buy a seven-dollar salad and leave one hundred dollars."

Since the disaster Maddy had been living in the basement of his brother's house with four dogs, two cats, and another couple. He put his wedding plans on hold, until his boss offered to cater the affair for free. Donnie Bennett knew what it was like to marry in the midst of great tragedy. He had met his wife, Karuleen, after insurgents in Iraq attacked her ride home from work at a store that served U.S. soldiers. They killed everyone in the van except Karuleen, who was shopping for bread. She found a note tacked to her front door when she got home.

Karuleen's eyes glazed with the memory. "The note said, 'If you come back to work for the American army, you're going to get killed. Not just you, but all your family, too.'"

The job of keeping Karuleen safe fell to Captain Donnie Bennett. His outpost, Camp Cuervo, was six miles south of Sadr City, one of the poorest and toughest neighborhoods in Baghdad. He persuaded the army to open a coffee shop on base and let Karuleen run it. The job came with a protected place to live.

"I only got to see my mother once a month," Karuleen said, but Bennett looked after her family, too, so she decided to learn English. The first words she spoke were "I love you." They married in Jordan a year later.

Bennett had served overseas for a decade, fighting in Kosovo and Baghdad. After his father died, he decided to return home to be closer to his mother. He retired from the army and took his bride to the safety of America's heartland.

The couple restored an old building and soon filled a fading block on Joplin's Main Street with laughter and good food. They named their new restaurant Caldone's to honor a friend who had been forced from the road in Iraq and shot in the back.

Captain Bennett won a Bronze Star in Baghdad for distinguished service in the face of "continuous and dangerous hardship," but the devastation caused by the tornadoes that struck his hometown was worse than any he'd seen during the war. A dozen houses exploded around their home, but the Bennetts' house still stood. Their business was spared, too.

Karuleen and Donnie Bennett survived because they'd decided to take their two boys, Kaden and Kolton, on the family's first vacation just two days before the storm hit. They rushed home to help their neighbors.

"When you see death on a scale that's typically not normal," Bennett explained, "your priorities change in life."

That's why they were determined to rebuild their community, one neighbor at a time. Bennett found Tina Lingard standing in disbelief amid the rubble of her medical weight-loss clinic.

"He drove up in his truck," she recalled, "pulled up as far as he could to the building, and said, 'What can I do?'"

The seventy-year-old needed a place to quickly reopen her clinic so she could support two daughters whose jobs were also victims of the tornado. Bennett gave her an office above his restaurant—for free.

"To me," Lingard said, "he had a halo hanging over his head."

The Bennetts believed their business had been spared to shelter those who were not as fortunate. Caldone's became a place where people came for rest and a kind word, to listen to live music and eat fine food. It cost them nothing, but they left four thousand dollars to help Kyle Maddy and two other employees who had lost much more.

"See those coins down there?" Bennett said, pointing to the restaurant's wooden floor. The change he had in his pocket when he left Iraq was scattered about. Donnie's four-year-old son, Kaden, bent to pick one up.

"Stuck," he said, looking up at his dad.

"I glued them to the floor," Bennett replied—a reminder to his family of their good fortune. Someday the Bennetts will tell their two boys about this incredible saga. What will they say when the children ask, "Are you sad that all this happened or happy to have been spared?"

"Not saddened or lucky," Bennett will tell them. "I feel blessed."

Blessed like the wedding dress that survived the tornado. Kyle Maddy beamed as his bride approached on their wedding day. Two little dots—water spots, practically invisible—were all that remained on her gown to remind them of that terrible night.

"It's great to see her wearing it," Kyle said, unable to stop smiling. He turned to gaze at his neighbors gathered under a quiet sky. "Couldn't be happier," Kyle told them, leaning down to kiss Kelsi.

Officiant LeeAnn Langan took their hands and raised them above their heads.

"Ladies and gentlemen, the loving couple, Mr. and Mrs. Kyle Maddy!"

Her announcement was greeted with a full-throated roar. On Kyle and Kelsi's big day, the city had something it needed as badly as rebuilding—a cry of joy and not pain.

Bliss can be powerful. I've seen it change lives. Its promise pulls us through the dark moments, beckoning us toward happiness. It fills our world with dreams, some of which are a bit older than others.

When John Suta was young, he wanted to be an opera singer. He taught himself five languages, studied the piano, and mastered the harmonica. But what made him happy could not pay the bills. So he raised two sons on a pipe fitter's wage and waited for his bliss.

One day after Suta retired, he saw an old French horn in a second-hand store. It reminded him of his dream deferred. Suta bought the tarnished instrument for seventy-five bucks and set out to make it as beautiful as the music he hoped to play. His retirement pay left little extra for lessons, so he found another way to learn the instrument.

He went to Roosevelt Middle School in Eugene, Oregon, and asked to join the beginners' band. Principal Dan Barron thought it was a great idea.

"What an opportunity for our students to see a grandpa starting at point one, learning how to play," he recalled. The kids thought it was funny until they heard the seventy-four-year-old's first sweet note.

"He's good," a kid with a clarinet admitted.

Suta held the note so long that the trombone player next to him lost his grip on the slide, letting it clatter into a music stand. Laughter tumbled down the risers. Principal Barron shook his head and marveled: "That man has lived with music all his life. He's lived it and he's watched it lived a whole bunch of times."

Suta started with the sixth-grade band. For three years he rarely missed a practice despite heart trouble and nerve damage that made it difficult for him to walk.

The morning we met, Suta shook my hand and said, "I'm a real eighth-grader now." Just another thirteen-year-old with sixty-four years' experience at being thirteen.

Bandleader Josh Mack, in his first teaching job, couldn't bring that kind of perspective to class, so he encouraged the kids to turn to the old guy with the French horn for guidance.

"You might make a mistake," Suta told them. "You might be disappointed, but you're doomed if you don't try."

The old pipe fitter connected those kids to the music he loved, becoming the band's heart in the process. Every day he toddled in to class wearing two shirts and a smile. The kids could not imagine the band without him. When he stumbled in the little house where he lived alone and fell on his French horn, crushing its bell, they were as devastated as he was.

"You know," Suta said, "it's not just a piece of metal; it's an extension of how I feel."

He took the horn to a music store for repairs, but after it was fixed, he realized that he could not pay the bill. Reluctantly, the store's owner hung a For Sale sign on the instrument and put it in his window.

The next day a grieving Suta walked past the store. His French horn was gone! Had it sold that quickly? He hurried into the repair shop. His horn, now polished and gleaming, was propped on the counter. The bill that dangled from it read "Paid in Full." On the back was a note from his fellow band members.

"These kids all chipped in," Suta said, his eyes shining as brightly as that polished old horn. "That's—that's what they did." He sighed. "What a gift, huh? What a bunch of nice kids"—to help an old pipe fitter, still hammering away at life and getting the best of it.

What was it about that creative mind that kept him working long after he set aside his tools? The urge to create never left him because the kids in that band wouldn't let him retire. They did what was needed to help him. That's part of the American character. Like the music they learned together, it echoes from one generation to the next. People are the sum of such moments—good and bad, seen and unseen.

Chapter Five

Stories Hiding in History's Shadow

You don't bounce around this country as long as I have without discovering fascinating stories that never made it into our history books. Such tales, however little known they may be, are important in bringing to light the choices that earlier Americans made when faced with difficulties like those we confront today. Knowledge of the past helps us plot a more informed course into the future. We all know what is and what ought to be, but few remember what was. It always involves more than we think we know.

World War II was a gathering storm when a young Jewish architect named Alfred Preis fled from the Nazis. The newlywed left his home in Vienna, Austria, determined to get as far away from war as possible. He and his wife chose Honolulu, Hawaii. Police picked them up in the first long breath after the Japanese bombed Pearl Harbor.

"We were brought down into a darkened city at a snake's pace," he recalled. "Dead silent. Interrupted by shots from time to time."

Preis thought they were needed as translators to help police interrogate suspected German spies, but instead he felt a sharp, cold object against his back.

"A bayonet," Preis said, wincing at the memory or it, "and a voice said, 'Go ahead.'"

He was pushed through a door into a darkened room, where he was surrounded by little glowing lights, all at different heights, which he soon realized were people sitting on bunk beds smoking cigarettes.

The former conductor of the Honolulu symphony was there, as were most of the chefs of Hawaii's great hotels. They were all U.S.

citizens from Germany, Italy, and Norway who had been rounded up as possible spies.

The next day Preis and the others were herded onto Sand Island.

"No floors," recalled Preis. "Cots without mattresses. Mud on the ground. When we lay on the cots, they started to sink and kept on sinking."

Preis caught a glimpse of his wife, who was being held with other women behind a chain-link fence on the other side of the island.

"The guards heard me trying to yell to her," Preis said with tears in his eyes. "They took my wedding ring away. They told me they didn't want me to use it to bribe someone for a chance to be with her."

To keep mentally active, prisoners formed a university on Sand Island. This was no ordinary group. One of them knew—by heart—nine of Anton Bruckner's symphonies, and could hum and analyze each one. Another prisoner, a violinist from Germany, added to their knowledge. Others taught city planning and anatomy, and during the blackouts the group studied astronomy.

The camp eventually became so crowded that some of its inmates were transferred to detention centers on the mainland. When they pointed out that few other Italian Americans or Austrian Americans were being held, they were released. But soldiers met them at the gate, transported them back to Hawaii, and locked them up again. During the war, the islands were under military rule, so it was all perfectly legal.

"From Sand Island, I could see my house," Preis said. "By the time I was released, months later, I had lost it because the mortgage went unpaid."

Alfred Preis stayed in Hawaii after the war, even though the architect could only find work digging ditches. Eventually, he was hired to design something special. Twenty years later, not far from his island prison, Preis offered a simple tribute to those who fell at Pearl Harbor. You might know his work: He is the architect who designed the USS *Arizona* Memorial.

We puttered toward his masterpiece one morning on a harbor boat filled with sailors who wanted to reenlist at one of the navy's most sacred spots. The aging architect sat in the bow, gazing at his creation as we chopped through the surf. He was dapperly dressed—blue sports coat, white slacks, and an ascot. Seabirds soared and dipped, seeming to lead the way. Off to the east, dawn's first light framed the monument in a halo of pink.

"Do you know who that man is?" I asked the sailors, pointing at the figure hunched in the bow of the boat. No one did. "That's his inspiration," I told them, motioning toward the memorial. Our skiff cut across another craft's wake, sending a spray of salt water onto Preis's coat. He was lost in thought and didn't seem to notice. As we passed Sand Island, where he had been detained during the war, I said, "Let me tell you his story . . ."

When we docked at the *Arizona* Memorial, Preis waited for the sailors to climb the ladder first, but instead, they lined up to shake his hand. Their commander came last and, saluting Preis, asked, "Did anyone in government ever apologize for what we did to you?"

"No," said Preis, his eyes shifting away at a question that clearly made him uncomfortable.

The commander gently took Preis's hand and helped the old man up the ladder. At the top, the architect walked away from the sailors and went to watch the oil bubbles that still escape from the sunken ship beneath the memorial. The sailors followed, and their commander held out his hand once again.

"On behalf of the United States Navy," he said, "I apologize." Another voice echoed his: "I apologize." Then another, until a chorus of apologies cascaded around Preis, who stood stunned and speechless. There is no word in the dictionary for what happened to him. They're going to have to make one up. I hope it's easy to spell, because people are going to try to explain it for a long time.

Another architect was scrambling through dust and rubble the day America was attacked again, this time on 9/11. Joe Fuchida watched the planes crash into the World Trade Center from his office window in New York City. His father had been at Pearl Harbor and spent the rest of his life trying to blunt the kind of animosity that would lead to another such tragedy. Mitsuo Fuchida was the pilot who led the Japanese attack.

Memory is too fragile a thread from which to hang history. Most of us no longer recall or have ever even learned what America did in retaliation for the destruction at Pearl Harbor, but it changed our world as surely as the events of 9/11. Eighty Americans volunteered to do the unthinkable: to set out on a secret mission to bomb Japan and give America its first victory of World War II, knowing that their planes didn't have enough fuel to return safely. They would have to ditch behind enemy lines.

"I was too big a coward to back out," Jake Deshazer said. He was nearing ninety, one of the few who could still tell the story firsthand.

On April 18, 1942, Deshazer was an army corporal, standing on the deck of the aircraft carrier *Hornet,* desperately trying to keep his bomber from sliding into the sea.

"A big wave came up," Deshazer said. "The front end of that airplane went way up in the air, and the tail went down with nothing to stop it."

Sailors came running with ropes. One of them, standing next to Deshazer, backed into a spinning propeller and lost an arm.

"He looked up at me and said, 'Give 'em hell for me.'"

No one had ever launched a bomber in so short a distance—450 feet.

"My pilot, Bill Farrell, said, 'Jake, can you row a boat?'"

The planes soared over Japan, flying close to the ground. Deshazer, a bombardier, dropped his load near Nagoya, then the plane headed toward the coast of Asia. The bomber flew until it ran out of fuel. Then, one by one, the crew bailed out. Deshazer landed in a Chinese graveyard in Japanese-held territory. He and seven other flyers were captured, condemned as war criminals, and sentenced to die.

Three prisoners were killed, but Deshazer was spared.

"I don't know why I wasn't executed," he said.

Instead Deshazer spent thirty-seven months in solitary confinement, most of it sitting in a five-by-nine-foot cell, with only a small window above him. In the gloom of that pit, he was given a Bible and read a line that changed his life:

"Love your enemy . . ."

He wondered, *Boy, Jesus doesn't expect you to love those real mean ones, does he?*

Deshazer did more than pray for them. After the war, he astounded his former comrades by going back to Japan as a minister. He remained there for thirty years and started twenty-three churches, including one in Nagoya, the city he had bombed. Even after so much time had passed, the idea still seemed incredible to him, but as he insisted, "My boss, God, said, 'You bombed 'em. Now try to save them.'"

Deshazer went to Tokyo to testify in support of some of the Japanese accused of war crimes. A fellow dressed like a farmer approached him while he was waiting on the station platform for a train to take him home.

"Are you that crazy guy who built a church in the city you bombed?" the man asked.

"Yes," Deshazer admitted.

"I'd like to talk to you about that church," the man said. "I'm the pilot who led the attack on Pearl Harbor, Mitsuo Fuchida. Your story of forgiveness has moved me."

Later Fuchida would say, "I was very lost after the war, but Jake Deshazer's story inspired me to get the Bible." He was later baptized in his old enemy's church, and the two men spent the rest of their lives trying to weed out the hatred that infests the human heart and causes war.

We all make deals with our hearts from time to time, redoubling our efforts when others drop away. Sensible voices tell us to stop, but we don't. The Abele brothers, John, Bruce, and Brad, spent a lifetime searching for their father's submarine, long after the U.S. Navy gave up and historians closed the book on one of World War II's biggest mysteries.

Their dad, Jim Abele, commanded the *Grunion,* a navy sub that disappeared off the coast of Alaska in 1942. Military planes crisscrossed its last known location but never found where it sank. The brothers from suburban Boston kept looking, a quest that cost them a bundle.

"If this were an official navy project," John Abele said, "I would guess that the taxpayers would be paying about ten times what we're paying."

"How much have you spent?" I asked.

He waved off the question with a flip of his hand. "That's a secret." In 2006 they began crisscrossing the Bering Sea, probing its depths with sonar. The brothers caught a break when a Japanese historian found a lost account of the *Grunion*'s last battle, which mentioned a confrontation between a cargo ship and the sub. The freighter's crew spotted two torpedoes bubbling toward them, the first of which missed; but the second exploded and stopped the engine. Terrified, the Japanese seamen turned a deck gun on the sub, firing eighty-four times as it began to surface.

"There was a dull 'thud' noise and a little spout. Presumably oil, we don't know," John said. Their dad's sub slid into history's shadows, and seventy men were never heard from again.

The sea holds many mysteries, but few detectives were as dogged as the Abeles. In 2007 the brothers circled close to the site of the sunken sub. Twelve miles north of Kiska, Alaska, at the western tip of the Aleutian Islands, Kale Garcia, the captain of their search boat, looked up from the sonar screen and said, "We've passed over the wreckage several times. It's down there."

Somewhere in the murky darkness a mile beneath the boat was their father's grave. The Abeles lowered a remote-controlled camera to probe the side of an underwater volcano. Half a mile down they found "skid" marks in the deep darkness and followed them. Lights on their undersea cameras scattered brightly colored fish.

Suddenly, John shouted, "To the left!"

The underwater camera swung left, spooking a red jellyfish.

"Oh, yeah!" John gasped. "Wow!"

There, in front of them, was an open hatch, which held a big clue.

John explained, "The sub's crew could not have opened that hatch if there were more than a foot of water over it. That means the sub had to be on the surface when it sank"—just as the Japanese freighter captain had reported. "The account of the Japanese freighter captain was accurate."

They had solved the mystery of what happened to the *Grunion*. It sank at a steep angle, perhaps forty-five degrees, and then ski-jumped off an underwater volcano, breaking its bow. The sub then slid down a steep slope, gouging a trail still visible after sixty-five years. "It looks like a road in the woods," John said excitedly. "See those two tracks?"

Everyone on board the boat huddled around the video screen.

"What's that?" Captain Garcia gasped.

A huge crab sat atop the sub's crumpled conning tower. Scattered all around were bits and pieces of the boat. The remote-controlled camera slid down the hatch but found no bodies inside.

"At that depth," John explained, "even bones would dissolve."

But not memories.

The last time the Abeles saw their father was at Sunday dinner at his sub base in Groton, Connecticut. Wartime secrecy prevented him from telling them he was leaving. He slipped away without a kiss or a wave.

Bruce Abele told me, "We only knew he had gone to sea when a neighbor called and said she had seen the sub leave."

Four months after his departure their mother got a telegram: Commander Abele was missing. A letter with a Navy Cross enclosed arrived next, citing him for valor. It came with a check, but she sent it back. She put her sons to work making wooden puzzles for elementary schoolchildren while she taught violin. Mrs. Abele never remarried. The boys never forgot their father.

"How did you finally grieve for him?" I asked Bruce.

He thought a moment and then answered in a voice as full of pain as that of any kid who has lost a father. "I used to shoot baskets in the backyard. This is hard to say, but if I could make five at a time, I'd say, 'Jim's coming back!'" He choked up. "But he never did . . ."

"Bless their hearts," Caroline Surofchek said, squeezing my hand. We were sitting together at a memorial service a few years later for the families of the men who went down with the sub. At ninety-one she was the only wife still living.

"Those Abele boys weren't nothing but little kids when they lost their dad. Thanks to them I've outlived the mystery of what happened to my Steve."

Steven Surofchek was just sixteen, a big boy who lied about his age when he joined the navy. A dozen years later he disappeared with the *Grunion*. His wife, Caroline, never moved so that he could find her if he ever came home. She looked for him every day.

"I'm still watching," she said.

Even now, knowing what happened.

"I'm still watching," she repeated, and showed me a picture of Steve.

"Did you fall in love with his wavy hair or his pretty eyes?" I wondered.

Caroline Surofchek laughed. "I guess I fell in love with all of him."

Besides, the man could cook. He served seventy men on a sub for a dozen years.

"Did he do the cooking at home, too?" I asked.

"Lots of it," she chuckled. "The only thing is, he made too much."

Donna Frances's dad was a newlywed the day he shipped out on the *Grunion*. Don Welch died without ever meeting his only child.

"In one letter," she said, "he asked, 'Whoever said, "Parting is such sweet sorrow"? I'd like to ask that person, What's so sweet about it?' "

"Somebody in the world had to know where they were," Mary Bentz insisted. Her uncle Carmine was aboard the sub. "Those sailors are alive to us. Maybe that sounds quirky, but they are alive in our memories."

While the brothers searched for the sub, the crewmen's relatives looked for one another. The boys' mom, Kay Abele, had kept them together for years, writing notes to the other sixty-nine families, week after week, until she died. Then they drifted apart, losing track of one another. The last relative was located the morning the *Grunion* was found.

"I love you," murmured Caroline, hugging John Abele's neck. Love is the thread that pulled the *Grunion* families back together one last time to hear the navy read the names that surfaced from the sea.

"Ship's Cook, First Class, Steven Surofchek . . ."

A ship's bell tolled as Caroline stepped out of her wheelchair and marched to the deck of a submarine similar to the *Grunion*.

"I feel like this is finally good-bye," she said softly. Caroline kissed the flower she held. A bugler began to play "Taps." She tossed the white rose into the water where it joined seventy others and slowly drifted off.

Memories frozen in time still have the power to move. At a moment like this, years do not flow back into the past, but gather invisibly around us. These men of the *Grunion* were no longer a list of long-forgotten names, thanks to the three little boys who grew old looking for their father. They found the man who had never left their minds.

The keys to history's treasures are often discovered in unexpected places. One of them turned up in a tiny Kansas town, unlocking a story half a world away.

Megan Felt snapped on a light in a darkened room and pulled a letter from a drawer. Megan and her friends were putting together a play for their Uniontown High School history club and had found a brief mention of a woman who saved children from the Nazi death camps during World War II. They wrote Irena Sendler a letter. Several weeks later an envelope arrived from Poland. Megan sliced it open and slid out Mrs. Sendler's tightly scrawled note.

"My dear and beloved girls close to my heart," she read. "My parents taught me that if someone is drowning, one needs to give a helping hand and rescue them."

In 1940 the Nazis walled off a neighborhood near Irena's home in Warsaw and pressed almost half a million people into an area the size of New York City's Central Park, with not enough food to keep them alive. Five thousand died each month. Sendler, a public health service nurse, warned the German guards that their health was at risk, too. Barriers and guns might keep her Jewish neighbors trapped inside the Warsaw ghetto, but not their diseases. The German commander gave her permission to treat their illnesses, but she did much more: Mrs. Sendler devised a daring plan to save the ghetto's children.

"I lost no time reflecting," she wrote the Kansas teenagers. "I knew in my heart that I had to come to their rescue."

But how could a woman less than five feet tall fight an army? Mrs. Sendler returned to the guard post with a bulging medical bag and a German shepherd dog by her side.

"Papers!" shouted the sentry.

When she reached into her satchel, it seemed to squeak. "Oh no!" Sendler gasped. Her hand had disturbed the sedated baby hidden inside. As the guard leaned over to see what was making the noise, Sendler stomped on her dog's foot.

"Nurse, control that beast!" the sentry cried, jumping back from the howling animal. She hustled past him and disappeared into the darkness. Sendler took the baby girl to a Catholic family who had agreed to raise her as their own, but first she wrote the girl's old and new identity on a cigarette paper and put it in a glass jar, vowing to return the child to her Jewish parents after the war.

Back she went the next day for more babies, carrying them out in gunnysacks. She led their older brothers and sisters though sewers to safety. Many of the kids were placed with Catholic mothers who had tried to become pregnant but could not. They were willing to raise the Jewish children at great personal risk. If the Nazis found them sheltering these youngsters, they could be killed, but Sendler's glass jar was stuffed with thousands of names. She buried it beneath an apple tree in her backyard, across the street from the German barracks.

Eventually, the baby carrier was betrayed.

She was arrested, both her feet and legs were broken, and she was all but murdered; still, she never revealed where she'd taken the children. At war's end she quietly dug up the jar and—true to her word— began returning them to surviving relatives.

Irena Sendler saved twenty-five hundred children from the Nazi death camps. She did not reveal the full extent of her story until sixty years later, when four Kansas teenagers asked her why she'd risked her life. Sendler wrote them a series of letters to help them write their history play.

The girls from Uniontown went to Poland to meet her. She lived in a small apartment, looked after by one of the children Sendler had carried out of the Warsaw ghetto in a carpenter's box. White hair haloed her face. The old woman hugged each of the teenagers and settled into a comfortable chair to tell them the rest of the account.

A number of the children she saved could not be returned to their birth parents, who had been murdered by the Nazis, so Catholic couples continued to raise those kids as their own. Some never knew who their real parents were until later in life, when they came to Sendler and asked her about them.

She had a question, in turn, for the girls from Kansas: "Why do you care about all this, when you come from a place that doesn't have a Jewish family for miles and miles and miles?"

Jessica Ripper replied: "Race, religion, creed—it doesn't matter to us. What matters is that good can triumph over evil."

"I could only follow the need of my heart," Sendler told them, and then offered a bit of advice.

"Become like the farmers back home in Kansas," she said. "Don't sow seeds for food. Sow seeds for good. Try to make the circle of good around you grow bigger and bigger every day."

They left her staring out the window, watching them leave. She raised her hand and touched the glass. They would carry that image home with them, the radiant face of a tiny woman who had stood up to history's worst.

The curtain never came down on that play, not even after they graduated, got jobs, and married.

"We are trying to repair the world," Megan said, "by telling her story."

Norm Conard, their high school history teacher, has watched them perform in hundreds of schools.

"They're reaching over the walls of bias and prejudice that adults could never attempt to reach over," he said—and telling the tale of a ninety-seven-year-old woman that might have been lost forever, had it not been for some small-town kids intent on rescuing the rescuer's history.

People often ask me how I find the wonderful stories I feature. I get tips, of course, but that's not enough: I have to listen closely. Almost everyone has something significant to say. I overheard this exchange in

Walmart between two older men, one a customer and the other a greeter offering him assistance:

"Can I help you?"

"Sorry," said the customer, pulling out a cart. "I don't hear so well." He pointed at his ear. "I flew combat during the war."

"I served, too," said the greeter. Carl Grossman, an affable little guy, played his trump card in this game of "Me, too." He leaned in, touching the customer's arm. "Eight of us brothers were in uniform during World War II. Six saw combat."

His kid brother Mickey worked building the ship on which he later served and helped shoot down the Japanese suicide planes that tried to blow it out of the water.

His brother Hy was an officer in the Army Air Corps. Hy's roommate was Clark Gable. Brother Shimmy liberated an American POW camp in Germany and found a friend who lived down the street in their Pittsburgh neighborhood. A German grenade all but blew off his brother Eyo's right arm. Doctors decided they would have to amputate.

"Eyo said, 'I play piano. I love to play piano. If you take that arm away from me, I might as well die.'" Eyo came home, his arm partially paralyzed, but performed until his death at eighty-six.

And Carl? "I crash-landed two planes evacuating the wounded. I had a tooth knocked out. One tooth. That's all." He'd bumped it on a box of hand grenades. "Man, I got off that plane, I kissed the ground!"

Grossman served as a medic in the Pacific, fighting in nineteen battles and saving hundreds of lives. All eight Grossman brothers made it back alive.

Grossman shrugged. "We were blessed. Blessed."

Even the brothers who were too old to go to war served their country. One was a cop and the other worked on a top-secret project he said looked like a large metal lightbulb. After the last battle he was given an award for helping create the first atomic bomb.

Carl Grossman thought all his wartime medical experience would get him into medical school, but without a college degree he didn't have the heart to fight for admission. He followed his brother, Saul, into the car business. He sold Chevys in Detroit for fifty-one years but then fell on hard times, like the auto industry itself.

"I don't have much money, but I'm still blessed with a wife of fifty-eight years."

To save cash, Freda Grossman made the lunch Carl took to Walmart. His commute was thirty-five miles a day. I listened to all this in jaw-dropping wonder. The customer shook Carl's hand, started to leave, and then turned back. There would be one more surprise today.

"I'll be eighty-three soon," he told the greeter.

Grossman good-naturedly tapped the customer's shoulder, "Oh, you're a teenager. I'll be ninety."

Ninety. All his brothers were gone. Carl Grossman was the last of the Fighting Grossmans, still struggling with the American Dream.

"Did you ever think you'd be punching a time clock at ninety?" I asked.

"Never! Never!" Grossman said. "But it doesn't bother me. I'm glad to work. It's good for my mind."

He turned to joke with an old friend who had come into the store, grabbing the guy's tie and pretending to blow his nose in it. Old friend, old joke, but still good for a laugh.

"What happened to the golden years?" I asked as the yucks faded.

Carl Grossman chuckled, "They got tarnished." But he's still polishing them with his smile.

Every veteran carries in his mind the faces of comrades who did not return from war. Roby Albouy and I were walking through the Aspen meadows of Colorado one summer day when he pulled a yellowing snapshot from his pocket and showed me the ones he can't forget.

"I helped these fellows escape from the Germans when I was with the French," he recalled. "They were the downed crew of an American bomber. The Nazis were chasing them. That was thirty-nine years ago today."

He spent just forty-three days with them, yet there was something so vivid about their time together that no marriage, no job, carried the intense colors of those moments on life's edge.

July 19, 1944, was to have been their last mission, their forty-fourth flight. They were known as a hard-luck crew, but they had a passenger that day. Photographer Mike Beesick requested that flight because somehow, this crew always came back.

Over Munich, Germany, their big B-24 was riddled with flack. They edged their way through the Alps, looking for Switzerland, but lost power and searched desperately among the tall peaks for a flat place to land. Finding none, the crew decided to bail out.

It was tail gunner Ted Turback's twenty-third birthday.

"I was making all sorts of promises to God on the way down," he said. "My parachute opened up inside the plane. I stood there cradling an armful of white. I had never parachuted before."

Only one man on the crew ever had.

"I always wondered if I could," Turback said, pointing to the ground, "but it's easy to jump out when you know where the airplane is going."

Bombardier Joe Bossick said a Hail Mary after his chute opened. The silk pulled him from the dying plane. He landed just twelve hundred feet from the crash site, halfway between two German garrisons in occupied France. A farmer led him to safety.

"He picked me up in his arms," Bossick said, "and carried me while I regained my breath."

Pilot Ken Sorgenfree had a smashed face, and Ray Swizinski twisted his ankle, but the rest were unhurt. The French whisked them away before the German soldiers arrived. The Nazis grabbed a young doctor and asked where the fliers had gone. He refused to tell them and was killed.

The war changed for those airmen the moment they bailed out of their crippled plane.

"For the first time, we saw the results of war up close," Bossick said. "It was devastating."

French Resistance fighters took the Americans to a secret hospital where they cared for their own wounded. It didn't stay secret for long, however, and German soldiers soon attacked. The bomber crew threw injured Frenchmen on their backs and scrambled up a mountain. The rescued became the rescuers.

"The plan had been to send us to Switzerland," Paul Peterson said, "but we just said, 'No more.' We needed to help them escape, too."

They did—all but one.

"We made a place for him in the rocks," Noel Monod said. "It was really like digging a grave, but the French soldier was still alive. Barely. We just lowered him in there and patted a little snow so he could lick something. His lips were parched. He had a high temperature. Airman Paul Peterson acted as the minister. We were all around. The moon had just come out. Paul said farewell to him. Then he said to me that he wanted to be alone with the man for a moment. I wanted to give that French soldier my revolver, but Paul said, 'No, keep it. Christ did not believe in suicide.'"

During the war downed fliers and Resistance fighters seldom exchanged names. It was safer that way. Allies were often anonymous. But forty years after that American bomber crew flew through a hurricane of smoke and steel, those former French Resistance fighters found them again. At a reunion in Bismarck, North Dakota, Paul Peterson was still stung by the pain that the man they left in the rocks could no longer feel. Noel Monod handed him a note. Paul unfolded the note and read three words in English: "I am alive." The Frenchman Paul thought was dead had survived. Another wounded Resistance fighter found him after the German soldiers had given up the chase. The two stumbled out onto a glacier. One fleeing figure could barely walk; the other could hardly see. Together, they escaped.

On another icy field, far from war, a lone figure faced the wind. His white hair filled with blowing snow. Motts Tonelli still had the loping swagger of a seasoned athlete, as he crunched across the out-of-season football field, heading for the end zone.

His happiest memories were of events that had take place there. In 1937 Tonelli was a fullback at Notre Dame University, a player with dazzling speed. The quarterback handed him the ball with two minutes left in a game against their archrival, the University of Southern California. Tonelli juked past several defenders and raced for the goal line.

Five, ten, twenty yards.

Everything in the stadium seemed too slow for him. Defenders fell away, and Tonelli scrambled on.

Thirty, forty, fifty yards.

Fans were on their feet, doing what seemed impossible—screaming and holding their breath at the same time. The fullback blazed past leaping cheerleaders in blue and gold.

Sixty, seventy yards.

Finally a Trojans defensive back managed to run him down at the thirteen-yard line. Two plays later Tonelli high-stepped over the goal line, dragging a defender into the end zone.

"Touchdown!" screamed the radio announcer in the press box high above the field. Final score: Notre Dame, 13; Southern Cal, 6.

Tonelli knelt on the turf and listened to the cheers for his victory. He could still hear them on that frosty morning years later. The winter of life stirs memories, but he was not reliving the glory of that moment. Standing in the end zone with me, he turned his face to the crystals drifting out of the clouds and recalled a kindness shining in a dark place.

After graduation Tonelli enlisted in the New Mexico National Guard and shipped out to the Philippines to play with an army basketball team. The day after Pearl Harbor, he traded his ball for a gun. The Japanese attacked Manila, too.

"We knew we couldn't win," Tonelli recalled. "We didn't have much ammunition, and the ammunition we did have was old and many didn't fire. There were duds."

Only two grenades in twenty-five exploded. Sergeant Tonelli fought hard, but eventually gave up, along with twelve thousand other GIs, the largest single surrender in American history. Japanese soldiers forced them to walk seventy miles to a POW camp. Tonelli was in good shape, but many of the U.S. soldiers had been wounded and living on short rations for months. For them, it was a death march. Ten thousand American and Philippine soldiers died.

"You'd see them get shot," Tonelli said, dusting snow from his letter jacket. His gaze turned inward. "You'd see them get killed."

Some Japanese guards stabbed prisoners who were too weak to crawl. Others took anything of value they saw. One demanded Tonelli's class ring.

"He kept pointing at it," Tonelli said with a fierce new light in his eye. "I said, 'No, I'm not going to give it to you.'"

The guard pressed his bayonet into Tonelli's neck, forcing a life-and-death battle of wills. Soldiers marching nearby yelled, "Give it to him, Sergeant! He'll slice you sure." Tonelli hesitated a moment longer. Blood trickled down his neck as the guard pushed the tip of his bayonet deeper. Slowly, Tonelli slipped the ring from his finger and dropped it into the guard's hand. The Japanese soldier grunted and let him live.

The Bataan Death March was not known for any acts of kindness, but there was at least one because of that last-minute run Tonelli made in Notre Dame Stadium. It was a moment one University of Southern California student from Japan would never forget. Five years after that game, plodding along a narrow road, the student, now a Japanese army officer, recognized Tonelli.

"You beat my team!" he shouted.

"What?" Tonelli sputtered.

"When USC played the Irish in football, I was there," the officer said. "You scored the winning touchdown and destroyed our hope of victory."

Oh, boy, Tonelli thought. *This guy's going to kill me.*

But his enemy did something unexpected.

"You are a samurai," he said, in tones of respect.

Tonelli was stunned and speechless.

"Did one of my men take something from you?" the officer asked.

"Yes," Tonelli answered. "A soldier took my class ring."

The officer reached in his pocket and pulled out a circle of gold with a black onyx inset.

"Is this it?"

"Yes," Tonelli gasped, as his enemy grasped his hand and pressed the ring into his palm.

"The lieutenant said, 'Put this ring where my soldiers won't find it.' I swallowed it several times on that long march," Tonelli said. "Want to see it? It's been washed."

That Japanese officer did something special because he remembered one glorious run. Tonelli got back a piece of his life.

"When you talk about war," Tonelli said, "you're talking about life. I never saw him again, but he gave me an extraordinary gift."

It helped Tonelli do something most of his buddies did not: He survived the ordeal—with a ring and the memory of a single act of kindness.

Half a world away, Xiamara Mena stood among an army of soldiers who did not make it home. She threaded her way through their tombstones, beginning the long, slow business of learning how to live alone.

Her son, Andy Anderson, was buried in Arlington Cemetery. He died fighting in Iraq.

"The first year was pretty hard." Mena sighed, wiping away a tear. There was something more that she did not tell me: The Army Reserve was sending Andy's twin brothers, Rafael and Randall, to Afghanistan.

Xiamara Mena stood apart from the other mothers who had come to visit their sons' graves that day. Beth Belle kissed a nearby headstone and then hugged it. Her embrace said silently what could not be put into words.

Belle was planning her boy's coming-home party from Afghanistan when Lance Corporal Nicholas Kirven was killed on Mother's Day. He so loved the marines that Beth and her husband allowed him to enlist at seventeen.

"He was always a peacemaker," Belle pointed out—the kind of kid who, when he touched someone's life, they shined. In Afghanistan the infantry rifleman passed out Beanie Babies and rebuilt houses before he died chasing insurgents into a cave. That was three and a half years earlier.

"The first thing any new mother here at Arlington Cemetery asks is, 'Does it get better?'" Beth paused, lost in thought. "I have to tell them no. Time does not heal all wounds. It just gives you a few more seconds before the loss begins again each day."

Paula Davis rose from her son's grave and joined Mena and Belle. She, too, understood the public smiles and private tears of a mother who has lost a child. A mortar shell took her only son, Army Private First Class Justin Davis. She left a new picture of him at his grave every week, even though technically that's not allowed.

"I want people to realize that this is a human being. It's not just a number. It's not just a name." She paused and looked down. She took a deep breath, then said fervently, "I want them to see the person who lies here."

Davis's heroes were God, Dr. Martin Luther King Jr., and Bruce Lee. He loved kung fu movies, and even shot one of his own—on the front lines in Afghanistan. He said he wanted to be an actor.

A quiet scene played out near these three women. The men of Marine Lance Corporal Eric Herzberg's fire team were gathered with his mother at his grave. They were sent back to Iraq the day before his memorial service. On the second anniversary of his death, the buddies gathered at home to finally say good-bye.

"When we are weary and in need of strength," Eric's mom recited a prayer. "We remember them," the marines responded. Another mother, Gina Barnhurst, choked back a sob and read passionately, "They are a part of us."

Her son's story ended at age twenty. Two years later, Barnhurst still sat by his grave and wrote letters to her son. They felt like arrows to her heart.

"How do we keep having birthdays and Thanksgivings and Christmases without being able to hug you?" Her voice caught. The paper in her hand shook. "How do we keep living our lives without you?"

Barnhurst hung twenty-two stars in a tree near Eric's headstone to mark what would have been his twenty-second birthday.

"You have this emptiness you cannot fill," she said, "and I just felt like I had to be where he is."

"What did you say to your son the last time you talked?" I asked.

"Oh, that's a hard one." She swallowed with difficulty. "He said,

'Mom, don't worry about me.' He gave me this big smile that he always had and he hugged me, then went off to help load a truck. They always asked for volunteers, and he was always the first one to volunteer. You want to have a longer conversation, but you don't get a chance to do that."

"What would you have said?"

"I want to say, one more time, how proud of him I am. And how much I love him. And miss him. And what a deep hole there is in our lives."

Eric Barnhurst died on October 21, 2006, while on patrol in Iraq. A sniper shot him through the neck. He was buried, like the others, in Section 60. Death there is too fresh for the simple stones that mark the resting place. People leave all sorts of mementoes. One mother, who does not live near the cemetery, asked Beth to take twenty-six cents to her son's grave.

"Since he was a little boy, she never ended a letter without 'a quarter for a call, a penny for your thoughts and all your momma's love,'" Beth sighed.

The mothers don't talk about coming to the graves. They simply visit their sons, watching over them, just as they did on playgrounds long ago. Pride, anger, and grief flash across Gina Barnhurst's face.

"You feel like you should've just jumped across the ocean and been there to hold them that last minute."

Paula Davis reached out and squeezed her friend's hand. The mothers had formed a special bond, offering one another—and any new mothers who joined them—something other friends and family could not.

"I can take off my mask that I wear when I go out to face the world," Paula Davis said. "When I come amongst my friends here, I can be myself. They know exactly the feelings I am having."

"We don't have to be the actors that we so often have to be," Belle agreed.

"We look into each other's eyes and we instantly hug. You cut through to that deep connection because you feel each other's pain," added Gina Barnhurst.

The first grave in Arlington National Cemetery was dug to remind a Civil War general about war's human toll. The graveyard was once Robert E. Lee's plantation. Eighteen hundred men rest forever in his former rose garden. During the wars in Iraq and Afghanistan, there were as many as thirty burials a day. Nearly one in ten who died fighting rest in Arlington cemetery, the highest percentage from any war.

Beth Belle's son Nicholas was the first to be buried in a new row of graves. Three years later, five more rows stretched beyond his headstone. Belle dropped to her knees one last time before leaving him, hugging his headstone, pressing her cheek against his name.

Not far away, Michael Najarian found his name chiseled on a list of war dead. His was one of more than fifty-eight thousand names on the wall of the Vietnam War Memorial in Washington, D.C. Najarian served in Vietnam, but was still very much alive.

"I just sort of sank on the ground," he said, shaking his head. "I was stunned to see my name among the lists of the dead. I couldn't believe it."

Najarian had been an air force sergeant; the Najarian on the wall served in the navy. They were born one year and one day apart.

"Only a middle initial separates us," he said, leaning to touch the engraving. "He's Michael Anthony. I'm Michael George Najarian."

They grew up on opposite sides of the country and are not related. One man died at twenty-one. The other was given the gift of growing old.

"I read something the other day," Najarian said, pausing to dip a brush into the bucket he'd brought to the memorial. "'A veteran is a person who wrote a blank check to this country.' Our nation withdrew everything that guy had."

Perhaps that's why the Maryland veteran rose before dawn, drove to the memorial, and cleaned the name of the other Michael Najarian, a task he'd carried out for fifteen years.

"That war is never over for anyone," Najarian said, growing emotional. "Not for me or anyone else. Period."

He eventually persuaded other vets to join him. So many now come to the wall that it is washed every week for free.

"I use it as my Wailing Wall," Bill Gray said quietly. The former army lieutenant lost five men in his platoon.

"One of them, Gene White, was a young sergeant about my age. He had just come back from R and R in Hawaii with his wife," Gray said. "He was killed by an incoming mortar round with only a month left to go."

Gray's company commander also died.

"The new C.O. would have written the parents of the dead in my platoon, but it would have been a form letter," Gray said, so he wrote the letters himself. "My letters had dust on them, the dust we had in the central highlands."

When North Vietnamese soldiers overran Bill Gray's outpost, he recalled, "I was hit in the right leg and was afraid I was going to bleed to death." But he got all of his injured men out first and was awarded the Silver Star for gallantry.

At first Bill Gray came to the wall at night, taking pictures. He was still crouching in the darkness of his mind.

"I suffer from survivor's guilt. Cleaning this wall is an opportunity to wash that away."

Gray stretched to reach the names of the dead in his platoon.

"You realize there are so many families who have been affected by this," he said, gazing at the army of names. "I try to see the thousands of people that they left behind, the wives, the parents, the kids, the unborn."

Cleaning the Vietnam War memorial is not a job for these old soldiers. It is an honor. Every day that they go down to the wall and pick up a brush is Memorial Day. After all, what does a soldier who survived war fear most? That people will forget. That's why most of them have a dusty box or two tucked in the back of their closets. Some are filled with happy memories, and some with pain.

"My brother was a good leader," Brad Zucroff said, pulling a picture out of a trunk of his brother's things. He had not gone through this box in thirty-five years.

"Steve died horribly," Brad said, tapping the photo of a young man with old eyes. A land mine blew apart Marine Corporal Steven Zucroff during the Vietnam War—on the day after Mother's Day, in his twenty-first year.

Three decades later Stacey Hansen, a firefighter in San Jose, California, found Steve's dog tag while vacationing near Da Nang. It was lying in a pile of U.S. military dog tags on display in a dingy Ho Chi Minh City museum.

"This is such a personal thing," Hansen said. "I couldn't believe that they were just lying in the bottom of an old glass case! Who are these guys? And where are they now? Did they make it out alive? Why are their dog tags still here? Would they want them back? I couldn't leave them behind. Those were all my American brothers."

She bought the dog tags for about two dollars apiece.

"How did you know they were real?" I asked.

"Well, I didn't know one hundred percent, but if they weren't, I was just contributing to their poor economy."

It was clear to Hansen that her unplanned purchase might have been more than a mere impulse buy. Each tag represented an individual's life—and those of a family and countless friends—affected by war.

Maybe this is why I went to Vietnam, she thought. *Maybe it's more than just a vacation.*

Sorting through all those rusting bits of metal, she wondered how they had been lost and if there were more. Her vacation became a quest. A taxi driver wrote her a note in Vietnamese to help her explain her search, and the note became her calling card. Hansen traveled all over the country for five weeks, clearing out her savings account, and came home with 562 tags.

"Why were you so passionate about this?" I asked. "A war that you don't remember, people you've never met?"

"So many of them were teenagers or young men, and they never had their life," she replied, "so if I can bring some type of closure or healing to those families, I'm willing to do that."

Back home in California, Hansen began to have second thoughts. Finding all those GIs or their families seemed too daunting a task, so she put her pile of dog tags on a closet shelf. She could not leave them there. They had been forgotten for too long. Six months later she pulled them down and started searching.

"I wasn't looking for anything in return," she said. "I was just looking for people to send them to."

Most of the people she contacted lived too far away to visit, but Steven Zucroff's brother, Brad, was just an hour away by car.

They met in a park overlooking the Pacific near Hansen's home. Brad Zucroff brought the old box with his brother's things. "You've seen his name," he said, as the two walked across the bluff and sat on a bench. "Now you should see the person."

He lifted the lid and pulled out a picture. It was not the image of a weary warrior that Hansen had expected.

"That's my brother on the pony," Zucroff said. A sunny six-year-old dressed up like a cowboy stared at them from the photo.

"That's him?" Hansen asked, shading her eyes from the setting sun. "Awwww . . ."

She popped the lid on the box she carried. "I want to give you something," she said, handing him a small present wrapped in paper. Joggers ran past as Zucroff began to unwrap his gift. Far below, a family on the beach rolled up their towels and headed home. This was not a moment in life many historians would record, but it had great meaning to the two people on that park bench. It marked the end of a journey that spanned thirty-five years and fifteen thousand miles. Neither distance nor years had paled Zucroff's memory of his brother. Finally, he touched the last thing Steve wore in life.

"That's really amazing," Brad said, choked with emotion. "Thank you, thank you, thank you."

Stacey took his hand.

"You're so welcome."

Torn, tarnished, history sometimes has a way of finding us. People like Stacey Hansen are strong and genuine in a world that sometimes is not. They remind us that we all are citizens of history and should help where we can. They journey a troubled road, dreading the darkness, guided by other people's pain. I was blissfully unaware of the depth of such sacrifice until it crash-landed on my doorstep.

Even for believers, what happened on 9/11 seemed unbelievable. On that day a little chapel survived the hell that toppled nearby skyscrapers of concrete and steel. I was standing outside St. Paul's Church, one block from Ground Zero, on the terrible day terrorists smashed planes into the World Trade Center in New York City.

A dozen modern buildings toppled as well, but St. Paul's—pieced together with rock and timber—stood without so much as a broken window. The Reverend Dr. Daniel Matthews, rector of the Parish of Trinity Church, walked with me through the church's graveyard, which was covered in ash. The dust of the dead had settled in the chapel cemetery.

"You know what everyone in the neighborhood is calling St. Paul's, don't you?" the minister asked, stopping to dust off a headstone. "The little chapel that stood."

"The most astounding thing for me," he continued, "was not the soot and the dust, but the paper. There must have been ten million pieces. Everybody's desk wound up flying out the window."

Four hundred sixty thousand tons of debris from the Twin Towers alone had landed nearby: enough concrete to build a five-foot sidewalk from New York to Washington, D.C., enough steel to build twenty Eiffel towers. Sixteen acres of rubble, some of it nine stories deep.

Reverend Matthews figured St. Paul's was spared to shelter those who were not. "It is a symbol," he said, "of where we have been and where we are going and what we have to do in the future."

The little church is the oldest in Manhattan. It opened in 1766, a decade before the Declaration of Independence. Almost every president has prayed here, beginning with George Washington, who came to St. Paul's after this country's first inauguration.

On the day I showed up, Dr. Kathy Fallon was in the president's pew. "I'm sitting where George Washington and his family used to gather for church," Fallon explained. "Fixing feet." She was running a foot clinic.

"It's appropriate to be in a church," another volunteer said, "because, in a way, we're saving soles."

St. Paul's was a place where workers at Ground Zero could rest, or get a foot or back rub, a quick meal, and a kind word.

"It's like a M.A.S.H. unit for the soul," Matthews said. "These volunteers did a great job."

A thousand of them served twelve-hour shifts. They came from all over. The day the towers came crashing down, Dr. Fallon rushed to Ground Zero, driving two and a half hours from her home in Armonk, New York. En route Fallon realized she would miss a celebration. Her husband, Jim, would have to blow out the forty-two candles on his birthday cake without her, but then came another realization: "Oh, my God, my baby is four months old today!"

"I need to be here," she insisted. "When my son, James Edward, grows up, he'll understand what happened on September eleventh, and I think he'll appreciate that his mom was down here, trying to help out."

Whenever we leave home we all tell our kids, "I'll be right back." After 9/11 some children no longer accepted that. Victoria Alonso's mother, Janet, went to work at the World Trade Center that morning and never returned. Her dad was left to care for a two-year-old daughter and a baby boy born with Down syndrome.

"If I was to tell you I did this by myself," Robert Alonso said, "I'd be a liar. I'd be a flat-out liar. I got my mom, my aunt, my pop to help."

But he never returned to work at the pizza place he owned in Stony Point, New York. His family covered for him.

"I owe it to my children to be around," Alonso said. "If I buried my grief in work, my kids would lose both their parents."

He no longer put off anything that brought them joy, either.

"If we're lying on the floor, and all of a sudden, Victoria says, 'Daddy, I want to go to the park!' I'm like, 'Oh, I don't want to go to the park.' That's what I'm thinking, but I say, 'Let's go. We're going to the park.'"

"Hang on, guys!" Alonso shouted as the kids squealed with laughter. They were riding in a grocery cart, careening across the lot toward their big SUV.

"Why should I deprive my children from going shopping?" he said.

"I see all the other mothers going shopping with their kids. Why can't I do it?"

He raced alongside the grocery cart, jumped on its rear axle, and pushed with a powerful leg. The children exploded with laughter again.

"When my kids smile," Alonso said, "the terrorists lose. The people who killed Janet wanted to destroy our happy lives. They lost. We won."

Since 9/11, Alonso has taught his children to treat every moment like an unopened gift. "I don't want to be the rain cloud in my family," he explained. "I want to give my kids the incentive to do things and go forward."

He coached Victoria's softball team to the New York State championship the year she turned twelve.

"The games were so tense, all of us went out and bought rounds of Lipitor," he chuckled.

He toasted his son Robby, too. The ten-year-old had learned to walk and read before most kids with Down syndrome because his dad played with him every day.

Robert and Janet had waited a long time for their family. After trying to conceive a child for ten years, they gave up. Two months later, she was pregnant. They considered it a victory, so they named their daughter Victoria.

These days, when Victoria looks in the mirror, she sees her mother.

"She was special to me," Victoria said, even though she can barely remember her mom. "I love her. People need to know that."

They are much alike. Victoria is an honor student. Janet had studied nights and weekends for years, graduating from college in her late thirties. She worked as an e-mail manager on the ninety-seventh floor of the World Trade Center. She had just gone back to her job at Marsh & McLennan after staying home to take care of her second baby, Robby. Janet Alonso's body was found seven months after 9/11, on her son's first birthday.

"God works in funny ways," Robert Alonso sighed. "Hearing the knock on the door and the news that Janet's body had been recovered from Ground Zero—that was the most difficult. It really knocked me out. It was like September eleventh all over again."

I visited the Alonsos on the first Mother's Day after 9/11. Robert scooped up his kids and carried them out on the back deck. "Come on," he told them, "let's say hello to Mommy in the stars." That day would have been their parents' thirteenth wedding anniversary.

As Victoria neared her thirteenth birthday, I asked her, "If your mom were sitting here today, what question would you ask her?"

She stared off across her backyard, lost in thought, and then turned to me.

"I'd ask her, 'What would you want to do with me today?'"

Good times keep bad memories at bay. The Alonsos spent that 9/11 in the park where they played near a memorial that their neighbors built to Janet and all the other parents from their New York City suburb who went to work that day but never came home. Robby wandered to a wall filled with names, as his father and sister played catch nearby.

"Right here," he said, pointing to Janet Alonso's name etched in marble. "This was my mommy."

The little boy leaned over and scraped his fingers back and forth across the stone. His father watched and gulped back a tear, then rubbed his own hands together, as if he could scour away painful thoughts. Robby drew his fingers to his mouth, kissed them, and gently pressed them on his mother's name.

"Momma," he said softly.

We all think about 9/11 and how it has changed our lives, but the Alonsos live it every day. I was on or near that terrible pile at Ground Zero for six weeks after the attack, knocking on doors, talking with people, trying to put a face on the faceless thousands who pitched in during the rescue efforts. Most didn't say much, as they needed all the oxygen they had just to get through their day.

My task was to find hope in all its many forms. I spent the first few hours wandering on foot with families who were clutching photos of their loved ones, trudging to one of the twenty-one hospitals in New York, standing in line to be told all of the injured were simply John or

Jane Doe. Their wallets and purses had been lost in the Twin Towers. Their injuries were severe.

One morning amid the clatter of machinery at Ground Zero, I came across Eric Ortner, a volunteer emergency medical technician from Scarsdale, New York. He was also an NBC News producer at the time, one of the first on the scene. Eric did something journalists seldom do: He delayed his own coverage by two days, leaving the biggest story of his life and his camera crew behind so that he could spend the next forty-eight hours looking for lost lives.

The twenty-six-year-old had volunteered to lend his local ambulance crew a hand, while completing an eight-hundred-hour course to become an emergency technical crew chief. Eric took night classes in medicine and studied journalism during the day, earning his degree from the University of Rochester. When our worst nightmare happened, Eric Ortner was there for more than a story.

"We first got a call to help a man trapped ten feet under the rubble at Ground Zero," he said. "It was so smoky, you couldn't see more than five feet in. We grabbed firemen, hip by hip. Made a human chain to where this person was trapped. Firefighters laid a hose line. They put in just enough water to make the hose rigid. We followed it like bread crumbs. Our human chain went deep into the rubble where the person was trapped."

Rescue workers clawed at the concrete, trying to free the man. They lowered Eric into the hole. He took no camera, no notebook; he conducted himself with a doctor's sensitivity but could not save him. Eric would not talk about what the man told him.

"He thought I was a doctor. It wouldn't be right."

Lenox Hill Hospital in New York City experienced a mini baby boom on that dreadful day. Fourteen children were born instead of the usual six. Mothers who couldn't reach their own doctors wandered in off the street. Cries of joy mixed with those of pain.

Ira and Leandra Pintel wondered what they would tell their daughter, Sarah, about being born in a time of great sadness, but sadness does not linger in a place where there is such joy.

Svetlana Debelli lifted her baby to me. "This is New York's future right here," she said. "Still going strong."

Svetlana was late for work on 9/11, stuck in a commuter train, on her way to the Blue Cross/Blue Shield office in the World Trade Center. Her mother had already arrived, but made it out alive and in time to see the birth of her first grandchild.

Birth is the victory of life over death. Time and again we rebuild our lives with second chances. Twenty-five thousand New Yorkers were homeless in the days after the 9/11 attack. Most families faced the prospect of no power or lights and left the area around Ground Zero, but there was a block where people stayed, just a short walk from where the World Trade Center had stood.

Only one person who lived on Duane Street left, saying he did not want to live next door to three thousand corpses. The rest turned the terrible into routine. Martha Nishida pedaled off on her bicycle to her job selling rugs the very next day, though with the police barricades in her neighborhood, she didn't expect many customers. Gil Friedman, a sculptor, swept away the dust in his studio and added more of his own.

"I want to make sure that the terrorists are not successful," he said. "That they do not destroy our feeling of democracy."

Citizenship had seemed an almost quaint term until that terrible day. Marita Merriman and Madeline Lanciani, both mothers, fed rescue workers with food they bought after walking their children half a mile to the nearest working subway station so that the kids could go to school. The job of mothers, they said, is to try to make life normal again. Marita pointed to a simple note scrawled on the dusty hood of a car that showed the resolve of this battered neighborhood: "We will survive."

Americans open their hearts and wallets all the time, but rarely do we read about what the world gives to us, and that seems just as important. On the eve of 9/11 there were some villages in Newfoundland, Canada, where unemployment hovered as high as 50 percent, but that remote island in the North Atlantic—Canada's poorest province—set a mark for charity worthy of the history books.

After the attack on the World Trade Center, pilots flying from

Europe were told to put their planes on the ground as soon as possible. Thirty-eight airliners with more than six thousand passengers ended up in Gander, Newfoundland.

School bus drivers were on strike, but they left their picket lines and worked twenty-four hours straight to take the stranded travelers to nearby towns. Passengers feared that they were being dropped off at the end of the earth, but they couldn't have been made to feel more at home.

The tiny coastal town of Lewisporte canceled classes so that visitors could use school computers to send messages home. Because their luggage was still locked on the planes, passengers were given coins to wash their clothes at the Laundromat. Those who needed prescriptions were taken to pharmacies for free medicine, while some townspeople worked through the night, baking them fresh bread. One hundred seventy-six people slept on church pews. Honeymooners got the choir loft all to themselves.

If the passengers had simply stayed in that church until their planes were ready to leave, there wouldn't be much of a story. Lots of towns help in times of crisis. But the people of Lewisporte took the travelers out, sailed them around the bay in their boats, and invited them to sleep in their homes.

Susan and Trevor Tetford took in two New York City couples with babies. Trevor tossed his keys to a total stranger and told him to use his car. They became close friends even though they were together only three days during that terrible week in September.

When their Delta flight 15 was finally able to leave Newfoundland, passengers passed the hat. Two hundred eighteen fliers pledged thirty-five thousand dollars to start a scholarship fund for Lewisporte's children. At that time, only a quarter of Lewisporte's kids graduated from high school, so the money was awarded not just to a star student or two but divided among every senior who made straight As—all this because some people in a faraway place were kind to strangers who happened to be Americans.

Chapter Six

What If?

My dad had always hoped I would take over his optical store. My grandfather wanted me to follow him into law. Nearly everyone in the family worried about my poor choice of careers. I started my professional life at the St. Louis Zoo, announcing an elephant act—Alice, Pummy, Trudy, Clara, and Marie. It's where my hometown CBS radio station, KMOX, sent me after I was turned down for a news job. That may be one reason I spent the rest of my career working for NBC, but I did give the zoo my best shot—literally. Let me explain. In those days the St. Louis Zoo produced three free animal shows—one featuring elephants, another with lions and tigers, and a third featuring chimpanzees. That last act was the most popular because trainers dressed one of the chimps, Little Pierre, to look like Batman. The hairy Caped Crusader entered high over the crowd on a wire between the announcer's booth and the stage. Unfortunately, the wire was accessible to a big chimp called Captain Bozo that wanted to escape showbiz, so the show's director gave me a rifle that fired tiny little sponges and told me to shoot at Bozo every time he came close to the wire.

"You won't hurt him," he insisted, "but Bozo weighs one hundred and twenty pounds. We can't have him dropping on the kids."

All summer long I annoyed the big chimp, popping him with the sponge gun. At last, late in the season, my sound engineer and I were playing a hand of poker while the show progressed. By this time we knew the routine so well that we didn't have to watch it.

"How 'bout a big hand for him, boys and girls!" I shouted into the microphone, while slapping down a card.

Suddenly the audience gasped: There was big ole Bozo, looking like King Kong, climbing the wire and already halfway over the moat that separated the audience from the stage. I grabbed the sponge gun and leaned out of the announcer's booth.

POW! POW! POW!

Bozo dropped into the water. The audience applauded as if they thought the popgun fire were part of the act. He bounced back on stage, unhurt, but I had already been picturing the newspaper headline in my mind: "Zoo Announcer Shoots Beloved Chimp."

Sometimes when you climb the ladder of success, you find it's been leaning against the wrong wall. As was the case with Bozo, showbiz was not for me. Luckily, it is possible to fail your way to the top, if you have another job waiting. Cattle were the only animals in sight the day I drove into the parking lot at the NBC station in Oklahoma City. They were grazing beneath the television tower and I was thankful that no one asked me to shoot them. I arrived before my new boss, Ernie Schultz, heard about the Bozo incident. He hired me to be a reporter/ photographer, but let me anchor a local newscast. The microphone I wore that morning was as big as a hot dog. I struggled to snap the cord, which hooked with a T-clasp, like a necklace, around my neck. The announcer's voice boomed in the studio:

"Here's Bob Dotson . . ."

CLUNK! My mike fell on the floor, and I ducked down to find it. The director asked the cameraman, "Where'd he go?"

"I don't know," the cameraman muttered under his breath.

"Well, find him!" the director yelled.

He pushed the camera toward the anchor podium, tilted up and over it, and caught me searching for the mike on the floor. My rear end was on TV longer than my face was.

Afterward I skulked back to the newsroom. Schultz pulled me aside and said, "Bob, they don't pay us to look silly."

Somewhere that chimp, Captain Bozo, was hooting. I wondered if I could get my old job back at the St. Louis Zoo. That night, when I called my mom, she laughed but assured me, "Honey, whatever holds you back will push you on."

My mother knew me well, but she knew something about performance, too. Dottie Bailey had sung on NBC long before they offered me a job. When Eddie Cantor's popular network radio show came to Kansas City during World War II, my mother drove a hundred miles from her hometown in northeast Kansas to audition. Like any *American Idol* hopeful today, she wanted the nation to hear her beautiful voice.

Later, Mom performed at the summer opera in St. Louis, filling in for the lead actress in *Show Boat*. One night when she sang one of the musical's best-known numbers, "Bill," my dad, Bill Dotson, who was in the audience, thought she was singing directly to him. He waited for her at the stage door and came back four nights in a row with roses. Mom finally went out with him because, she joked, "I liked his mustache, his black wavy hair, and his green Packard convertible, not necessarily in that order." It was the end of her singing career and the beginning of my brother, Bill; my sister, Suzi; and me.

I often wonder what my life would be like today if I had gone back to the zoo. Nothing is preordained in America's history. The paths it takes twist and turn with the lives of every one of its citizens, and with the arrival of each new immigrant. Many of the latter come with incredible stories, seeking the second chance our country could offer them.

There once lived a prince who became a pauper, and then lived happily ever after. He's an old man now, painting his life on plastic, a life that would have been filled with pomp—if the circumstances had been different. Andrew Romanoff was born into Russian royalty, a prince raised in a castle. That's usually a recipe for a grand life, but he lost his kingdom in the Russian Revolution, only to find a fairy-tale ending in northern California. The day we met, all that remained of his royal past was baking at three hundred degrees, distant memories shriveling on plastic.

Romanoff sounded anything but regal when he said, "Well, it's really cool, man. I enjoy painting pictures on Shrinky Dinks"—a children's toy made of large, flexible waxy sheets. When heated in an oven, they shrivel to tiny images. His illustrate a fascinating tale about a boy who would be king in a country that didn't want one. Andrew's parents fled to England during the Russian Revolution. His grandfather was one of the last czars. His great-uncle, George V of England, took them in.

"One day, I was riding my bicycle around the Windsor Castle grounds," Romanoff recalled. "I happened upon the young princess Elizabeth, who would later become queen, and bumped her with my bike. I said, 'Excuse me, I'm so sorry. I bumped into you.' But her dad, the king of England, called my dad, the former Russian prince, and said, 'Look, when my daughter's out bicycling, keep your boy out of the garden!'

"The British royals, despite their generosity, generally kept their distance" from their relatives without a throne. Fortunately the castle had lots of places where a kid could find some fun. Romanoff's family took him mushroom hunting "with all the good linen and silver"—for a picnic, a welcome break from breakfast in bed.

"My nanny set a table for me on my pillow every morning for twelve years," he said. "Brought me tea and biscuits." But this luxurious life would not continue. Eventually the little prince was sent to school with commoners. Money was tight, even for royalty, during the Great Depression of the 1930s.

"I was walking outside the palace grounds, holding my nanny's hand, on the way to my first day of school," Romanoff remembered. "We passed a long line of people waiting for food in a breadline. I asked Nanny who they were. 'Oh,' she said, 'those are people you've never seen. They're poor.'"

Years later he would pay back Britain's royal family for the help they had given his parents. Romanoff joined the British navy during World War II, where he served so well in battle that the king invited him to dinner. The little princess he had bumped with his bike was there, too. It was the future queen's birthday.

"The king said some very kind things about me at that dinner, then leaned over and spoke into my ear, 'We're going to play games after the meal. Let Elizabeth win.'"

After the war Romanoff came to America on a freighter, hitching a ride on a ship carrying stud horses to be bred for the Kentucky Derby. He decided to head for California, and rode there on a Royal Coach called Greyhound. Looking out the window, he thought, *This place is heaven,* but once again, Romanoff's life collided with fate. He married, but then lost his young wife in a flu epidemic, and struggled to raise two young sons. In time he met Inez Storer, a woman who had four kids of her own.

"We just combined the families about a year later," Inez said with a smile. "It was the Brady Bunch."

Their neighbors in Inverness, California, were thrilled. Carla Steinberg told her friends, "Daaaawlink, I'm living next door to the prince!"

Romanoff became a kind of king in that community of artists, leading by example.

"He wasn't going around saying, 'This is the meaning of life!'" Sym Van der Ryn said. "He just lived his life well! And if you were paying attention, you learned from that."

The little town's "royalty" inspired Marty Knapp to take splendid pictures.

"I may still have become a photographer, but I might have had a harder time becoming an artist," Knapp said. Things might have turned out differently if Romanoff had not chosen to live like them, taking care of his neighbors as he did his garden.

I wondered what he had gained with the loss of a crown.

"Independence," he answered, "and a life of freedom, living in the United States."

Andrew Romanoff earned nobility, a quality that is not only a birthright of monarchs. During the American Revolution, kings ruled most of the world. They believed they were divinely chosen. In America the first presidential inauguration changed all that, but what if George Washington had decided to become king? It could have happened; he was asked to assume that role. The popular general turned the suggestion down, however, and made it clear he never wanted the subject mentioned again. Just suppose he had been a Royalist at heart. Who would be our king today?

George and his wife, Martha, had no children. After he died, the succession would have passed to the descendants of his two brothers, Augustine and Samuel. Sam married five times. Today he and his brother have more than eight thousand descendants, fewer than two hundred of whom still bear Washington's name. During the U.S. monarchy's first century, two men named Bush would have been king. Bushrod Washington the First would have reigned during the War of 1812, Bushrod the Second between the end of the Civil War in 1865 and the start of World War I in 1914. There also would have been two King Spots, no doubt causing their White House dogs endless confusion.

When the son of King Spotswood the Second died in 1994, the crown would have passed to our current king, Paul the First, the retired manager of a building-supply company based—where else?—in Valley Forge.

"I doubt if I'd be a very good king," Paul admitted. "We've done so well as a country without a king, I think George made the right decision."

Around Leon, Texas, Paul's son, Bill, was affectionately known as Prince William.

"Somewhere along the line we lost the height," Bill chuckled. "George Washington was six feet three inches, and I guess from the love of little women over two hundred years, we gradually got smaller."

William's older brother, Richard, would be next in line. Dick couldn't have cared less about his hypothetical birthright, but Bill's house looked like Mount Vernon's gift shop. His family has known for years how closely it is related to the man who could have been king.

"The French Revolution started right after our country's revolution," Bill pointed out. "They were beheading noblemen left and right. It probably wouldn't have taken very long for something like that to bring us down."

At least one Washington actually did achieve royalty: Katharine Willis, George's great-grandniece, married the Prince of Naples. The rest of us, more than one hundred million Americans, have family ties to at least one of our presidents. Before George Washington, the authority vested in one man was the measure of greatness. The man who could have been king insisted that voters should decide whom to grant power to, and that changed the world. We celebrate this great victory for common sense every Fourth of July, but what happened to the losers—no, not the British, but the Americans who fought with them?

Our revolution was a civil war. Even the founding fathers' families were split. Benjamin Franklin's son William defied his father and remained royal governor of New Jersey until his arrest in 1776. Upon his release two years later, William fled to England; he and his father were forever estranged.

By the spring of 1783, a massive exodus of refugees was under way. At a time when the total population of America was about 2.5 million, an estimated 100,000 Loyalists, as many as 2,000 Indians, and perhaps 6,000 former slaves were forced to leave the country.

The largest number, perhaps as many as 40,000, sailed for Canada. One Loyalist refugee described her arrival there: "I watched the sails disappearing in the distance, and such a feeling of loneliness came over me that although I had not shed a tear through all the war, I sat down on the damp moss with my baby on my lap, and cried bitterly."

This fascinating tale took me to Shelburne, Nova Scotia, a little town northeast of Maine.

"We've all got the same names as your names," Patrick Melanson pointed out. "It's all the same faces. It's all the same history."

Fifty-three American regiments fought alongside the British during the revolution. Who knew? One in five bet on England to win. At war's end, King George offered a powerful incentive to emigrate to Nova Scotia: The people who fought a war over taxation would be given a tax break.

Lorraine Chapman gestured to the rocky coastline.

"Most of them expected homes to be here and land to be prepared," she said, "and none of that happened."

Some of the women wouldn't come ashore until houses were built. Others faced their first Canadian winter living in tents. Surveyors quickly laid out an exact replica of the place many of them had left: Philadelphia. Their new town, Shelburne, Nova Scotia, became the fourth largest city in North America.

Barely two years after the American Revolution, another boat arrived in Canada bearing a battle-scarred man who walked with a slight limp. Everyone knew his name: Benedict Arnold.

"Oh, the traitor, eh?" asked a man who looks remarkably like him.

Steve Arnold is Benedict Arnold's closest living relative—his great-great-great-grandson.

"There isn't a sitcom that hasn't taken a potshot at Benedict," Arnold pointed out. "Even Homer Simpson tried to pass himself off as the old turncoat."

History may have been too tough on the old traitor, Arnold insisted. "The biggest history lesson is that there's more to the history."

The British gave Benedict Arnold a deed to nearly fifteen thousand acres in Canada. He set up stores, warehouses, and wharves, and even managed, through middlemen, to sell goods in the United States. Within fifteen months of his arrival, he was the most successful trader in the colony, but controversy followed him to Canada. When the British army pulled out, the economy tumbled, and Arnold went broke. He hounded his neighbors to pay their bills, once again becoming the most hated man in the country.

"By giving people credit," Steve Arnold explained, "he was just setting himself up."

Benedict Arnold left his son to look after things and sailed back to England, where he died penniless.

It's amazing that Benedict Arnold stands at the crossroads of so much American and Canadian history.

"He has had a huge impact," Steve Arnold agreed.

Benedict Arnold left an astonishing legacy. Today 10 percent of Canada's population, some 3.5 million people, are direct descendants of Americans who lost in our fight for independence. Those original hundred thousand Americans might never have gone to

Canada if Steve's great-great-great-grandfather had succeeded in his treachery.

If America had lost its revolution, a lot of people living in Australia today would have ancestors in the state of Georgia. Our American Revolution deprived England of its dumping ground for convicts in that colony. Since they could no longer be sent there, King George shipped them off to Australia. It was a grueling journey, months at sea.

One family that arrived safely started a diary to remind future generations of this providence. These would-be Americans, named Warwick, invited me to read some of those old ledgers. Hundreds of them were stacked from the floor to the ceiling in a weathered old barn nestled under an ancient pepper tree.

One entry from 1839 recorded the death of a shepherd boy named George. It noted that he was buried in the family cemetery, and included a reminder to call the next child George so that the name would carry on.

The family built an extraordinary life on not much more than hope. Their ranch was in the Australian Outback, some of the driest country on earth. In order to make a modest living they farmed 125 square miles, a vast estate that held seven thousand sheep. On the morning I visited, Richard Warwick rode off on a motorcycle looking for a flock. His sheepdog rode on the back so that he wouldn't be worn out before they found the sheep.

When the Warwicks first settled in the Outback, they built a small town. It had a minister, a doctor, a postman, and a schoolteacher for its population of fifty. Most of those buildings are gone. The countryside around the Warwicks' homestead looked like an abandoned battle-field, with monumental lumps of machinery lying broken and rusting in the landscape.

The town's inhabitants tried raising wheat, but the land was too dry. Corn—too dry. One by one the people left, convinced that a dead heart lay at the core of their continent. The Warwicks stayed, however, even though they had to care for their sheep with only one hired hand.

Their kids' closest friends lived six hundred miles away. The children dressed up on Halloween and described their costumes to their pals over a shortwave radio.

For nearly two hundred years—ten generations—not a day had gone by without a Warwick on that land. It was only willpower that held them, and that was poor sustenance.

The afternoon sun slanted through the eucalyptus trees when Grandfather Warwick led me down to the family's cemetery. It was a beautiful spring day in October. Richard Warwick's mother stopped now and then to pick tiny purple flowers called "Salvation Janes," named for the colors of the Salvation Army.

When we reached the iron gate and entered the cemetery, Grandmother Warwick turned to her husband and said, "Frank, do you remember when we first came here?"

"Yes, Mary," he said. "It was the day we got engaged and came down here to pick out our plot."

No Warwick is ever really alone out there. Family is all around them, reminding them to make a difference, no matter how life changes their plans. Such extraordinary people build this world.

The Warwicks wondered what their lives would have been like had their ancestors been sent to America. We all ponder from time to time, "What if?" How different would my life have been had I let the lure of exotic places lead me into dangerous stories. That happened only once.

Images of lightning flashed across the plane's radar screen, which was covered in circles, pinpointing storm cells, so many it looked like a bowl of Cheerios. We were riding an invisible roller coaster, dropping thousands of feet. Drinks were on the ceiling; our stomachs were in our throats.

"Are you worried?" I shouted to the pilot.

"The storm clouds? No," he yelled, wrestling with the controls. "What concerns me are those mountains, the cumulus granite!"

We were flying through mountains in Costa Rica, looking for a landing strip in the jungle.

"When we touch down, I won't be able to shut off the jet's engines," he called over his shoulder. "We'd need help getting them started again, and there are no facilities out here. You'll just have to roll out, and we'll pull away. We'll toss you your gear after we turn around for takeoff."

The plane bucked on, while down below was total darkness. I had left Dallas with television cameraman Henry Kokojan and sound engineer Bob Eshbaugh, heading toward Guyana, where a cult leader named Jim Jones had ordered his followers to commit suicide and hundreds did. Halfway there, flying over Costa Rica, word reached us that they all had died. The foreign desk at NBC News had another assignment for us: to land and relieve George Lewis, an NBC correspondent who had been with the rebels who were trying to overthrow Nicaragua's dictator, Anastasio Somoza Debayle. Their camp was down there somewhere. Lightning scratched past us, touching a plateau.

"Look!" Eshbaugh shouted, one hand clutching his sound gear while the other pointed to lights lining a makeshift runway.

"I see it," nodded Kokojan, rubbing his Miss Piggy keychain. He hung it under his lens so that kids he filmed would stare at the Muppet and not directly into the camera.

"Hold on!" shouted the pilot.

The jet made a tight circle beneath the towering mountains and touched down, bumping on the hard earth. We opened the door and dove out and away from the engines, cradling our gear. As the plane spun around, out came our suitcases—and on board leaped George Lewis, who yelled, "I left you a jeep!"

A moment later the plane was airborne again, disappearing into the storm. The landing lights blinked out. We jumped into the jeep and drove to the little hotel where George had stayed. When I dropped my bag on the bed, there was a knock at the door.

"Welcome, señor!"

"Who is it?" I asked.

"I come from Commander Zero."

The leader of the rebels, Edén Pastora, did not want to be numero uno, so he insisted his men call him Commander Zero. Apparently the double meaning was lost on him, but I was in no mood to chuckle. The man at my door was carrying a machine gun.

"Have you been listening to what's been going on down in Guyana?" he asked.

"Yes," I said. "That's where we were originally headed."

"All those poor people drinking poisoned Kool-Aid," the man sighed.

"Just terrible."

Cyanide and bullets had killed 918. Not until 9/11 would more American civilians lose their lives in a single incident.

"Well, if it's all the same with you," I said, "I'd like to wait until morning before we head into the jungle."

He shrugged and, shifting his weapon, said, "Suit yourself. I'll drop by at breakfast."

Another flash of lightning and he was gone.

At sunup Henry, Bob, and I were finishing *huevos al gusto* (eggs as you like them) in the inn's dining room when the soldier walked in, reading a newspaper.

"Señor Dotson, did you sleep well?"

Was that a smirk I noticed? "Short night," I replied.

"Why have you come? Your colleague, George Lewis, was just here."

"My assignment is to find out if you will be attacking Nicaragua this week. If so, NBC News would like me to go along."

Please, please! Say no, I prayed.

"Señor Dotson," he said, "I have just been reading about that tragedy in Guyana. What that madman has done. All those dead people."

"Yes, sir. We lost an NBC correspondent, Don Harris, and cameraman Bob Brown. They were doing a story on the Reverend Jim Jones. His men shot them."

"Sad. So sad."

Outside, a flatbed truck idled, and more armed men stood waiting. I made a pact with myself in that moment: If I got out of this okay,

I'd stay home and look for people who offered solutions to problems that didn't require bullets. I pointed out the window at the truck and said, "I hear the NBC crew rode one of those to their deaths down in Guyana."

Henry and Bob shot me a nervous glance.

"Not to worry, señor. We won't be going anywhere. We won't attack this week." He tapped his newspaper. "With all that's going on, our fight wouldn't make page thirteen."

Many of the people who are constantly in the news know the business and its limitations better than the correspondents who cover them. Journalists have little time these days for in-depth reporting. Most are expected to constantly tell what they know as soon as it happens. If reporters are riding in a car and the right front tire goes flat, they typically hop out, glance at the tire, and then start tweeting. Maybe they come back a few months later to lament the fact that the right front tire is still flat. I became determined to examine all the tires, to find out why some were still rolling. To do that, I had to stop chasing headlines. That's why I decided to stick to stories that would address a list of long-overlooked names, seeking drama and dimension in the lives of ordinary Americans.

A full chronicle of our country is not recorded in the news, but is tucked away in our attics and basements, waiting for each succeeding generation to find. That's why I poke around in those forgotten corners, tapping into people's hopes that their lives hold something of value.

How different would my life have been had I not stumbled across some old film stuffed into a crawl space between the ceiling and the roof of my first office? It was shot by a Pathé newsreel photographer named Bennie Kent who worked in Oklahoma from 1904 to 1945. He sometimes filmed scenes his bosses did not ask for: pictures of women wearing more than bathing suits, Native Americans not wearing feathers, African Americans dressed in suits—all of them examples of individuals who were rarely photographed during Bennie Kent's time. The film had been rescued from a projection room and was soon forgotten.

Looking at what Bennie Kent thought was important enough to film, I began to realize how much of our American story is disregarded. Nuggets of wisdom are often buried in tattered diaries, their tales told only if someone bothers to rescue them. That's why I started a quest to save those unnoticed stories of people who never became famous, who never did anything that would get their names in the news. Yet few have ever affected more lives with acts of kindness and bravery than some whose deeds have largely been forgotten.

Chapter Seven

America Works Best with a Level Playing Field

The real story of this country is not what we see in movies or on TV. It is people, inspired by a common dream, who band together to overcome great odds. The struggle for racial equality began in one of the most diverse places in America. No, not New York or California, but Oklahoma. The state once had twenty-eight all-black towns scattered throughout thirty-seven Indian nations. For nearly a century Oklahoma was primarily a land of the red and the black, a checkerboard of Indians and ex-slaves who very nearly got their own state, until thousands of immigrants from around the world joined them seeking free land—land they got in a single day.

I stumbled upon this extraordinary tale when I was just twenty-five years old, searching for a man named Charlie Ellison, who I'd been told could sing the traditional sacred harp spirituals, hymns that date back to slave days and are sung unaccompanied.

I found him sitting in a field of daisies, his legs splayed out in front of him, with a tattered hymnal spread open upon his knees. Charlie Ellison looked to be past ninety. His head was tilted back, and his eyes were tightly shut as he soaked up some sun.

It was a brilliant, warm spring day and Ellison seemed rather formally dressed to be sitting on a hillside of flowers. He had on a sports coat. His chin covered his bow tie, and his collar points soared upward. The ninety-year-old had a neck that fights buttons.

A weathered church perched on the hillside behind him, its parishioners long dispersed to Sunday suppers. Ellison preferred to sing his songs outside, and he was singing one as I approached.

"There is a melancholy place
For those who have no God . . ."

The voice was clear, deep, and perfectly pitched. His finger tapped time on the page.

"I can't sing it by myself, hardly," Ellison said softly. Crickets picked up the chorus.

Ellison was a black man who looked like an Indian. When I asked him about that, he admitted he was one of the first Americans, and then he said a curious thing.

"You've never seen the world through the looking glass of my mind. I'm a mix of native people and black folk. Our history has always been there, but you must look through the looking glass, darkly."

Then he led me to a handful of friends, who told me a tale seldom told.

"When Andrew Jackson had all the Indians on the Trail of Tears, whether the history books show it or not, some of those people were black people."

Percy Alexander, a farmer about Ellison's age, was full of memory. He paused in his work and leaned against a fence.

"A lot of the colored, you see, ran off from the plantations, and them Indians, they harbored them in. All up and down the Mississippi River was just a dark swamp. And they could never get them colored folks out of there. They stayed in there.

"Them Indians had the awfullest time," Alexander said, pulling on his hoe. "I heard my mother and them talking about it. I was a boy about seven or eight years old. They would beat 'em. They shot 'em. They killed 'em. They just murdered 'em all kind of ways, and run 'em on back across the Mississippi River. Back into Oklahoma. The United States gov'ment just decided to let 'em have this place. Give 'em this and never bother 'em about it anymore.

"The Trail of Tears treaty said as long as the oak and ash would grow, as long as the water'd run downstream, they'd never be bothered about this country."

No one knows for certain how many African Americans came to Oklahoma on the Trail of Tears. Census takers in those days didn't knock on doors, and runaway slaves weren't answering any roll calls.

"Slaves would go back, slip out at night to old Marster's and them's farms. Kill a hog and cut it all up. On the way home, they'd start a song."

Alexander began beating time with his hoe.

> "Way back, way back . . .
> I'm going to my shanty, way back.
> The houn' dog's on my track
> And the chicken's on my back,
> But I'm goin' to my shanty, way back . . ."

His old eyes strayed across the meadow to focus on chickens cackling somewhere in the distance.

"The slaves would get turpentine and put it all under the bottom of their feet to keep the dogs from trackin' 'em. The property owners would come out with the hounds and go and run 'em in the woods. Probably catch a whole lot of 'em. Every time they caught a slave, they got seven hundred dollars for that slave. That's the way they made their living."

Not all of the runaways found freedom among the Indians. Some of the tribes in the South had plantations of their own. A black back was the going thing in a cotton field, no matter what color the field's owner happened to be.

"All of them Indians from northern Georgia, Tennessee, and all, when they moved out West, they carried their slaves with them."

Antoine Fuhr picked up the story. He was dapperly dressed, sitting under a honeysuckle bush with two friends, Jim Simmons, a successful rancher, and the Reverend Charles Davis. The three had just come from a funeral. All were in their eighties. All had faces you might find on an Indian-head nickel.

"Some of the blacks, of course, married into the Indian families. That's why there were so many black Indians, Creek and Seminole Indians."

David Wisener held an aging picture of himself. A small black boy wearing buckskin, furs, and feathers stared out of the picture. Wisener, a deacon, was the same age as the others. As he pursed his lips and examined the photograph, Antoine Fuhr continued.

"Many of the Indians that ranked very high were black people. Most people don't know that Osceola, the chief of the Seminoles, was half Negro. His mother was a Negro woman, but his father was a chief.

"Look at Jake Simmons over there if you want to. He's about two-thirds Indian. But on the tribal rolls, he's a black man. All right, look at Reverend Davis. He's about a quarter-breed, but the rolls say he's a Negro."

Wisener passed his picture around, then said, "Bud and Ed Cox were well-known Creek Indian citizens, black freedmen. They operated a big ranch out there, five miles west of Wetumka. Every summer they would have a branding festival. They'd get out and round up the cattle. Maybe a thousand or fifteen hundred head of them at a time.

"All the ranching business was done by colored. All cowboys were colored. The Indians and the colored owned all the land."

Few of the men who rode after cattle kept accurate journals. As a rule, they wrote history with their horses and punctuated it with their six-guns. And yet with passing references in diaries and letters, it is clear that no fewer than three thousand black cowboys passed through Oklahoma. One of them originated the most popular event in rodeo.

Clarence Christian added this memory to the field of daisies.

"Speaking of Mr. Pickett, Bill Pickett, I knew him not intimately, but I knew him real well. He was grown, and I was a child. It just so happened that, as kids'll do, I kinda caught myself a little sweet on his granddaughter. This enabled me to be around him quite awhile.

"Mr. Pickett had some livestock on a little acreage he was working. Occasionally, they'd get out, and this would kind of irritate him. He would have to hunt 'em down at night, and the neighbors would squawk. One day, one of his cows got out. His wife called him, told him the cow was gone, and he'd have to find it."

Christian smiled like a man with a secret.

"Mr. Pickett wasn't too good with a rope. He could ride real well, better than average, but his roping left something to be desired."

He stopped to let that sink in.

"Well, he chased that cow and he couldn't get a rope on him. Seemingly, through a fit of anger, he decided just to manhandle this cow. He rode alongside him. He leaned over between his horns and bit the cow on the nose.

"This threw the cow off balance. The cow stumbled. Mr. Pickett just held on with his teeth and fell over on his head.

"When he hit the ground, this sudden jerk threw the cow. To his amazement—he wanted to know if it was just a freak thing or whether it was something out of the ordinary—he tried it again. And it worked again.

"So according to him and his daughter, Miss Nellie, that's how the rodeo sport of bulldogging was really originated."

Congress gave black men the unpopular task of keeping the peace in Indian Territory. During the Civil War, troops were removed from the western edge of Oklahoma, and Plains Indians began to raid the herds of the Chickasaws and Choctaws, two of the "civilized" tribes to the east. Bootleggers and horse thieves entered illegally, and encroaching white settlements threatened to set Oklahoma on a warpath.

Six black army regiments were formed and sent west. Two were to be stationed in Oklahoma. General George Armstrong Custer was asked to command one of them, but he refused, and in so doing set his path to the Little Big Horn ten years later.

Officially, those who patrolled the Oklahoma border were known as the Ninth and Tenth cavalries. but to those who knew them best—the Cheyennes, Comanches, and Kiowas—they will always be remembered as the Buffalo Soldiers, because the black men's curly hair reminded them of buffalo hide. And the name, evoking both fear and respect, stuck. For twenty tempestuous years, the Buffalo Soldiers protected Indians from Indians and whites from renegades, and themselves from both. They fought in every major Indian war in the Southwest. They quieted the frontier, and in the process won twelve Congressional Medals of Honor.

·   ·   ·

The Reverend Charles Davis hoisted his cane for attention.

"Bass Reeves!" he shouted.

We looked at one another for some clue as to what was to come. The only sound was an industrious bee in a honeysuckle bush.

"I can tell you more about him than perhaps you ever heard."

Davis paused dramatically and then proceeded in a big, booming voice.

"The officers of the law, the chief ones among us in Indian Territory, were known as U.S. marshals. Bass Reeves came in from Arkansas as one of those United States marshals. Bass was a brave man, mentally and physically strong. He could whip most any two men with his fists. He was a man that, when he went after a group, now, brother, he'd bring you in. But he was kind and sympathetic. He never barged in and caused trouble.

"I have seen him come to a community on Sunday and have a warrant for somebody. Call him out and say, 'I've got a warrant for you. Would you mind coming into Muskogee to the marshal's office tomorrow morning?' He'd say that nicely. 'I don't know what it is, but you'd better go see about it. If I have to arrest you, you see, they'll have to take you to Fort Smith, and you'll be away from your family.' And he got lots of his work done just that way.

"His son, Benny, grew up here. Married a native woman. They had some trouble and he murdered her. Leo Bennett was the head marshal. He was arming his men. He got word that the boy was determined not to be taken alive, threatened them not to come to his house because he wasn't going to be arrested.

"Bass went to the office, Leo Bennett's office, and asked him not to go.

"'You might get killed,' Bass said. 'Let me have the warrant. I'll go up there and do exactly what the warrant says, bring Benny in dead or alive.'"

Charles Davis and his friends followed Bass as he approached Benny's house. They peeked out from under a wooden sidewalk as Bass yelled to his boy.

"'Now, Benny,' he said, 'you no more my son. You committed a crime, and I have a warrant in my pocket that says to bring you in dead or alive. I'm going to take you in today one way or the other. That's all there is to it. You can come out with your hands up or your whole body will be down.'"

Davis rubbed his cane handle, relishing the moment.

"Benny came out. The people standing around hollered to him, 'Don't raise your gun, because Bass will kill you sure. He was sent to get you, and he means to do it.'"

The old man slowly lifted his walking stick, aiming it like a rifle to emphasize his words. After a while he dropped it.

"Bass arrested Benny and took him in. Benny went to the penitentiary."

"You see," Reverend Davis continued, "to commit a crime was something awful, and whoever did it, he wouldn't like it, because it would be remembered forever. They would announce it all around that they were going to whip a certain man on a certain day for committing an offense. The people would come from far and near.

"There was no certain whip to be beaten with. The officer'd go to the nearest woods and cut down a limb. Trim it up nicely. Bring in two or three of them for the whipping that day.

"If a fellow was caught again, it was a hundred lashes by two officers. That's right. One, fifty lashes, and the other one, fifty lashes. One man would count so there wouldn't be any missed or give too many.

"Well, now, the third offense was death. There was no bond, no reprieve, no renewal of the case or nothin' of the kind. He was 'shot at sunrise,' that's what my old stepdaddy would say.

"'You've had your trial, you've had your witnesses. The jurors have found you guilty beyond a reasonable doubt. I set your execution at sunrise next Thursday morning. That settles it.'

"They had no chamber of death. They didn't hang by rope. They had a block set up. They would set the prisoner there, tie a white cloth across his chest about where his heart was. Two officers would take a rifle and step off according to the presiding officer. Thirty feet. And then turn at his command."

Davis demonstrated with his cane.

"I've seen that right at the old Lee courthouse."

There was growing public pressure to open new homesteads in the West, and this threatened Indian Territory. Americans who saw the frontier closing watched their dreams of free land slip away. Many who had no property felt the "civilized" tribes—the Cherokees, Chickasaws, Choctaws, Creeks, and Seminoles—held more than they needed.

Indian Territory belonged to the tribes as a whole. The government set up the Dawes Commission in the late 1800s to assign Indian land to individuals, in hopes that some would sell to white settlers, as indeed they did. The commission was also instructed to prepare a list of the members of each tribe. This roll was to include the Indians' ex-slaves, the black freedmen. Not all of the blacks got an even shake, but Creek freedmen got more than anybody else because of the twinkling eye of Judge Reed.

Antoine Fuhr allowed as how he had never publicly told what he was about to tell, because Judge Reed was a prominent man, and there was no percentage in embarrassing prominent men. But the judge had long since passed away.

"Judge Reed was an honorable man," Fuhr said. "A black man who interpreted for all the chiefs. When they got to the allotment of the land, and the chiefs sat down with the Dawes Commission, the commission said, 'Now, we can give each Indian a hundred and sixty acres.' At least that's what Judge Reed interpreted to the chiefs. 'Indians all get a hundred and sixty acres.'

"Well, they asked what the Indians were going to do about those black people in their tribes. 'What do they get? Don't they get something?' And the chiefs said, 'Nothing. Give them nothing.' The Dawes Commission asked Judge Reed, 'Now, what did they say?' Judge Reed said, 'Chiefs say, give 'em the same thing.'

"The commission depended on his interpretation!" Fuhr said gleefully. "That's how our folks got homesteads in Oklahoma."

The Reverend Davis chuckled, brushed the sleeve of his rumpled blue suit, and tapped his black round-toed shoes with his cane. When the laughter died down, he noted:

"I grew up on the through-road going west. Some of the pioneers would camp overnight, and I'd hear my mother talking with the womenfolks. They said they were on their way to the Promised Land. I didn't know what that meant."

He smiled.

"They were going to homestead the original Oklahoma."

Sidney Cline Church cleared his throat. He was big and rawboned and about eighty. His voice blared like an old bugle as he began telling the story of Paul Sykes, who arrived in Kingfisher, Oklahoma, with six hundred former slaves.

They came from Alabama the year before one of those big land runs offered free homesteads out west. Paul Sykes's wagons rolled in with very little food. It was November, too late to plant. The former slaves had no money, but Sykes had an idea.

"The old gentleman would come down here and meet the trains," Church said. "There would probably be three or four trains a day. He had his cane, and he was stooped a little bit. He would start to sing like this."

Church stood, leaned over, and began to bob up and down. He was then about the same age as Sykes was when he first saw him.

> "Ol' ark's a-movin', a-movin', a-movin',
> The ol' ark's a-movin' right along . . .

"After the train had stopped, people then, of course, would throw a little money out to him. Sometimes maybe they'd throw a dollar, fifty cents, but mostly it was probably nickels and dimes. Sykes kept a lot of people alive that first long winter with the money he collected at the train station.

"Traveling salesmen also dropped off hogs and turkeys. One or two gave him a cow. Indians, blacks—and whites—came to the feasts he set out."

Sykes continued to sing on the Rock Island Railroad station platform, and for many years thereafter he would feed two or three hundred people three times a month. He became so well known that the railroad wanted to set him up in Chicago, but he declined. He decided to stay in the city he saved.

Church paused to let his memories catch up and then pulled a picture from his pocket of a young man in uniform.

"In World War I the boys all left here and enlisted in the old Oklahoma National Guard. I signed up, too. I'd been hiding here. I was a Welshman who jumped ship in Galveston, Texas. Hitchhiked to Oklahoma. America had been good to me, so I fought for her.

"We finally got overseas. We ran into the lines. We lost a lot of good boys. I got knocked out pretty bad.

"Now I'm on the platform in Paris, France, and I'm waiting for the train to go to Le Havre to cross the English Channel to go home. A Frenchman asked me what part of Oklahoma I was from, and I said, 'Kingfisher,' and he studied a second, and his brows knitted.

"'Ah,' he said, 'the black man, he dance, he sing.' I looked at him in amazement, and I said, Yes . . ."

The fellow had been one of those salesmen who passed through Kingfisher. Of all the sights and sounds he'd encountered in America, the French salesman remembered an elderly man in a derby hat and a long black coat singing on a railroad platform. Until Paul Sykes died, he fed folks who were waiting for better times.

Logan Jackson, a retired carpenter, spliced his thoughts with laughter. He wanted no one to think he was complaining.

"In 1892, when I first came here, there were two frame buildings, and the rest was tents and dugouts. Those that had horses and cattle, they made it. But you take a person like me, come here with nothing, just his bare hands, well, he had to dig things out for himself."

The fact that Oklahoma was one of the few places where blacks actually owned land was, from the beginning, a fact not lost on either blacks or whites. It was a seed of power and contention.

For years a move had been under way to make Oklahoma an

all-black state. In 1890 Edwin McCabe, a black man who sought appointment as territorial governor, was convinced that power lay only in numbers. McCabe had been state auditor of Kansas, but when his party refused to let him run for a second term, he came to Oklahoma. For ten years, his newspaper, the *Langston Herald*, was distributed throughout the South and urged settlement in Oklahoma's all-black towns.

Antoine Fuhr drew a circle with his hand.

"There was between fifteen and twenty Negro towns within a thirty-mile radius of Muskogee. Absolute Negro towns. These colored folks, they'd hear about that. Some of them would come to see. There was a Negro postmaster. They'd take them on down and introduce him. There was a Negro mayor. Yeah. 'Call a meetin'!' There was a Negro councilman. A Negro marshal, town marshal.

"Black folks come here to Muskogee, they couldn't hold one of those offices. They couldn't even get to be dogcatcher!"

The leaves crackled. Jake Simmons rocked forward in his chair.

"I remember the first white man I ever saw. His name was Ed Hodd. He gave me a dime and gave George Drew a nickel. Well, I looked at the size of money and said, 'Now, here I'm getting the short end of this thing.' So I traded with George. Traded my dime for his nickel."

He boomed a big, hearty laugh.

"I didn't know any better until I spent it for some candy. See, I didn't get but five or six sticks, and George got ten."

Antoine Fuhr was tickled.

"That was the first white man you ever saw?"

Simmons smiled broadly and replied, "Yes, that was the first white man. Foreman of the Seavers ranch."

Davis tapped his cane.

"That's right, I knew him."

Simmons sat back and slapped the arm of his chair.

"The first deal I made, I got stumped!"

The old men shook with laughter.

.   .   .

Several women now joined our little band beneath the honeysuckle bush. Mrs. Andrew Rusworm ran a funeral parlor. Mrs. Blance Harper was twisting the lilac chain that held her glasses and recalling happier times growing up out in the country.

"We'd play together. We'd run. Go over to the white girl's house. Spend the night. She'd come stay the night with us. We didn't think no more about it. We'd visit back and forth as though we were one."

Farmwork was not segregated. People needed one another. Pigment made no difference in the dust at baling time.

As Mrs. Rusworm remembered, "If one wasn't busy and another was fixing a fence, he'd come over and help him. And when his fence needed fixin', Dad would go over and do the same."

But black homesteaders were outnumbered. G. I. Currin, the only black elected official in Oklahoma Territory, lasted one term. He proposed the first civil rights bill. It did not pass.

"You couldn't vote unless your grandfather voted in eighteen and sixty-six."

Birdie Farmer, a retired schoolteacher, was nearly one hundred, a quarter century older than Oklahoma.

"Of course, that prohibited all Negroes from voting, because no Negro's grandparents voted before the Civil War."

Strips of deep lavender began to appear at the edge of the sky. The first feathered shadows fell on the daisies. Approaching darkness stirred Logan Jackson's memory anew.

"Dan Porter was an old Civil War veteran. I was a little boy. At the time we met, they were enforcing the Jim Crow law, which said black men could not vote.

"Man told Dan Porter, says, 'Don't you go in there and try to vote.' Says, 'You can't read.'

"Porter says, 'That don't make no difference. I'm one of the men who made General Lee surrender!'"

Logan stared into the faces around him, "You don't know who

General Lee was, do you? He was a general in the Civil War. Yeah, an old soldier. Well, Dan, he voted."

Oklahoma's statehood in 1907 brought new laws. Overnight black people were told where to sit, where to walk, and when to learn. For those who had come west with the frontier spirit, it was a bitter, lonely ride into the future.

"In the fall of 1906 my husband and I would go down to the courthouse and go into the judge's chambers and listen to political speeches."

Birdie Farmer could see this scene clearly in her mind.

"C. N. Haskell was running for the Democratic nomination for governor. Anytime his name was mentioned, we'd have quite a crowd. The white folks were in the courtroom, but I was in the chamber.

"In one of his campaign speeches, Haskell made the assertion that they were not to mention anything about the Negro or Jim Crow or anything until after the constitution was signed by the president, who was then Theodore Roosevelt. Because if they did, Theodore Roosevelt would certainly not sign it, and they couldn't become a state. They would wait until after the first assembly of the legislature to pass any kind of laws against the Negro, then they could do as they pleased.

"And, oh, that pleased them!"

Birdie Farmer clapped her hands.

"They gave vent to their feelings by throwing up their hats and just hollering and whooping.

"They didn't mention anything about restrictive laws at all. It was only after the first house and senate met, they did the dirty work, so to speak. The first senate bill was separate coaches. 'There shall be separate coaches for Negroes and whites.' And the separate coach the Negroes were put in was just a little place right in front of the train. Right next to the baggage car. It was not comfortable. It wasn't kept clean."

The old woman's face looked tired. Her shoulders sagged.

"It made you feel that you weren't human, that's all."

Clara Luper picked up the thread of the conversation. Mrs. Luper, a history teacher, had led America's first sit-ins.

"In order to bring about changes, real changes, I think we had to go back to the Scripture, which teaches us plainly that 'a little child shall lead them.' Our children helped us win the right to eat in restaurants, sleep in hotels. But more importantly, we used our children to remind people what America was all about."

She, too, stopped to ponder, her dreams scattered about her like the daisies.

"The thing that hurts me most was not the fact that I went to jail twenty-three times trying to eat in an all-white restaurant, not the fact that once a man spit in my face. It was the day that our local amusement park opened to blacks. I was so happy because as a mother I wanted to take my child to the park. So when I found it was open, I immediately contacted my daughter and said, 'Marilyn, I would like to take you to the park.' But Marilyn looked at me and said, 'Mom, I want to go to the park, but I'd rather go with my friends.'

"And I realized that although I had spent my life trying to open up that park, I would never have the pleasure of taking my own children."

The group sat in silence until a night wind flipped a page in Charlie Ellison's hymnal.

"Well, that's it," he said. "Yeah, that's it. My eyes are about gone. Yeah, they're too old. Too old, I can't see no more to tell."

How that diverse group of Americans succeeded in living together made an extraordinary difference for the millions who came after them. Of course they had racial problems, and still do, but the way they worked them out holds lessons for our own time. This country's struggle for equality is filled with tragic, unrecorded skirmishes.

One of them took place on the U.S. Navy destroyer *Truxtun* in February 1942. That day the ship was plowing through the North Atlantic, surrounded by a wind that sounded like hell's idea of music. The blizzard blew in biblical proportions, bullying the *Truxtun* onto the rocks, offering Lanier Phillips a terrible choice: Stay and be washed overboard, or try for land and be lynched. His captain had told him that black sailors might not be welcomed in foreign lands.

Phillips already had lived a childhood of desperate fear. The Ku Klux Klan burned down his school in rural Georgia. Growing up in the segregated South he saw no future, so he joined the navy, even though the only job it offered a black man back then was that of a servant.

Phillips's ramrod posture bent with emotion. "I felt I was the lowest, the least, and the last, because that's the way I had been treated all my life."

Now, dangling above those frigid waters, Phillips shouted to the three other black mess attendants, " 'You're going to die if you stay on board!' Ice was forming on all our bodies. Every time a wave would come, it would wash ten to fifteen people overboard."

Phillips dropped into the last raft, but the other mess attendants remained behind.

"Well, they all froze to death," Phillips said. The men died along with 107 other shipmates.

Forty-six members of the *Truxtun*'s crew survived because villagers from Saint Lawrence, Newfoundland, rappelled down ice-covered cliffs to save them.

"These people took a chance on losing their lives to come down and help us," Phillips recalled, shaking his head in wonder. "We needed help."

One of the rescuers, Levi Pike, agreed. He was eighteen at the time, working in a mine behind the cliffs.

"Some of them were in terrible shape. Terrible, terrible shape. Sometimes you'd run out to get one and you'd miss him, because the sea had drawn him back again. You had to run back yourself to keep from getting carried away."

Phillips, coated in oil, was taken to a makeshift hospital.

"When I woke up, I was stark naked"—and terrified.

Charlotte Kelly and a friend, two white women, were frantically trying to scrape the oil off his body.

"I can't get you clean," Kelly said anxiously. "I can't get you white." Lanier looked up and said, "No. You can't get it off. It's the color of my skin."

"I was the first black man they had ever seen."

Kelly stayed up all night heating stones on her stove and wrapping them in Phillips's blankets to keep him warm. The next morning, navy medics came and took the survivors away. A lifetime would pass before the sailor returned as an old man to Saint Lawrence. Phillips and I stopped at a weathered house with a view of the ocean. The inside was just as Phillips remembered it.

"The stove was here," he said, pointing to a corner just beyond the kitchen. "The bed was back there behind that old wood stove. That's where I slept the night."

Charlotte Kelly still lived in the house, but said the friend who had helped her had died.

"I didn't even get a chance to thank her," Phillips murmured—or to tell her how he'd lived the life she saved. He decided to be more than a mess attendant and applied to the navy's sonar school. Although he was turned down repeatedly, eventually Lanier Phillips became the first African American in the U.S. Navy to earn a rank that took him out of the kitchen. He opened the door for thousands of men and women the navy had excluded.

Phillips retired in 1961, but not from the sea. He worked with French explorer Jacques Cousteau, helping to locate a lost nuclear bomb. Later he faced down bigots with guns while marching for civil rights. That plunge into the icy waters off the coast of Newfoundland left him fearless, and he believes that his life really began in Saint Lawrence.

"When the *Truxtun* collided with the cliffs in Newfoundland, I collided with my destiny."

The man who had desperately needed a hand now offered his. The town's mine had closed, and half its population had left, but Phillips did something for the sixteen hundred who remained: He cashed in his life savings and built a new playground.

"Something came over me," Phillips told a young couple who were pushing their children on the swings. "What your grandparents did etched in my mind a valuable lesson. I learned that not all white people were racists. Caring can come from unexpected places. Your people, they didn't just save my life—that's a minor part of it—they changed it."

Forever, with a simple act of kindness.

Some people endure the worst of life's punches and still prevail. Their struggles are etched on their faces, leaving marks of lessons learned, not defeats. None of them long for a return to a time made innocent by lack of detail. They build better days for all Americans. We find new freedom, largely because of these unknown people who charted a course that changed the country's culture.

Chapter Eight

They Never Let a Handicap Handicap Them

Successful Americans embrace failure. Fear of failing paralyzes progress; learning from mistakes pushes the country forward. Rachael Scdoris taught me that lesson. She was about to race a dogsled team eleven hundred miles over a treacherous trail she could barely see. Rachael was born with congenital achromatopsia, a rare disorder that left her sight fuzzy and without color, but she figured the biggest barrier to her success was "being blond." Her stunning good looks caused some to underestimate her ability.

"People say my eyes are a huge disadvantage, but I'm an athlete," Rachael said, strapping her dogs into harness. "I can easily jump off the sled and run up a three-mile hill, if I have to."

Scdoris's huskies had jogged fourteen miles the day we first met. They needed to run two thousand more to qualify for the Iditarod, an incredible race through the Alaskan outback, across a wilderness so vast it would stretch from Maine to the tip of Florida.

While some of the other mushers questioned her ability, Scdoris simply shrugged and stepped back onto her sled runners: "Quitting is just not something I'm really into."

She was eighteen, sleeping under the stars with her dogs, getting them comfortable with life on the trail. Her dad, Jerry, said Rachael had grown up listening to his huskies sing lullabies. "Dad used to take me on runs when I was a baby to put me down for a nap," she explained.

She started raising her own team in second grade.

"Rachael camped outside with her puppies for an entire year," Jerry Scdoris said with an incredulous smile.

Race rules require that she harness her huskies without help, slip protective booties over tender paws (a total of two thousand times), and dish out three tons of food and water. "They'll burn eight to ten thousand calories a day out there," Rachael explained, requiring her to stash pallets stacked with food along the eleven-hundred-mile trail.

"Winning the Iditarod is basically who can take the best care of their dogs—the fastest," she said, wiping ice from a puppy's paw.

The only concession to her blindness was an extra pair of eyes: Rachael's dad became her practice spotter, driving a sled ahead of hers and using a two-way radio to alert her to dangers.

"There's a boulder up ahead . . ." he warned, and Rachael swerved to steer around it. To her, the beauty of the Alaskan outback registers as only a black-and-white smudge, but she won't let anything hold her back.

"If there's a barrier," she said, "I'm determined to break it."

Scdoris would be the first musher in Iditarod history to be allowed a spotter: Paul Ellering, five-time Iditarod champ. Veteran racer and four-time champ Martin Buser remained concerned for her dogs' safety, arguing, "If you had a blind person driving your school bus you would probably yank your kid out of that bus." Scdoris had already proved her competence. At fifteen, she finished a five-hundred-mile dogsled race over mountain passes with tricky turns and blowing snow, the youngest ever to do so. She started with sixteen huskies and finished with all sixteen. None were injured.

"My dogs come first," she said. "Anything that will keep them safe, I'll do it."

The biggest races in life begin far from the starting line. That's why Jerry Scdoris maxed out his credit cards and drove twenty-five hundred miles—to the top of the globe—in the dead of winter to help his daughter chase the dream she cannot see. He did not ask her to reconsider.

"Not allowing her to accomplish her goals would be a setup for failure in life," he said, loading the last dog into his truck. "Hopefully she will make it easier for the next young person who comes along"— one who has a dream stronger than life's problems.

Scdoris raised most of her team from puppies at her home atop a forty-acre hill near Bend, Oregon. Second-graders who were now studying in her old classroom marveled at what she had accomplished since she was their age. The day before she set off for Alaska, one of them asked, "How is it being legally blind?"

"It's pretty difficult to be all the way back here and have your lead dogs over there by the wall. You can't see exactly what's going on."

Just getting to the starting line was a victory for a woman who sees only possibilities. Scdoris pumped her fist as she passed through a tunnel of screaming fans.

"The important thing is that I'm here," she said as she skidded to a stop. "I don't worry about falling anymore, because I've fallen before. So I just deal with whatever's out there."

"Five!" cried the race starter. The dogs began to yelp. The crowd roared.

"Four!"

"Whoa!" Scdoris yelled, stomping on her snow brake, holding back her team.

"Three!"

"A lot of people tell me I'm crazy," she said as she smiled over her shoulder.

"Two!"

Paul Ellering slid his team into the spotter's position in front of Rachael.

"One!"

Four little girls stood on tiptoes to see Scdoris pass. "GO!"

"Hi! Chee!" Scdoris shouted. Her dogs skittered off into a fog of ice. She was heading into some of the deepest snow in decades. The mushers ran through a crystal swamp, bone-chilling ice that pulled at legs and made each day's trip seem like two. Scdoris successfully navigated the most treacherous sections of the Iditarod, but after reaching the Eagle Island checkpoint (732 miles into the 1,200-mile race), her dogs got sick with a virus they had picked up along the way. Rather than risk their health, Scdoris dropped out.

"The pride of Norway!" cried the race announcer, as Robert Sorlie schussed into Nome, Alaska, winning the Super Bowl of sled-dog races. Rachael was heartbroken, wondering, *What am I doing out here, in the hardest race on earth?* But then, her toughest race had been the one she had set for herself. Her dream seemed foolish only to those who dared not try.

A year later, on March 18, 2006, Rachael Scdoris passed under the Burled Arch in Nome and slid into the history books, becoming the first legally blind athlete to finish the famed Iditarod. It took her twelve days, ten hours, and forty-two minutes. She was seventh out of the twenty rookies who started the race.

History is not just for winners. Sometimes there is more to remember than merely who crossed the finish line first.

You don't need perfect eyesight to have the kind of vision that builds America, just a determination to break down barriers. The country owes its success to those who are willing to try regardless of disability, people willing to risk their lives for country, family, even strangers.

One morning on his way to work in Durham, North Carolina, Marty Revelette saw someone trapped in a burning van. "Out of the corner of my eye I caught a red coat," he recalled, which turned out to be worn by eighty-six-year-old Elma Sneddeker.

"The car started smoking," she recalled, "and every once in a while it would shoot up in flames."

Fire so hot, it melted the battery and sizzled toward the gas tank.

Sneddeker thought, *This is it! If it hits the gasoline, I'm a goner.*

To do nothing is in everyone's power. As other drivers sat watching, Revelette—a man born with no arms—steered his car to the side of the road with his feet. He dashed through the smoke and found a face pressed against glass.

"He shouted, 'Open the window!'" Sneddeker was frantic. "I tried to press the buttons," she said, "but I couldn't open the window."

The electrical system was dead. Smoke from the engine swirled around her.

Revelette shouted, "Lady, watch your eyes!" and hit the window four times with his foot. The fourth time shattered it.

"I tried to grab the latch to unlock the door, but a foot doesn't work like a wrist; I couldn't get to it."

"Smoke and flames started burning the front seat," Sneddeker recalled. "Woosh! Woosh!" Her face lit at the memory. "I knew I was going to die."

But Revelette wrapped his leg around her and pulled her through the window without a scratch—or a moment to spare. Good stories like that begin with a lump in the throat, something you feel compelled to tell. The man with no arms never revealed why he did what he did that day. Real heroes seldom believe they are heroes, but it's clear that someone very special stopped at that burning car. He had grown up in an orphanage after his sharecropper parents abandoned him because he had no hands to help them pick. As an adult, he started his own business—"Hands Free Landscaping."

"I wasn't born without arms for no reason," Revelette said. But it took him almost thirty years to discover his calling.

On another road in his past life, Revelette could not save his own son.

Four-year-old Marcus had begged his father to let him ride in the back of their pickup. When the truck hit a bump, though, the boy bounced out. Revelette hit the brakes and ran back, but without arms could not give his son the mouth-to-mouth resuscitation he needed. A police car finally stopped, but the officers were too late to save his son. Revelette stood there, stricken, a frustrated father who had been unable to help.

"They zipped up the little green body bag, and I said, 'Marcus, I know you're still here. Forgive your daddy for what happened.'"

Thirty-three years later, Revelette found redemption in rush-hour traffic. Elma Sneddeker owed her life to Revelette's resolve never to find himself so helpless again.

"Here I am," Elma said, "a healthy woman"—with a face no longer lit by fire but glowing from the inside out, smiling because of a man with no arms, but a lot of heart.

I often find that heroes are in the corner of the eye. Storytelling is a search, not a certainty but a hopeful journey during which I am constantly looking for something better around the bend. I'm on a quest that hasn't changed since the first caveman killed a mastodon and came back to paint an account of his adventure.

On a beautiful fall day in Cleveland Heights, Ohio, I was admiring leaves that looked as if they'd been dipped in paint. I noticed a young man who was doing that, too, his nose two inches from a berry.

"Butterscotch," I heard him say.

The woman standing next to him asked, "Do you think that is a color you need?"

"Yes," he said emphatically.

I watched him push through the shrubs. He was handsome, smartly dressed in a long coat. Probably not the gardener. The woman with him was old enough to be his mother, and as it turned out, she was. He had not said more than a sentence to her in nearly a quarter of century.

Seth Chwast cannot hold a conversation or express a complex thought. At age two he was diagnosed with autism. His mother, Debra, said, "I tried for five years to conceive. I never wanted anything more than I wanted that child."

She was determined to give him a normal life. Chwast tried every therapy that might open his world. Nothing changed except her marriage, which ended.

"I could start weeping now, thinking about it," she said.

A counselor suggested that Seth consider mopping floors for a career. Instead his mom enrolled him in one last therapy class at the Cleveland Museum of Art. Suddenly the boy who barely spoke began to communicate. His mother was blown away.

"I had no idea he had any talent," she marveled.

We usually talk about the challenges of autism. We seldom consider its gifts. Seth began painting thirty hours a week, filling the entire house with his work. He took me on a tour, rattling off the names he had given his paintings like a four-year-old quickly turning the pages of a storybook.

"Northern Lights Are in the Sky, Fantasy Red Horse, Blue Whale with Flippers and Tail, Northern Lights with Peanut Butter and Jelly Mountains."

Seth trotted down the hall to his studio, picked up a brush, and without a pause began to paint.

Debra Chwast stepped up behind me, as her son pressed his face close to the canvas. "He has incredible focus," she said. "He lives only in the moment. He is as certain in his painting as he is lost in reality!"

Apparently Seth sees the finished painting in his head before he even starts.

"Head, then neck with body," he said, leaning back, revealing a beautiful blue horse, work so vivid and varied, it mirrored the great masters Van Gogh and Chagall.

"There is no limit to what Seth will do now," his mom said. He now has a world of artists who understand him. Art professor Michael Cunningham became fascinated with this man who could see beyond what's normal.

"It's a stunning example of someone who has pathways of communicating with us—sharing with us—that are not traditional," the professor explained.

"What is Seth trying to say through his painting?" I asked.

"Maybe it's his way of saying, 'I count. I'm real,'" Chwast suggested. "Maybe it's like Pinocchio. He became a real boy, you know, instead of a wooden boy."

Music drifted from their living room. Seth was now dancing fluidly, and his mom joined him.

"Don't assume anything's over," she said later. "It doesn't matter if an autistic child is five or twelve or twenty. As a parent, you may not get what you want, but you may get something better that you never even dreamed of."

A happy son who can show us what only he can see.

Have you ever felt that you could create if only you had a season of quiet in your life—that you could paint if you lived with a lovely view? The Sangre de Cristo Mountains north of Santa Fe, New Mexico, have been an inspiration for generations of artists. Each morning as the sun slips over the horizon, the paint pot tips and spills, casting its beauty on the people below.

Life in the valley flows in rhythm with that beauty. Sculptors work the morning light, moving with the sun. Michael Naranjo had lived in those mountains all of his life. He, too, was an artist, but for him the sun's beauty was only memory.

Naranjo is totally blind.

"I live in a sheltered world," he said, "where all I see is beauty."

The Indian dancers of his boyhood are fading in his mind's eye, but dozens of them still exist as vivid images of his Indian heritage. Naranjo grew up on the Santa Clara Pueblo. His mother was a famous potter, and Naranjo was a promising painter, until he went to fight in Vietnam. The last thing he saw before he lost his sight was the Viet Cong soldier who nearly killed him.

"We just looked at each other," he recalled. "Just gazed into each other's eyes. I shot. He tossed a hand grenade. I started to turn toward it. It exploded."

Locked in the darkness of his mind, Naranjo asked for a bit of clay to pass the long hours in an army hospital. With his one good hand, he made an inchworm. Then he had a grander vision: He would build a twelve-foot statue, all by touch.

"I was sitting in my living room," Naranjo remembered, "and saw this gray shadow moving across in front of me. It was my mind's eye that was looking at it. And, suddenly, the shadow formed. It was an eagle dancer. When I looked close, it disappeared. But I had seen it, so I could bring it back."

He worked with the three fingers the explosion had left him on his left hand, and a withered right hand.

"I knew it was going to be difficult to create with my left hand," he said. But he was determined to learn.

Museum officials in Florence, Italy, built a scaffold for the blind artist to help him study Michelangelo's *David*.

"I knew his face was in front of me," Naranjo said. "I touched a thousand places," he said, so that he could feel what the rest of us see in the blink of an eye. He discovered something we tourists can't see from below.

"Hearts. Hearts!" he said fervently. Even now they were vivid memories. "I couldn't believe the *David*'s pupils were hearts."

Touching Michelangelo's statue changed Naranjo's art.

"I could see farther into the stone," he said. "I could see inside, where before, I felt the surface."

His work improved, and soon he was invited to present pieces to the White House and the Vatican. His sculptures now reside in major collections around the world, but one feature is always missing: None of his human figures have eyes.

"I decided if I was blind, they were going to be blind, too," he explained. "These sculptures are my children. I struggled with them in thought and in their creation. They were very strong within, and they had to come out."

He wanted us to view them as he did—with his hands.

"Close your eyes," Naranjo told a little boy.

He guided the child's fingers over a statue of a GI carrying a wounded comrade.

"Cool," the kid said. "This sculpture is better than the ones I see."

Naranjo chuckled. After a lifetime of blindness, he knew we can tell more from a touch than from a glance.

I left him holding hands with his wife, Laurie. The artist had never seen her or their two daughters, but he said, "I'm happy. My life is full. I really don't think I would take sight over the life that I have today."

It's amazing what an artist can see, when he can't see.

Michael Naranjo is one of those people who hold a mirror to our lives, reflecting who we wish we were. When Evan Light looked into that mirror, it was held by Nick Ackerman, someone who understands his desire to be the best athlete in the land. Neither Evan nor Nick cared they had no feet.

"Elbows in!" Ackerman commanded, throwing an arm over Evan's back, and they began to wrestle. "Palms out. Drive. Drive. Drive!"

The two crabbed around the mat, locked in each other's arms. Evan was eleven that day, short for his age, an olive-skinned kid with a shock of dark hair. Nick Ackerman, his coach, had once been a farm boy who still flashed an aw-shucks grin. They couldn't have been more different in appearance, but they had many things in common. While growing up in Colfax, Iowa, Ackerman tried all sorts of sports— baseball, soccer, even football—on artificial legs.

"I was the only guy to break his leg in the first half and play in the second," Ackerman recalled with a grin. "My dad went home and got a different set of legs, an old set, and I put 'em on and went out there and finished the game."

Evan played football, too, as well as golf, tennis, and basketball. Now he wanted Ackerman to teach him wrestling. "I don't think I have any limits," the boy told him.

Ackerman's mom, Cindy, allowed him to take risks.

"I didn't want him to be stopped from doing things," she explained, "so I went to the teachers, to the coaches, everybody I could, to tell them, 'Let him get hurt.'"

She figured bumps and falls could be fixed, but not letting Nick try could do permanent damage.

"I always thought I was the normal one," Ackerman said. "I used to break the legs off my G.I. Joe action figures, to make 'em cool like me."

Ackerman's legs were the center of a life-or-death battle when he was a baby. At eighteen months, he contracted a deadly form of meningitis that put him into a coma.

"By the time we got to the hospital," Cindy recalled, "his skin was black."

To save his life, doctors had to amputate his legs below the knee.

Evan lost his feet in a traffic accident that also took his mother's life. The Light family wanted a little boy after three girls, so they adopted him from an orphanage in India and brought him home to Indiana.

"What do you tell the other kids," I asked, "when they ask how you lost your feet?"

A smile dawned on Evan's face. "Shark bite."

Humor was the rudder that helped him steer past problems. Evan wanted to meet someone who had sailed through life's storms and excelled, someone like him, so his dad drove him to Nick Ackerman's office. The trip took four hours. Randy Light didn't care.

"God picked up Evan from the other side of the world, from Calcutta, India, and put him in our home in South Bend." Davenport, Iowa, he said, is not that far for a beacon of hope.

"If I had an opportunity to have my legs," Ackerman told Evan, "I wouldn't take it. I wouldn't! I like where I'm at," he said. Even though he is not living the life he dreamed of.

Working outdoors seemed the logical choice for Ackerman, who grew up in the country. He planned to become a park ranger after graduating from high school, but instead spends most of every day indoors, designing and fitting artificial limbs. He crafted a customized pair of wrestling shoes that cushioned the ends of Evan's legs.

"All he had before was a set of duct-taped foam pads," Ackerman laughed—not good enough for a national tournament, Evan's first. Ackerman playfully slapped him on the chin, urging, "Get loose! Shake it out!"

Wrestling mats covered an entire football field at the University of Northern Iowa, where Ackerman and Evan joined hundreds of other wrestlers and waited for the referee's whistle.

When his turn came, Evan toddled to center mat. He slapped hands with his opponent and was promptly pinned. Afterward, Ackerman huddled with Evan and told him, "The best advice I can give for getting off your back is to not get there."

Ackerman spoke from experience; he had lost a lot, too, admitting with a groan, "I was awful."

Until finally he wasn't. In 2001 the Simpson College senior wrestled his way to the NCAA championships. He fought a fellow who had not been beaten in sixty-three matches. No one without legs had ever won. Nick did. The NCAA picked him as the outstanding college player in the country, and during the NCAA's centennial, his win was named one of the twenty-five defining moments in our sports history. The list also included Jesse Owens's four world records in 1935, Doug Flutie's Hail Mary touchdown pass in 1984, and tennis great Arthur Ashe's big wins in 1965.

"Everybody has some obstacle to overcome," Ackerman told Evan. "You and I just have ones that are more visual."

He wrapped the little boy in a bear hug and then leaned back and held his gaze.

"I'm proud of you, buddy," he said intensely. "You did well."

All dreams worth following come with long odds, but Evan works hard, is determined, and is lucky to have found both a family who loves him and a coach who cares. His time will come, for to surrender a dream means to leave life as it is and not as it could be.

I'm fortunate to have encountered many Americans who refuse to see limits but instead see only opportunities. Ed Lucas decided he wanted to broadcast baseball games after watching the first nationally televised playoff on October 3, 1951, when New York Giants outfielder Bobby Thompson hit a walk-off home run to win the National League pennant. Ed ran outside to celebrate this legendary moment in the sport's history. The twelve-year-old fired a fastball to a friend with a bat.

"The ball came back and *boom,* hit me right between the eyes." The injury destroyed his retinas, leaving him totally blind.

It seemed to be the end of the world. What could he do? Ed was enrolled at St. Joseph's, a boarding school for the blind in New Jersey. One snowy afternoon his dad showed up to take him home for the weekend. When his father knelt down to help him put on a pair of galoshes, a nun touched Ed's shoulder and said to his father, "He's only blind. He's not handicapped. When he puts them on himself, you can leave!" An hour and half later, they left. After that, anything seemed possible.

The twelve-year-old was determined to stay close to the game he loved, but memories take you only so far. Soon he was grown with two sons of his own to raise alone—their mother had left them. The boys thought their father had superhuman powers. He used to read to them at bedtime with the lights out. Yankee Stadium became their second home, as Lucas interviewed players for New Jersey radio stations. Despite the injury that caused his blindness, he still loved the game.

Baseball took his sight, but baseball also gave him a life, as well as another chance at love. Yankee Hall of Famer Phil Rizzuto set him up on a "blind" date, where Lucas met Allison Pfeifle, a fan with failing sight. He helped her with the slow business of learning how to live a new way. They talked on the phone for six years. Then, one evening, Lucas came into her flower shop and asked her if she wanted to go to a movie.

"We can hear what's going on," Lucas assured her. "When they're not talking, they'll either be walking or kissing. We can figure that out."

Lucas admitted that when it came to Allison, it was love at . . . well, you get the idea. They got married in the fairy-tale setting of Yankee Stadium, with Lucas standing where his heroes all have stood—at home plate. As always, his sons were at his side. Chris Lucas told the gathering that his dad had gone through a very dark winter being blind, "but he's had a great spring, a great summer, and now in the fall, he's going to have a lot of fun."

Yankee Stadium holds a lot of special memories, but none like that—the day a blind man stepped up to the plate and won the game of life.

Broadcasting was my dream as a boy, too.

For a child growing up with a bad leg, TV was a picture window. Nothing seemed impossible on that little screen, not when your heroes all wore white hats and rode horses. Roy Rogers and the Lone Ranger could lift me off the couch and let me ride my imagination to a better place. Andy Devine's squeaky voice yelling, "Hey, Wild Bill, wait for me!" was a siren song. The Polio Kid could become the Cisco Kid. Everyone could tell by my outfit that I was a cowboy.

My grandfather Bailey, who had lived in the old West, watched those TV cowboys with a bemused expression and tried to set me straight.

"How many times," he wondered, "did the Cisco Kid shoot that revolver without reloading?"

I counted fingers on both hands.

"Ten."

"Ten?" he snorted. "I counted twelve." Grandpa was big on addition. "Problem is, that pistol only holds six bullets."

Pointing to the Lone Ranger's horse, Silver, galloping after bad guys, he said, "We seldom ran horses like that on the open range. They might step in a prairie dog den and break their legs."

I turned up the volume on the TV. Grandpa turned it back down.

"Most of us," he continued, "couldn't afford our own horse. We'd rent them. Two dollars a day. A quarter off if you brought your own saddle. The rental horses were nearly always dirty brown and ugly, so you wouldn't be tempted to steal them."

On our TV set, Roy Rogers's horse, Trigger, tossed his golden mane and tapped his hoof to tell Roy how many outlaws had taken Roy's wife, Dale Evans.

"Those rental horses would never race after outlaws," Grandpa scoffed. "They were trained to walk five miles to the nearest stable. The only time they ran was the last fifty yards, when they could smell the feedbag.

"You pulled off your saddle and plunked it on another dull horse. We rode like that all day. At sunset on level ground, you could look back and see where you started that morning at sunup."

The real West held little fascination for a five-year-old with a cast on his leg, but because my grandfather had lived there, I asked, "Grandpa, were you ever Wyatt Earp's deputy?"

"He was before my time," he chuckled.

"Maybe horses ran faster back then," I said, smiling.

Family can be both handicap and help. We are forever measuring our lives against those who have gone before us, who set the benchmarks we constantly check. When was my brother allowed to go on his first date? How old was Mom when she got married? Was I making more than my dad did at this age?

Pepe Gallego said he was seventeen when the answer to that last question made him smile. He set out to earn some summer money at a sawmill in Glendale, Oregon, and wound up bringing home a bigger paycheck than his father. So he kept the job, dropped out of high school, and got married. He and his wife, Judy, raised four children, the last of whom was born with a disability—an inability to speak.

Gallego mortgaged his home, cleaned out his savings, and started a small grocery business on the side so he could make more money to care for the boy. Before he could get a loan, Gallego revealed something he had kept secret for twenty-three years: He had never learned how to read or write. He worried that that might cost him his job at the sawmill, but the owner, Bill Gregory, set up a small classroom to teach him. Gregory's father had dropped out of school, too.

"My dad went to the eighth grade," Gregory said, "and my mother just got through fifth grade. As a result, my dad was pretty limited in the jobs he could get."

For years Pepe Gallego had felt trapped. "My whole life was: get up, go to work, come home, lay down, watch TV, and sleep," he said. "Twenty-three years just slipped away." He feared his fellow workers would laugh when they found out he couldn't read, but some of them enrolled in the class, too, encouraging the boss to provide them even more. Gregory not only paid to teach his employees how to read but offered all sorts of educational courses. One worker even studied guitar.

"Well, sure," Gregory said, "I think that's great, being a guitar player myself. It shows good judgment."

What Gallego learned from Gregory's school made him a better grocer. His business flourished, and he eventually had seven employees.

"I don't know if I'm going to be as generous as Gregory," he said.

In fact, he eventually left the sawmill.

"If my employees do go somewhere else," Gregory said, "that's still much better than having a guy who stays with you and can't read or write."

For years, Gregory handed out five-hundred-dollar scholarships to every graduating senior in town who wanted to go to college. Many got their start at the sawmill school.

"He was our Santa Claus," Gallego said. "A Santa offering dreams."

No child ever asks what Santa would like for Christmas—a fact I was pondering while standing in a long line waiting to see St. Nick.

A little girl ahead of me sprang onto Santa's lap and announced, "I want a Barbie doll!"

"I want a Barbie!" her sister repeated.

"You want a Barbie, too." The bearded man nodded.

"And some doll clothes," the little girl added, poking his red coat.

"I want some doll clothes, too," her sister said.

"Oh, boy," sighed Santa. "We definitely have an echo in here."

Their parents laughed, and I did, too. Clearly, this was more than just another storefront Santa. That twinkle in his eye was the expression of love, not a sales pitch. After his shift at the shopping mall, he invited me to see his special workshop.

This one was filled with the glitter that kids desire, but rather than toys, its inventory was something far more precious: Santa and his pals were making electric wheelchairs. The first one he built was for a toddler in Vietnam.

"She had lost both her legs to a land mine," Santa said. "When I met her, the seat in her wheelchair was about shot."

Santa wore a different uniform then. He was Marine Major Ed Butchart. By the time we met he had built more than a thousand wheelchairs. The first ones he built with parts scrounged from trash piles near his home outside Atlanta.

"I'd get in there among the coffee grounds and garbage," Butchart said, "and dig them out!"

If a child can find a wheelchair nowhere else, he can get one from Butchart for free. Ryan Mercer's parents watched as Santa pulled the little boy up on his lap.

"I've got something sticking out of my beard," Butchart said. "I wonder what it is? Is it a mouse?"

Ryan giggled and clapped his hands, then saw something that drew his attention to a corner of the workshop: a light glimmering off his new motorized ride. Ed lowered him into the seat and showed him how to get the wheelchair running. Ryan had cerebral palsy, but soon was spinning around the workshop. After several loops he suddenly stopped and looked up at the old man with the gray beard.

"You want to hug me for a minute?" Ed asked.

Ryan nodded. His first word that night was "wheelchair," murmured in Santa's ear.

It's never too late to have a happy childhood. Growing up with the aftereffects of polio taught me to view my handicap as a springboard. Whatever held me back also pushed me to achieve. We all approach success differently because of the limits placed on our lives. That's why most successful people "do their own thing." Their handicaps are not an excuse for failure. They are more often the edge that helps them succeed.

Chapter Nine

Where a Game Is Still a Game and Not a Bottom Line

I've never been much of an athlete. In this beefcake world, I'm a patty melt. But I love games, especially the kind where both sides are still smiling at the end. Games are particularly important in a nation filled with people who come from other countries. Sport is a common ground, a way to get to know one another. One of my favorites, Priests on Ice, never made it to ESPN.

These guys were to hockey what the Harlem Globetrotters are to basketball. Their goalie rode a horse named Penance. Their best player was a priest dressed as a nun, "Sister Mary Shooter," who would distract the other team's goalie by lassoing him with a twelve-foot-long rosary. Meanwhile, the priests would put Plexiglas in front of their net, so their opponents couldn't score. If, by some miracle, an opposing player did manage to make a goal, he was recruited on the spot, at center ice, given a cape, a candle, and a pail full of holy water in the face and then put in the penalty box for playing like a Protestant.

Father Vaughn Quinn captained this crazy team. He wore a beanie and carried a teddy bear. When Father Quinn was not playing hockey, he drove a fire truck. On sunny days you could see the good father racing his fire engine through stoplights in Detroit, hauling gangs of alcoholics who had never learned how to live life sober. Father Quinn ran the largest alcohol rehab center in the Midwest. The fire engine was part of his therapy, teaching drunks to have fun without drinking. If they fell off the wagon, he went looking for them in his 1925 Dodge hearse. Some sobered up inside reading the words Father Quinn had painted on the ceiling: "You ain't dead yet!"

The beanie-wearing priest had once been a drunk himself, which helps explain why his hockey team took their fun so seriously: It was their way of reaching people. Church attendance soared when the Flying Fathers arrived in town.

"You can't stay in the rectory," said Quinn, "and wait for folks to come to you."

After the game, dozens of people would drop by to talk hockey, and a number of them would say, "Hey, I could use some help."

On this particular day the crowd roared and jumped to its feet when Father Quinn skated onto the ice holding the tail of that horse named Penance. He was chasing Sister Mary Shooter. They raced down the ice and jumped on the other team's goalie. When the snow had cleared, there were four pucks in the net.

I'm not sure the scholars of Rome would comprehend all this, but Father Vaughn Quinn understood that nothing transforms human apathy quicker than a laugh.

I make it a practice always to follow a chuckle to its source.

In Kodiak, Alaska, I heard laughter echoing down Pillar Mountain. Two duffers were ice-picking their way up the snow-covered cliffs, carrying golf clubs. For these avid sportsmen, no course was too far away.

"A fine shot, sir," one of the duffers cried. "A fine shot!" They stumbled on in the snow. Pebble Beach it ain't, but it *is* a golf tournament— one hole, par seventy. That's right: one hole, par seventy.

"Oh, did you hear that clunk in the bushes?" Pogo Good shouted as his ball disappeared down a ravine. His partner struggled to find footing. "Are you ready? Fire away there, Scrim. Fore!"

The classic began during a cold lull in the fishing season. Scrimshaw Matthew bet Pogo Good and the boys he could beat them in a game of golf. Same rules as for the Masters would apply—sort of.

"Nice shot," Scrimshaw observed as Pogo's ball landed six inches inside a snowdrift. "Beauty!" He pulled out an ice ax. "Now we dig."

Players are allowed, without penalty, to dig out golf balls that land in snowdrifts. They can then tamp down the snow to make a level playing surface and hit the ball again. Each of the forty-four golfers had a caddy and a spotter who stood a couple of hundred yards up range to track shots.

"Right over your head. You see it?" Pogo asked as another ball took off.

"I heard it land," said Scrimshaw. "It could've landed anywhere."

There was nothing fair about that fairway. On the right was the "Ravine of Doom." Shank one over its side, and it would take a howitzer to get you out. There are bushes, sleeping bears, ice fields, and cliffs for nearly a mile. The course is fourteen hundred feet straight up from the valley floor to the "green."

"Body block. Body block!" Pogo shouted to his spotter as another ball careened back down the mountain. The spotter dove on it to stop it from rolling. (That's a legal move.)

"We had a ball take off," Scrimshaw recalled. "It probably went a mile. Kept going and going and going. It was gone," he chuckled. "Two-stroke penalty."

Rick Lindholm, the only two-time winner, was the man to beat that day.

"All right," Lindholm said as he took a perfect swing, looking as smug as a Presbyterian with four aces. "Another good one."

Pogo, who was busy plucking his ball from a snowy tree branch, asked, "Is that a bird's nest?"

Scrimshaw Matthews shot a twenty-two, but Rick Lindholm was white-hot. He finished five thousand yards—par seventy—in nineteen. Meanwhile, Pogo Good was sliding down the ravine in search of his ball.

"Okay," he huffed. "What we're going to try to do is to get out of the bushes." Before, he meant, they woke up the bears.

Even sleeping wildlife would not stop John Espinoza. He played golf all day, almost every day, on a course he and his father, Steve, built by hand, carving it out of the ten-acre woods around their Montana home, creating fairways wherever a ball hit a tree.

"Timber!" Steve shouted as another tall pine tree came crashing down. John's mom was not happy. "At first I thought it was just totally crazy," Juana told me. "But they just kept going and going!"

A hole a year, for ten years.

"What's the challenge on this fairway?" I asked Steve Espinoza as we approached the first tee.

"Clear the house," he said, pointing at the hazard. "Don't break any windows."

Their home lies directly in front of the green. Par three, if you're good. John is good. I am not.

"Look out!" John yelled.

"Oh, he hit the roof," Steve roared. "The ball is on the roof!"

John smiled and then concentrated on his swing. The ball hooked around the house and landed on the green—not bad for a guy who is nearly blind in one eye. John was also partially deaf in both ears and needed more than a dozen surgeries to drain fluid from them. He was born with Cornelia de Lang Syndrome, a congenital disorder that often causes mental retardation, but John was sharp and wanted desperately to play golf like his big brother, Mike.

"You know what was so hard?" his dad said, as he watched his son putting. "I didn't believe in him. I said, 'You can't do this like Michael.'"

That was grief talking. Steve's daughter died of a heart defect, and then Michael was killed in a car accident. Steve's best friend died in his arms in Vietnam. Haunted by these deaths, one day Steve kissed his sleeping wife, grabbed a gun, and went out, intent on taking his own life.

"I would have killed myself," Steve admitted, but at the last minute, he realized John needed him.

They began to heal each other. Steve has a disability, too: On some days old war wounds confine him to a wheelchair. On those days John mows the entire course. As we watched him from their backyard deck, his father said passionately, "This kid has self-pride. He can do it. He can accomplish it by himself."

An army of people heard what John was doing and began donating what he needed.

"It's a huge challenge," golf course superintendent Jim Peacock said. "There aren't a lot of golf courses around him in Eureka, Montana, and he started from scratch, not knowing what to do."

But that backyard golf course can't hold John any longer, not after he qualified for the Special Olympics in Dublin, Ireland, where the family that had lost so much finally won—a bronze medal.

"He became a champion," Steve said proudly. "He's as good as his brother. He doesn't have to live in his brother's shadow anymore."

John Espinoza opened his golf course to anyone with a disability. They play for fun, and for free. His dog, Zing, retrieves the shots they don't like.

"How has the golf course changed your life?" I asked.

John answered with one word. "Happy." He took another swing. His father watched the ball's flight and then turned to me and said, "If heaven is a place where dreams come true, then this is truly heaven, because this dream has come true."

It's hard to tell whether some children will excel later in their lives. The ultimate winners are not always the most obvious. Early on, the bright lights seldom find them, and they live far from the rest of us. A friend of mine played football for a West Texas town that was so small the players changed their uniforms at halftime and came back out as the band. There were so few girls that another town lent them cheerleaders. It made for some close relationships. My friend married one of them. She also played flute in the band and moved yard markers. That's the way it is with small-town football—a family affair.

The Dancing Darlin's of Gordon, Texas (population 478), may have had the most democratic pep club in America. Nearly every kid was a member—well, not everyone, as somebody had to play the game. Gordon had only a handful of available boys on the beautiful autumn afternoon I drove into town, so no matter how small they were, they were expected to suit up.

Football is more than just a game in Gordon. It is the rhythm of life. As sure as autumn follows summer, little girls grow up to be cheerleaders and little boys dream of Friday night heroics.

The town's antique fire engine led the pep parade that evening. It still drove fine, but its siren went silent at around the time gas rose above eleven cents a gallon. Little Lloyd Riblock was the replacement, sprawling on the hood yelling, "Whoop, whoop!" while a flatbed truck carrying the rest of the team bounced behind. Dozens of pickups followed. Most everyone in town wanted to be in the parade, posing something of a dilemma: Who would stand on the sidewalk and wave?

For as long as many people can remember, Gordon has closed the doors of its businesses in the golden sun of autumn to follow its teams. If you wanted a cinnamon bun or Band-Aid on the day of a game, you had to get it before Lloyd Riblock sang his siren song.

Just before kickoff, he hopped down from the fire truck and became just a little boy again, kicking dirt while people parked their pickups around the field. They backed in close and dropped their tailgates, so grandmas could watch the game from folding chairs placed in the truck beds. Across the field, football players were putting on uniforms in a shed they shared with the visiting team. Both sides knew there would be some confusion that night: Their school colors were the same.

Tiny Texas towns like Gordon had formed their own football league, fielding six-man teams. In six-man football only three players went to the line. Anyone could catch a pass, a rule that could blow a game wide open. If either side got more than forty-five points ahead, they called it quits and went to the American Legion hall for sodas.

I hesitate to use the word "cozy" to describe the game I attended, as it seems so out of place when discussing football, but that evening was, well, cozy. Families huddled together in the backs of those pickups, watching players dart down the field. Carrie Teichman, not much bigger than the football, cuddled in her father's arms and waited for the band. She loved to hear the drums at halftime.

"My favorite part of the night," she giggled.

Carrie was blind. She nodded off when the band hustled back to the shed to become football players again.

A lot of us enjoy watching big-time football players seeking professional careers. Folks in Gordon, Texas, enjoyed the game for other reasons. I do, too, as I'm a big fan of people who play for pure pleasure. One crisp winter afternoon in St. Petersburg, Florida, I stopped to watch Fred Broadwell waiting for a pitch, crouching over the strike zone, leaning into the wind, seemingly suspended. When the ball floated over the plate he chopped it toward the shortstop and shuffled off toward first base on stiff legs. It was a big day for Broadwell. A couple of years earlier he had been sidelined with pneumonia. Now he was back, at ninety-five.

"Go, Freddy!" yelled the crowd, as the shortstop stabbed the ball, fielding it on one hop and then stopping as his back stiffened. The third baseman grabbed the ball from the shortstop's glove and flipped it across the diamond. Freddy scuffed across the bag, a beat ahead of the ball. It was all in a day's play for the Kids and Kubs. Those two teams had been battling each other three days a week, sixty games each winter, since 1931. Nobody on the field was under seventy-five.

What's the matter with seventy-five, they chanted. *We're the boys who are still alive. Rah, rah, seventy-five . . .*

When these fellows talk about the great old players, they don't mean DiMaggio, Gehrig, or Ruth; they're talking about guys like Ed Forest, who stood on his head at home plate to celebrate his eightieth birthday, and Chappy Chapman, who got 144 hits one season. In the midst of winter these men had found an endless summer.

A roar went up from the crowd as a grounder dribbled between the right fielder's legs, and old Freddy shuffled toward home plate.

George Bakewell yelled, "How's that for a ninety-five-year-old man?"

Broadwell doffed his cap and winked as he scored. Sometimes there's no defense against experience.

"They can't throw out a ninety-five-year-old man?" Bakewell shouted gleefully.

Fans roared their approval. Broadwell was from that generation for whom a game is still a game and not a bottom line.

Twelve years would pass before I sat in the stands again to watch the Kids and Kubs. George Bakewell was now ninety-nine, catching for Pappy Hill.

"Okay, Pappy, right over the plate!" Bakewell said, adjusting his jaunty bow tie and flashing two fingers between his legs.

Pappy Hill, pushing eighty, slipped on a pair of glasses and leaned in for a look. He took off the glasses, put them in his pocket, and stung a strike into Bakewell's glove. It seemed to me that these guys had been taken off Father Time's mailing list. If Babe Ruth were alive, he would have been two years younger than Bakewell.

"You get better and better, George!" shouted a woman sitting next to me.

It was another gorgeous winter afternoon in St. Petersburg, and the start of George Bakewell's thirty-seventh season. He rarely struck out.

"Watch this!" George said, trotting over to the woman who had yelled at him. He kissed her. The two had just gotten back from their honeymoon hiking in Switzerland.

A fellow like that naturally attracts a following. "The Kissing Bandit," another woman called as she waved him over. He smooched her, too.

George's kissing fans don't fluster his new bride, Bonnie.

"Let him have them. I don't care. He's mine. They're not going to get him."

Some of the new guys would like to be in his cleats, but Pappy Hill didn't train like George. "I smoke fourteen cigars a day," he admitted.

At eighty-seven Bakewell jumped rope a couple of hundred times just to keep his blood pumping. He warmed up with an eight-pound iron bat.

"See that little egg?" Bakewell said, flexing his arm and pointing to his muscle.

Before the game he rode a stationary bike twenty miles. Some said he could circle the bases faster than the scorekeeper could keep score. (The scorekeeper was ninety.)

Every three days or so, whenever one side begins to score more than the other, club officials get together and trade players to keep the games even. A player plays whatever position he feels up to that day.

"You know, I wouldn't be opposed to hitting a ball and falling dead on the way to first base," Bakewell said. "I wouldn't be opposed to that at all. That'd be a nice way to go."

At season's end George Bakewell turned one hundred.

We talk a lot about sports legends, and "legend" is a word we tend to use easily. A team wins thirteen games—legendary. A guy tosses one good season of baseball—he's a legend. A single Saturday afternoon thrill—legendary. But what of the legends who build quietly, year in and year out, until they touch us all? For sixty summers Jimmy Porter gently coaxed the kids of Carrollton, Texas, to play the game he loved.

"Hi, Jimmy," said a father, holding his three-year-old son by the hand. "This is Jason."

"How you doing?" asked Jimmy.

"Say, 'Hi, Jimmy,'" the man urged the boy.

"Hi, Jimmy." The little boy's words were hidden behind the knuckles in his mouth.

"Jimmy taught me baseball," his father said. "You wanna learn to play baseball from Jimmy?"

The boy's face brightened. Kids took to Jimmy Porter like ants to a picnic. He was seldom more than a pebble kick from the nearest ballpark. He lived alone, and never married, but always knew what he wanted.

Porter had built his life around kids. For forty years he lived in a boxcar to be near their ballpark. When the boxcar was moved, he built a shack. When the shack was torn down, he found a house nearby. It was stuffed with clippings and gifts from the kids he coached.

"Some people say, 'Jimmy, you're poor,' but I say, 'I've been poor long enough to get used to it!'" He rolled his head back in a hearty laugh. "I just love baseball and I love the kids. I get so much kick out of playing with them."

Carrollton, Texas, named a park after Jimmy, though he seldom went there, as it was too far from the ball field he loved. His life each year began with the first warm days of summer when the kids returned to the place he had never left.

"When you get up here and start batting," Porter said, snapping his wrist to show a young ballplayer how to swat at a pitch, "don't go down, stand up straight."

The child listened closely. At eighty-one Jimmy Porter was a sports legend in Carrollton. Not because he had once played in the old Negro leagues with Satchel Paige—which he had—but because he got homesick for the kids and gave it all up.

"Pow!" yelled Porter as his Little League team gathered around him. "The ball bounced off my bat and knocked that pitcher out." He was telling them a tale. "The umpire said, 'You hit him!' I said, 'No, I didn't. I hit the ball. The ball hit him!'"

The kids laughed, and Porter shuffled off to his frayed folding chair behind the screen at home plate. A young girl watched her brother take the field and then turned and touched the coach's shoulder as the old man started to take his seat.

"You used to give out autographs, didn't you?" she asked shyly.

"Yeah."

"Jimmy . . ."

"Hmm?"

"My mom and I are going to try and come out to your house sometime this week." She had a hopeful look. "Maybe me and you can play some baseball?"

"Sure," Jimmy said, grabbing a glove from his old duffel bag. "You can practice with this."

My memory is a lot like Jimmy's satchel, where everything is jumbled up inside; people, places, and random images are all tossed together. I've seen many a beautiful place in this country, and met any number of unforgettable folks, but mention Mule Shoe, Texas, and I mostly remember a sign: "Taxidermist/Veterinarian—either way you get your dog back."

Same with Blue Eye, Arkansas, just across the border from Blue Eye, Missouri (a pair of blue eyes). Idling at a stoplight one afternoon, I read this in the window of a photographer's studio:

"If you have beauty, I'll take it. If you have none, I'll fake it."

That's as good a definition of portrait photography as I've ever read.

One of the great image makers who worked with me, Jim Mulligan, played a game each evening whenever we were eating dinner together on the road. He asked everybody at our table to look around the restaurant and locate people who seemed to be having a worse day than we were. My all-time favorite was the woman I overheard telling her date:

"Honey, the gutter ain't a step up from you."

People who find a way to succeed regardless of their troubles always intrigue me. Jennifer Annable (pronounced *ANN-a-bell*) was five months pregnant when she moved to Seattle with fifty bucks in her pocket. She worked long hours, struggling to become a teacher, until eventually she ran a school for children with special needs. Her son, Kasey, brought one of them home.

"How would you feel about Melvin Jones coming to stay with us?" he asked his mom. Kasey was Melvin's high school basketball coach at the time. "He's just been shoved out by two other high schools and he came to us with zero credits."

Melvin was sixteen, in his sophomore year, drifting on the streets of Seattle.

"Every time I took him home," Kasey said, "I was taking him somewhere else. We drove around to four or five different places, and there were no adults."

Melvin's mother was dying of AIDS.

"He was loved," Jennifer Annable recalled, "but not parented."

So she made up a room for him. Why would a divorced, single mother take on such a challenge? She'd opened her home to kids before—five when Kasey was a child. Annable's father had grown up in foster care, her mother in an orphanage.

"My dream was always to run an orphanage," Annable said. "When I was a little girl, I had a hundred dolls and I used to line them up on the back porch. Those were my kids."

Her mom came close to being adopted three times, but each time the couple returned her to the orphanage.

"To think that somebody would take in a child," Annable sighed, "and then give it back."

She was determined to help children like her mom, but taking in

Melvin was one of the hardest things she ever did, because initially he did not trust her.

Melvin stashed the groceries she bought him under his bed, afraid someone would steal them, and resisted her attempt to become his new mother.

"I did not like it at all," Melvin said. "I fought it."

Annable told Melvin, "I'm not trying to take anyone's place, but you need a mom," and assured him that she had love enough to help another child. Still, Melvin's little sister, Marika, was not happy.

"Why you wanna go move in with her?" she asked her brother. "That woman's not family."

"He was with me," Melvin's older sister, Lakesha Bousley, insisted. "I was trying to figure out why he'd want to go with someone else other than me."

Melvin simply wanted someone to show him how to study.

"Jennifer was like a gnat," he said. "Always in my face, and she wouldn't go away."

"In order to graduate," Annable said, "he had to go to night school and he had to go to summer school, every summer."

Melvin rebelled. "I tried to leave the house at one-thirty, two o'clock in the morning, and I'd get into fights with Jennifer."

Kasey, his basketball coach, was soon having second thoughts. "Melvin was putting so much strain on my mother that it was kind of breaking her," he recalled. Then Jennifer did the unexpected: She gave Melvin her ATM card and personal identification number.

"She never gave that number to me!" Kasey laughed.

"I didn't want to be responsible for Melvin not making it," Annable explained.

She figured that trusting him with her money might turn his life around. He could have taken cash and left. He did not. Now she had his trust, too. There could not be two more different people in the world and yet they clicked.

"Different on the outside," Kasey pointed out. "Not different on the inside. Once Melvin bought into the hard work, the long hours, the family, and the changes in his life, he made it."

That high school sophomore who came to Annable without a single credit graduated from college as one of the top students at Portland State University.

Lakesha smiled. "I call Jennifer 'God mom.' No one will ever be able to replace my mom," she said. But what Jennifer Annable did for Melvin made her family.

Melvin nodded, thinking of all the hands that had guided him.

"I've only got two hands," he said. "I could not have done it by myself."

Life twists and turns, just like basketball: Sometimes you simply have to close your eyes and try a long shot. Melvin Jones did. Once, in a college game, he tossed the ball seventy-five feet to win at the buzzer. In a sense, that's what Jennifer did, too. She helped him win the game of life.

"Jennifer threw a Hail Mary pass," Melvin said. "I guess I caught it."

And together—they won.

Teamwork can bring the impossible closer. It happens all the time.

Ordinary athletes who play well together are capable of beating superstars who don't. I was standing on tiptoes in upstate New York, trying to spot a woman who led such a team. She was supposed to be in the midst of twelve thousand runners, shuffling to the starting line. The announcer greeted the rippling sea of people over the PA system.

"Welcome to the Boilermaker Road Race!"

Some of the runners hopped. Some stretched. Some simply stared, wondering if they could finish a race that was a bit over nine miles. Vivian White jogged nearly that far five days a week. Suddenly, there she was, smiling and waving, only five foot one. No taller than an August cornstalk, but at age fifty-one she was determined to run nearly sixty-five hundred miles: the distance from her home in Illinois to her son's frontline army post in Iraq.

"Every mile that I jog," she said, "brings him that much closer to being home, at least in my mind."

So far, she had logged more than a thousand miles in the six months since Brian had gone to war. Friends and family quickly realized that she would need help covering the remaining fifty-five hundred. Word got around, and soon others who had kids in the military started walking or running and adding their miles.

Tammy Utley knew the pain of a life put on hold. She waited for her own son's return from Afghanistan. While Nick was at war, Tammy drove half a day to cheer for a stranger.

"Vivian's a military mom," Tammy said simply. "I know what she's feeling."

Both mothers raised small-town sons who had never lived away from home. Brian grew up in Charleston, Illinois; Nick in Gowanda, New York. Both young men turned twenty under fire.

"Brian has lost friends over there," Vivian told Tammy as they traded pictures of their kids. "There are not a lot of snapshots of him smiling."

Private First Class Brian Bales had trained as a radio communication systems security repair specialist, but he was stationed in Kirkuk and often saw combat. When Brian was growing up, Vivian was able to guide him away from danger.

"That's the tough part for any parent with children in a war," she said. "The feeling of helplessness."

"There is nothing you can do for them," Tammy added, gazing down at her son's photograph. "You can't be there with them."

Vivian agreed. "How am I going to wake up every morning and not know whether my son's alive or not?"

Tammy nodded. "You wonder, 'Am I going to see him again?' You sit and you worry. You turn on the news and see everything that's happening there. And you worry some more."

"How am I going to come home from work," Vivian wondered, "and not worry that there will be a government car parked in my driveway waiting for me?"

Especially after she read this letter from her son:

I was marching along the beaten dirt, a rocky path, weighed down by a heavy kit of gear, water and ammunition totaling a third of my body weight. Wind at my back. Rain in my face.

Despite the cool chill of mid January, my body was sweating as I took the point in our search for my enemy, walking slower and slower into the dark forest. I grabbed the cap off my thermal scope and switched it on to find the heat signature of our enemies, my heart beating more and more with every step. In the distance I see a white glowing figure emerging.

Shots rang out from the three o'clock flank. We hit the ground faster than the hissing and snapping of all the bullets ringing past our heads. I fired at the white figure in front of me. The human being fell to his knees, then to his face.

MEDIC called a man behind me. I had a new mission. Save our wounded. We pulled the casualty from the forest back to a Humvee and drove through the trashed swilled streets of a nearby city, scanning the alleyways with my M2 .50-calibre machine gun. "In the clear," I thought. "I made it. Its over."

AMBUSH! The words crackled through my radio headset. Shots ring out from all directions. I saw two figures with AK-47's in the top floor of a building and a third enemy with an RPK machine gun. He was peppering our trucks and turning them to Swiss cheese. We were under heavy attack. I swung around my .50 Cal and fired two hundred rounds, feeling the concussion knock the pouring sweat from my face, like a punching bag over and over. The insurgents fell. Four lives had ended by my hand that night and I was filled with questions. "Was it justified? How many did I save? Could it have been seen as the will of God? Who knows?" I tell myself as I walk into the shower later that night, still in full gear. "My military brothers are alive. My lungs are filled with life."

I just stood under the waterspout, pulled the straps from my vest and let sixty pounds of gear fall to the floor. I would live another day; drive on to honor our wounded and never look back until the war was over. Honor and Courage were on my mind when I finally lay down to rest, as if my mind will truly be at rest for the rest of my life.

"At those times," Tammy sighed, "when there's nothing else you can do, you start walking or running. We are protecting our emotions, protecting how we feel, because we can't protect our kids over there."

She managed a smile as she shuffled through her photographs. "This is Nick coming home from Afghanistan."

Vivian leaned in. "Wow!"

"That was the first we saw him." Tammy tapped the photo with her fingernail. It had been a long, dangerous journey back. Nick was a New York National Guard driver in Afghanistan. Two rocket-propelled grenades hit the right side of his truck.

"Those were the bloody shoes days," Tammy said. "You walk and you walk and you walk." She walked until her feet bled, because no words could convey the fear she felt.

"Take out my heart," Tammy said softly. "It could speak a lot better than my tongue."

She couldn't reach out and give him a hug, so she embraced Vivian instead and then added the 140 miles she had walked to Vivian's total.

Nick's National Guard unit came back from Afghanistan just as Brian's army division was shipping him to Iraq.

"My hope is that every mother's story is going to end like mine," Tammy said. "Their sons and daughters will come home. But in reality, that's not always the case."

So she kept marching. Nick had a mission, and now she did, too.

"I feel I need to still keep walking," she said, "and walk until we bring all the men and women home from war."

"There are days when you just don't feel like running," Vivian admitted. "Those are the days when I think about Brian and say, 'He doesn't get days off in Iraq.'"

Vivian fondled the words pressed into the dog tag around her neck that read: "Many miles may separate us, but know I'm always by your side. I love you." Brian took one just like it to Iraq. Vivian vowed not to take hers off until he came home.

"Does he think you and your army of moms will reach your goal?"
I asked.

"He once told me, 'Mom, it's not me that determines the outcome
of your race. It's you.' Sometimes when I'm running, I think of that last
mile Brian and I will do together."

Vivian kept a chart of her progress on a map of the world. Every
three hundred miles, she added a pair of new feet. That afternoon she
called Brian in Iraq and gushed, "We're at 14,867 miles."

"Whoa! Dang!" shouted Brian.

"Yeah, pretty cool!"

"I'm already home," he chuckled.

"Yes, you're home."

Three hundred people in forty-two states were jogging and walking and donating their miles so that one mom could feel closer to her
son. Mothers in Afghanistan, Egypt, Germany, Norway, Canada, and
Iraq also walked and ran, adding their miles to Vivian's total—a stag-
gering 183,811 miles by the time Brian Bales made it back from two
tours of duty in Iraq—unhurt.

"I think that's the power of a mother's love," Vivian said simply. Not
just the mothers with kids in the field of battle, but even those whose
warriors have come home.

Vivian White was one of those folks who clean our rusty motor of
hope. She favored hope because she lived through a time when she
had little else. Tyrone Curry lived there a lot longer.

For thirty-five years he started work every morning at four. He seldom quit before dinner, but the longtime janitor at Evergreen High
School in Seattle, Washington, was happy. He accepted that in life,
someone has to put out the folding chairs. Someone has to do the jobs
we all take for granted. Besides, it left him muscled like a man who
tilled the soil, and he liked that. Still, everyone wondered why he didn't
kiss his trash sack good-bye after he won the Washington state lottery.

"I was dumping garbage," he said, stopping to empty a bin outside
the cafeteria. "This is where I was when I found out I won the jackpot,
and I took off running."

His wife, Michelle, had his winning ticket—worth "I don't know," she said when she called him. "It's got a three, a four, and too many zeros. I can't count that high."

$3,410,000.

To celebrate, Curry went bowling, just as he'd done every Wednesday night for twenty-five years. His friend and teammate, Kevin Johnson, said that Curry hadn't changed at all.

His bank account may be bigger now, but not his life. "I'm just Joe Citizen," the quiet custodian said. He still lived in a tiny house at the end of a cul-de-sac with his wife, a two-year-old grandson, two stepsons, and two in-laws, a mother and daughter.

"Before I won the money, I struggled. Sometimes I fell behind, but I always remember my mom's words. 'You can have somethin', but that person next to you might not have anything. If you look out for that someone, they'll look out for you.'"

Michelle touched his hand. "We were in the middle of bankruptcy when we won the lottery."

That big check bought them out of debt. They signed up for a time-share in Las Vegas.

"They called us and said, 'When you gonna come visit?'" Tyrone chuckled. "It really isn't in our makeup. We don't even go out to dinner. We cook at home."

He did put a new heat pump in his small house, added vinyl siding, a fence, and a new driveway for the car that still carried him to work—five years after his big win. Most folks figured he'd quit, but Tyrone is not a guy to give up on a job. During the Vietnam War the former navy boiler tender shipped out to the fight—seven times.

"You could be sleeping at four in the morning," I laughed.

"Nah." He ducked his head and smiled. "You need to be doing stuff. That's my philosophy."

He has cleaned and fed thousands of schoolkids since he came home from war. Most people in his Seattle neighborhood don't have a lot of money.

"Sometimes the lunch I help serve here at school is probably the only meal they get," Curry said.

He wanted to be a teacher, but after budget cuts eliminated his teaching assistant's job thirty-five years ago, Curry stayed on as a custodian. He never went looking for another classroom because he found a better one—and a second job—out back. Curry also coached the Evergreen High School track team. That's where he decided to splurge.

"I'm getting excited!" he said, watching runners circling toward him on the school's old cinder track. He was building them a new one, state of the art. It cost him forty thousand bucks.

"I'm not done," he said. Curry bought more lottery tickets every week. "Our tennis coach, she has, like, a hundred kids tryin' to play on four courts." He dreamed of building more. Didn't care about the odds.

"Life is lucky!" he said. And when it's not, Curry felt it fell to the janitor to fix it.

Curry's team captain, DeVante Botello, was having a tough time. Just before graduation, the eighteen-year-old's mother died of a heart attack.

"We were really close," DeVante said. "Her death left a void at home. I slept in the living room after her heart attack and woke up waiting to go help her." But she was gone. "My family was in shambles. I was kind of floundering. I didn't know what to do."

The honor student was just dragging his pen across paper, until his track coach showed him how to play the game of life.

"He taught me perseverance," DeVante said. "How to hold on and deal with the cards you're dealt. 'Power through,' Coach said. 'Life is hard.'

"Whenever we talk, I think about his advice for nights and nights. Some of his words are almost haunting. He told me, 'Don't give up quite yet.' Coach has this soft chuckle and then a nod. That power nod gets me every time. He just wanted to let me know that he was there for me." DeVante's eyes glistened, and he swallowed hard. "Coach said I didn't have to feel alone."

When life throws curves, people often dwell on the terrible things that happen, isolating themselves in grief. Curry asked DeVante to pay attention to those who were willing to put their hands on his shoulders and help him get through the ordeal. The boy's father was not around. Curry offered to pay for college.

"When I was coming up, I just had my mom," he said. "So I'm here for him."

"Coach is probably the most amazing man I'm ever gonna meet," DeVante said. "He's my hero. A real hero." One who hasn't gone to the moon or scored a touchdown, doesn't have a reality show, hasn't written a book.

"Why do you need to write a book," DeVante insisted, "when you live the way he does? You reach out and affect so many lives. I wish I was as good as him. I work for it. I work for it every day. Whatever I do with my life is gonna be in honor of Tyrone. He is always gonna live on through my actions." He shook his head. "Tyrone Curry, track coach, janitor. I'm never going to forget him"—the millionaire who cared more for other people's dreams than he did for his own. The luckiest man alive.

We live in an age where sports heroes are measured by the size of their paychecks, but performance—on and off the field—is all that really counts. The best will be remembered for what they did and not for what they could buy. The most important sports heroes don't all drive fancy cars. They teach the games they love in an old-fashioned way, stressing teamwork over "Look at me!" talent. They've seen it win on the field and in their lives. It is, they say, the key to winning—the essence of America.

Chapter Ten

Homesick for Places
We've Never Been

We do not always travel roads of reason, but we set off on them any-way. There are places that will always call us, moments when we feel connected to shared landscape and experience. Traveling into the unknown is as American as a covered wagon.

Jim Mott has that pioneer spirit. He was perched on a picnic table, sketching a fading afternoon landscape near Osseo, Wisconsin, when we found him. The first chill of fall was in the air, so he wore a knit cap as wind gusts scattered leaves across his canvas. Jim gazed out over green pastures and red barns, brushed the leaves from his lap, then started mixing paint. Painting is how an artist discovers what he has seen.

Mott had seen more than most. The successful middle-aged artist had traveled the country trading paintings for hospitality, staying with total strangers. Certainly, most would be reluctant to do what Jim Mott did, but this shy, quiet man had managed to safely explore twenty-nine states while traveling fifteen thousand miles. It cost him nothing but gas.

"I'm excited!" Rebecca Crowell practically bubbled after exchang-ing a few nights in her family home for a view Mott captured with pig-ment and canvas. "It's astonishing," she said, shaking her head. "I can't imagine traveling around and staying with people I don't know and painting under a certain amount of pressure while people are watching."

Apparently, that scrutiny does stimulate Mott's creativity.

"I do about five or ten times more paintings on the road than I do at home," Mott said, "just because there's this supportive audience of people that are curious to see what I'll do with their lives."

That was the whole point of his trip, Mott explained, as he painted a piece of coconut pie to pay for the one he was eating at a nearby diner, the Norske Nook.

"Ordinary folks ought to have art, too," he said.

The owner beamed. "The next time you stop by, it will be up on the wall!"

Mott's art is worth more than a piece of pie. He has a master's in fine art. Most of his paintings hang where everyday people seldom go—they are sold in New York City galleries—but he has become like Johnny Appleseed, planting his pictures in unlikely places.

On this odyssey Mott seldom paints traditional landscapes.

"I try to focus on the setting wherever I happen to find myself with my hosts," he explained.

Rebecca Crowell pointed to Mott's painting of the plastic chairs in her backyard.

"He really captured something about the spirit of our place here," she observed. "It looks cozy, but there's a little edge of chaos."

Like the journey itself. Before embarking on this trip, Mott mostly stayed home in upstate New York. "I really don't like to travel!" he admitted. "For me, change is just watching a different cloud roll in over the same landscape."

"I was too disconnected from everyday life," he said. So he did something seldom done these days: He decided to wander without a cell phone, computer, or BlackBerry and forced himself to talk face-to-face with the people he met.

"Did there come a day when you second-guessed your decision?" I asked.

"Usually nights," he laughed. "One time I got put in a cabin in the woods and was promised the most peaceful evening of my life. There were rats in the ceiling. I put a little radio up in the attic and played country music." Hearing that, they left.

The only thing that terrifies Jim Mott is a succession of ordinary days.

"One particularly great day," Mott recalled, "I learned it's possible to trade art for a speeding ticket. The judge allowed me to pay for the fine with a painting because it was"—wait for it—"fine art."

.   .   .

My favorite drives in America take me far from the interstate high-ways. I like to route my trips through towns small enough to con-sider Dairy Queen gourmet dining. That's where I often find the unexpected—Amish kids wearing in-line skates or Civil War buffs fighting the battle of Gettysburg until the concession stands close. The lights and shadows of my life have left a rich load of impressions. I've climbed hillsides under dirty-ashtray clouds to see sunsets stain the sky. I've been to places so beautiful, I thank God every day that he gave me time to pack a bag. He's allowed me to spend my life with people who have no riches but their thoughts, whose eyes grow rusty when they realize that poverty is inherited, just like wealth, and then shine with renewed determination when someone helps them do bet-ter than they think they can do. When I was a boy, my grandfather Bailey was the only member of our family who had a college degree. He never missed a chance to walk me by his law school at the Univer-sity of Kansas, hoping that I would get one, too.

"You know, Bobby, my life changed because of that man standing on the pedestal," he told me, pointing to a statue in front of the law building that showed a dapper fellow with his arm slung over a stu-dent's shoulder. "That's Uncle Jimmy Green, the first dean of the law school. I knew him before he was a statue! He made me dream of places I'd never been."

Sometimes in life you have to get lost—to find yourself.

Roy and Anna Williams set out from their home in Florence, Ken-tucky, to circle the West in a car that runs mainly on dreams.

"It has a four-cylinder engine," Williams said, popping up from under the hood. "Forty horsepower and no air-conditioning. Just the way Henry Ford built it back in 1929."

The old Model A had been Roy's "other love" since the Vietnam War.

"It was nothing but a broken shell." He laughed, slamming the hood. Bought as a joke for a boy who was far away, fighting.

"The driver's seat was missing when I came home," Williams recalled. "Someone replaced it with a toilet seat."

He worked nights and weekends to restore the old car. Its plumbing was seventy-seven years old. Steam bubbled out of the radiator. "This is my radiator recovery system," Williams said, pulling a flat bottle from the Model A's trunk.

"A urine bottle?" I asked, leaning in for a closer look as he duct-taped it to the engine.

"Yep." Williams laughed. "I borrowed this from a friend who works in a hospital. Works great."

Williams could "MacGyver" anything. An old sock was his gas filter. Foil from last night's dinner became his heat shield.

He had only one windshield wiper. "And it covers just half the windshield," Williams admitted.

"So your wife won't get to see America?"

"No. Not when it's raining."

Anna Williams stepped up on the running board. As she dropped their lunch into the toolbox, I asked, "What do you think of the long odds that this car will hold up for six thousand miles?"

"I'm just real excited about getting back," she deadpanned.

Fortunately, Anna was no backseat driver. Well, there *was* no backseat. Every possible inch was stuffed with the extra parts they might need.

Williams dug down beneath the sandwiches Anna had deposited in the wooden tool chest and marked his checklist.

"We've got an extra water pump," he called over his shoulder. "Extra carburetor, extra distributor, and the most important tool," he said, standing up to show me his GPS. On the first day of their trip, that high-tech map got them so lost, he started calling it Amelia Earhart.

"If a couple builds a house together," I pointed out, "it can test their marriage."

Roy and Ann nodded their heads and smiled. "We've done that."

"How about a trip like this?"

"We will have been married thirty-five years," Ann said, then paused for emphasis. "If we make it back!"

They puttered off and managed to visit all the postcard places they planned to see without a mishap Williams couldn't fix. He even saved some Japanese tourists stranded in Death Valley on a day when the car's thermometer topped 115.

"You take money?" one of them asked, trying to stuff some bills in his shirt.

"No," Williams said, "don't need 'em," and handed the money back. "The gas tank on this old car only holds ten gallons, not counting the can strapped to the running board."

The best part of their trip was not the sights they saw along the way, as the couple had already seen many of them in their three decades together. No, the highlight was losing themselves in America to find what they wanted most.

"It's really cool to be a part of something epic," Anna said. "I know though this trip is not epic."

Roy finished her thought. "But in our world, it is!"

They longed to live a tale that would be told at family tables long after they were done.

"It's an odyssey," Anna said. "Something to remember forever."

They didn't need an epic poet to record their adventure. Roy and Anna wrote their own ending, the words right there on the rear bumper of their aging Ford, as they returned home. Someone had scratched through the line "California or Bust" and added, "Been there. Done that."

This desire to reconnect got me thinking about what has replaced the kind of face-to-face interaction Roy and Anna Williams craved.

Sometimes I think Twitter and Facebook are making us see only people who are far away, and the Internet is making us value only people we haven't met. Perhaps we should take more pictures and write more stories about people we meet in person. Maybe it would help us treasure what we can also touch.

Many Americans spend a lifetime searching for a place where their dreams can flourish. Home is not where they are, but where they want to be. Those dreams become their guiding light, leading them to places and linking them to people they'd never thought they'd know. That restlessness, that longing, has become part of this country's character and is one big reason why so many American dreams eventually come true.

Edna Lewis was not content to tend a garden in a small Virginia crossroads settled by slaves, one of whom was her grandfather. She married briefly, had no children, traveled extensively, and settled in New York City to open a restaurant. Before she retired in 1992, Edna Lewis had worked in some of New York's finest restaurants and received cooking's highest honors—not bad for a chef who started in 1949 with no formal training.

The summer she opened her first restaurant, Tennessee Williams wrote a play called *A Streetcar Named Desire*. Marlon Brando wanted a part. They met to discuss it over their favorite dessert, a dish Edna called Just Pie.

That pie helped to form the most important friendship of Lewis's life. She was seventy-four when Scott Peacock, a chef at Georgia's governor's mansion, was asked to assist her at a fund-raiser. He was just twenty-seven when she came to Atlanta that day, dragging a huge cardboard box by a rope. It was filled with one hundred pounds of frozen pie dough, hand carried all the way from New York City. Lewis was as particular about her pie as she was about her friends. She and Peacock, although separated in age by half a century and living a thousand miles apart, fell for each other.

"I didn't see it happening myself," Scott said. "I'm sure neither of us did. We're both very shy, very reserved and private people, loners, really."

Peacock grew up in Alabama, learning by heart what food is like when it's homegrown and prepared simply. That helped him become a celebrated Atlanta chef. It also attracted Edna Lewis, the queen of southern-style cooking.

The day I met them, he was lifting a cake out of the oven and turned and placed it on a kitchen table in front of her.

"Tell me if it's ready?"

Lewis didn't poke it or taste but cocked her head and lowered her ear to the dish. "It's fading away," she observed.

There was a reason she was inducted into the KitchenAid Cook-book Hall of Fame: She cooked by ear.

"Does that mean it's done?" Peacock asked.

"I think so."

"No one has ever understood me the way she does," Peacock insisted. So what followed seemed quite natural. Lewis lost her home in New York City when her apartment was converted to a condo-minium. Peacock proposed she move in with him.

"Without realizing it, really, or thinking about it, we became a family," Peacock said, "and I formed a life with her and I love her."

But that love posed a big challenge. Lewis became increasingly forgetful, and in her eighties she needed constant attention. Scott Peacock became her caregiver because "it would be impossible for me to say 'You're an inconvenience now.'"

You won't find that recipe for friendship in their cookbooks. As Peacock explained it, "You don't count the grains of salt that you pick up to put on something. Something just tells you it feels right. This is what you do"—no matter where life's travels take you or whom you meet along the way.

Scott Peacock looked after Edna Lewis until the day she died, at eighty-nine. That was his recipe for love.

Take it from a man who has listened to all sorts of folks: What people want in this country is simple. They want an America that lives up to the brag. The places that do are not always in guidebooks. I found one tucked under a hillside halfway across Nebraska, and I had to drive to middle age to get there. Monowi was once a bustling town but had now become a collection of old weathered buildings that tilted against the wind. Only Elsie Eiler called it home. She lived in the smallest incorporated township in the United States—population, one.

"I'm the mayor," Eiler announced.

"When you ran for office," I asked, "did you campaign house to house?"

She laughed. "I went from house to bar and the bar back to my house. There's only me!"

Eiler opened a pub for company. Some of her regulars drive eighty miles just to chat. "I hear you've got great hamburgers," said one woman, ushering in a vanload of kids.

"Best in town!" Eiler said. "This is probably the only tavern in America that has toys," she told me, pointing to a group of smaller children playing in the corner. "I have a lot of little customers!"

They come for her "magic" key. It unlocks a great treasure.

"Would you like to see it?" Eiler asked with a grin.

"Oh, that'd be great," a little girl said, clapping her hands.

Out back of that tiny, isolated tavern was a public library that held five thousand books. "I'll loan you one to read," Eiler told the delighted girl.

"I'm honoring my husband's dying wish," she said, watching her guest read along the row of book titles. "He always told me, 'There is never a book that you open, that you don't learn something from it.'"

Rudy Eiler must have learned a lot. This library held nearly every book he'd ever read. Their son, Jack, helped his dad build the place.

"He would have three or four books going at the same time," Jack remembered. "If he liked one, he'd mark it and go back six weeks later and read the same book again."

Rudy would read anything—kids' books, westerns, the classics. He loved everything but romance novels. He told his daughter, Rene, never to throw away a book. It could take her places he could not.

"You were never stuck in a snowbank in Nebraska if you had a book," Rene said, smiling at the memory. "He said, 'Reading pulls us out of ourselves and into the lives of others, no matter where we live.'"

Her dad was a busy guy. Before dying of cancer, he ran the grain elevator, delivered gas, and even farmed a bit.

Elsie and Rudy were married for nearly half a century. They met as children in Monowi's one-room schoolhouse and lived in town all their lives, except for the few months when Rudy was in the air force, serving in France, and Elsie worked for an airline in Dallas.

"I could move to the city," she admitted, "and have lots and lots of acquaintances, but here I have a lot of friends!"

She was past seventy when we met, and some of her friends

worried about her decision to stay in Monowi, but she wanted to keep the town alive and the library open. I left her standing behind the counter, stamping library books, but asked one final question at the door.

"Rudy left the town a library. What will you leave?"

She thought a moment while checking out the book the little girl brought to the counter. Eiler playfully tugged the child's pigtail and said, "I guess I'll leave a little piece of myself these kids won't forget."

She is an American who lives up to the brag.

Learning is a lasting frontier. Perhaps that's why I'm attracted to parts of America that many people will read about only in books.

Drive west of Amarillo and you'll cross Loving County, where the Texas border takes a left turn and heads to El Paso. Loving was once the largest, least populated county in the country, 640 square miles of nothing but sagebrush, rattlesnakes, and sand. One hundred ten brave souls lived in that vastness. The Labor Department determined they suffered from high unemployment.

Newt Keen, who ran the only café in the county, asked, "Would you live out here if you didn't have a job?"

Everyone here worked, even the kids, but the federal government wanted to help provide more jobs. It offered Loving County's two small businesses preferential treatment for loans. Well, Mattie Thorpe's gas station already filled all ten cars and trucks in the county. Newt Keen served all the beer he had in stock every day. He used to sell eggs, but said he'd seen so many eggs that he "couldn't look at the back of a chicken no more!"

Mattie and Newt turned down the federal government's offer. The following week, a check came from Washington to establish a new city park in all that emptiness. County officials couldn't get anyone to take it back, so they used it to buy some extra sleep with an automatic flag-pole that worked on an electric eye. Sunlight started an engine that pulled the flag from a hole in the pole and raised it to the top. On the day I arrived, the whole county was over at Newt Keen's café, placing bets on what time the flag would come out.

· · ·

America's story pulls me like a magnet. Much of it is legendary, even if not all of it is true. I bounced over the Black Hills of South Dakota looking for Louis Whirlwind Horse, a Lakota Sioux who was one of the last living members of a traveling troupe that shaped forever the way the world would think America's frontier was settled. I found him gazing out the front window of his small home, watching the afternoon shadows slide across the prairie.

"You the one who wants to know about Buffalo Bill's Wild West Show?" he asked.

"Yes, sir."

He smiled, then lifted a finger.

"Let me tell you how I helped Colonel Cody invent the Old West," he said. "We were playing at the old Madison Square Garden in New York City, which is neither square nor a garden," Whirlwind Horse said. "Bill directed us to ride our horses around a circled 'wagon train' so we could show off our riding skills. My role in the act was to grab a pioneer woman and take her into a tepee set up at the other end of the arena. She was supposed to scream until Buffalo Bill came and rescued her, but we Indians were doing the screeching. You see, we played gin rummy while we were waiting for Bill to come shoot us, and she sat in on the game. She was the best card player in the show. Beat us every time. We were supposed to be killing her, but her card playing was killing us!"

All that remains of Louis Whirlwind Horse's grand adventure with Buffalo Bill are a few tintypes preserved in amber and his memories, softly spoken. He was one of 640 friends Buffalo Bill took on a trail ride around the world.

"We performed for princes and kings," Whirlwind Horse recalled, "and had a grand old time. The show was so popular in Italy, Buffalo Bill made a modest proposal to the pope. He suggested that His Holiness might bolster the strength of the church by signing on as an attraction."

Buffalo Bill left a legacy that lives to this day. Louis Whirlwind Horse was the last to remember it firsthand. We sat together watching the sun set over the Black Hills, their color locked and dried by the heat, the landscape wrinkled by sandpaper winds. Only he could see the West of yesteryear. It had left with a traveling showman who sold it to the world.

"Oh, before you go," Louis said, "one last story you should hear."

I turned back to listen.

"You remember Sitting Bull, who helped defeat General Custer at the Little Big Horn? He was a great war chief of my tribe, but he was also a man who cared deeply about children.

"On his trip to New York City with Buffalo Bill's Wild West Show, Sitting Bull was moved by the orphans he saw on the streets. He spent his pay buying them food"—which he handed out in a back alley. Louis fell silent and I pondered his story. Finally, he looked up and asked, "Who's the savage?"

The old war chief's descendants have battled poverty and despair for years. The latest looks like Sitting Bull in blue jeans. Ron His Horse Is Thunder is Sitting Bull's great-great-great-grandson. He quit a private law practice to come back to North Dakota as president of the college that bears his ancestor's name.

"I just had enough of the big city," Ron said. "Didn't feel at home. Didn't feel comfortable."

Besides, he had a grand vision for a place where it is sometimes hard to see beyond the next day. Ron challenged Sitting Bull College kids to start their own construction company on the Standing Rock Reservation.

"We didn't want to educate them so they'd just leave and go find jobs someplace else," Ron said. "We need help here."

The company they began was soon making more than $1.5 million for the college every year and earned Terry Brown Otter a new home, which he helped build in his poor neighborhood.

"I'm still shocked that we could do it," Terry said, watching his wife and baby boy playing in the front yard. Sioux country had high unemployment at the time; three out of four adults were out of a job. Why didn't they just leave and look for work somewhere else?

Ron tried to explain. "This is the last little bit of homeland that we once had," he said, meaning a reservation ninety miles wide that sits astride the border between North and South Dakota.

Growing up he straddled two worlds, living where eighty-seven thousand Native Americans lived, in and around New York City. He was Ron McNeil back then, his stepfather an air force officer from Long Island named Joe McNeil, one of the first students to participate in the sit-in protests that launched the struggle for civil rights back in 1960. What are the odds that Joe and Ron would end up under the same roof, two ordinary people who would change American history?

At fifteen Ron left Long Island to live with his grandfather on the reservation, where he rediscovered what Sitting Bull knew long ago.

"Our tribe had scientists," Ron said. "We didn't call them scientists. We had doctors. We didn't call them doctors. We didn't use the terminology that they use today."

But the Standing Rock people have a rich history in solving problems. Like Sitting Bull, the war chief who cared for and fed New York's immigrant children, they challenge our deeply held beliefs about what makes us who we are. Childhood poverty could have scarred Ron's students for life. Most would have expected them to fail, and yet some not only survived but thrived. A four-year-old half a world away showed me why.

Mario Capecchi was the son of a single mom, a poet who thought she could defeat the Nazis with her pen. During World War II, Lucy Ramberg was snatched from their home in the Italian Alps and sent to a concentration camp.

"My mother had anticipated her arrest by German authorities," Capecchi recalled. "Prior to their arrival she had sold all of her possessions and had given that money to a farming family to look after me. For a year I lived on that farm near our home in Wolfgruben, and then the money ran out. It's not clear how it ran out. The family could not afford me, and so I was put on the streets."

"How could a four-year-old survive on the streets during a war?" I asked.

"Shelter was no problem," Capecchi said. "There were lots of bombed-out houses, but what you are really concerned about is food"—which he patiently tracked with a hunter's eye.

"You have to see who's guarding the food," he said, "and then see what their patterns are before you steal it."

Capecchi learned to solve problems with methodical determination and enormous concentration—but by the war's end, he was a sick and starving little boy lying naked on a hospital bed with no sheets or blankets.

"Scores of beds lined the rooms and corridors of that hospital in Reggio Emilia," he recalled, "one bed touching the next. The nurse, Sister Maria, promised me that if I could go through one day without a high fever, I could leave the hospital. She knew that without any clothes I was not likely to run away."

On his ninth birthday Mario had a visitor—his mother, Lucy Ramberg, who had searched nearly a year for her lost son.

"Frankly, I didn't recognize her," Capecchi admitted. She had aged enormously in the concentration camp.

She bought him new clothes, and "I had my first bath in six years!" Mario laughed.

Her brother sent them tickets to America, and two weeks later they glided past the Statue of Liberty. Capecchi's eyes misted with memory. "I'm sure if I had stayed in Italy, I'd be in jail somewhere, or else I'd be dead."

Mario and his mom ended up in a Quaker commune near Philadelphia. He was nine years old, couldn't speak English, and had never been to school. An ordeal like his could scar a kid for life, but one of his teachers—the first of many people who found a way to help him—gave him paint and let him communicate by sketching a mural.

"Giving a child an opportunity to have dreams and then to be able to go after those dreams"—Capecchi looked away, lost in thought—"that's what the United States gave to me."

He would repay America's kindness by becoming a scientist, working with Dr. James Watson, one of the men who discovered DNA. Watson told me that Capecchi's breakthrough studies will likely be the keys to conquering cancer.

Like many immigrants, Capecchi thought America's streets would be paved with gold. "And what I saw," he said, "was actually much more than that—opportunity." A chance, despite his ordeal, to save a lot of lives. In 2007 Dr. Mario Capecchi won the Nobel Prize in Medicine.

Storytellers, like scientists, are forever trying to touch the truth. That often requires falling in love many times with the same subject.

Milton Rogovin did that most of his adult life. He photographed families in his small Buffalo, New York, neighborhood aging over the course of half a century. He didn't just snap their pictures but let his subjects choose their own poses and backdrops. He never prettied them up, and thereby looked deeper for the people they were.

"By showing these individuals as they are," Rogovin said, "they were actually speaking out, and that is what I wanted to do"—ever since his father lost his dry-goods store in the Great Depression of the 1930s and died of a broken heart. Rogovin was drawn to the hard-working, hard-luck, and just plain hardened members of society.

"When I met Milton, I was a full-fledged addict," recalled Andres Garcia, as he showed me around the neighborhood's health clinic. "Now, I'm vice president of the company that runs this place."

Garcia paused to look out his window at the photographer framing a photo.

"Milton recorded the history not only of people but of a *poor* community." Garcia paused to reflect. "The forgotten people."

Before he began taking pictures, Rogovin was an optometrist with a successful practice on the edge of the neighborhood. Back then the street outside his office door was filled with the unemployed. He decided to speak out.

"I was trying to bring these people to the attention of the public," Rogovin said. "These people should not have had to suffer as they were suffering."

He didn't realize that was dangerous talk in 1957. Milton was ordered to appear before the House Un-American Activities Committee because of his alleged ties to the Communist Party. The optometrist was shunned. His neighbors wouldn't let their children play with his kids. Customers stopped coming to him for eye exams. Blacklisted and unable to find another job, Rogovin and his family survived on his wife's schoolteacher's salary.

To keep busy, he picked up a camera and taught himself to take pictures. The out-of-work eye doctor decided he could help people see in a different way. He lugged his camera around the world, focusing on individuals who often seem invisible, earning almost nothing. His work went largely unnoticed, but became his passion. He took photographs of men and women who get up every day and struggle. Time passes; their kids are born, grow up, go to work, grow old, and die. Life is lived.

The country that once scorned Milton Rogovin eventually became proud of him for preserving what others overlooked, and today the Library of Congress has most of his life's work. Johnny Grant, one of the neighbors Rogovin repeatedly photographed over the years, pointed to his picture, which is permanently displayed in Rogovin's old neighborhood.

"When I'm dead and gone," Grant said, "my son and his children will be able to see this and realize we weren't just an ink spot on the wall. We're important, too, even though we may not live under lights and cameras all the time."

Milton Rogovin grew old watching this neighborhood grow up, and shared the yearbook of its inhabitants' lives. He was still photographing them at one hundred, surrounded by neighbors who were now taking *his* picture—the "forgotten ones" who did not forget him. Most who came to America were homesick for places they had never been. They saw its promise clearly, and it pulled them to a land they had seen only in their dreams. They risked everything to make that journey. Often, after great hardship, they built better lives. One of the best brain surgeons in the world once lived underneath an old camper in the middle of a California field. The hands that would ultimately rewire brains picked vegetables for twenty-two dollars a day.

"Sometimes I would cry myself to sleep," Alfredo Quiñones recalled. "I asked myself, *What am I doing here?*

"I have a cousin who told me, 'You're never going to be anything but a migrant worker the rest of your life.' But that just ignited a fire in my belly!"

The future brain surgeon was determined to follow his heart. He learned dozens of jobs, with a blazing desire to be the best at whatever life offered him. Dr. Joe Martinez Jr. steered him toward medicine.

"I think what drove Alfredo was fear," he said. "Fear of failure."

It still does.

"It's okay to be afraid," Dr. Quiñones pointed out, "because you know what happens when you're afraid? You work like crazy."

Alfredo studied math and science because in those fields he didn't have to write perfect English to do well. He made it to Harvard Medical School and graduated at the top of his class. Quiñones tells kids who wonder if they, too, can beat overwhelming odds, "The one thing that this country absolutely values is hard work!"

On the day we met, he and his students at Johns Hopkins Medical Center in Baltimore were gathered around a patient's bed.

"Awright! Here's my team!" Dr. Quiñones shouted, breezing into the room. His lesson that day: Treat all patients as friends. "Don't forget the human side!" he urged them. "Never let your brilliance blind you to that."

His life, like the lives of the patients he treats, has had more than its share of uncertainty and tears. Many nights his mother could not put food on the table because his father had lost the family's gas station in Mexico.

"He used to tell me," Quiñones recalled, "'If you want to be like me for the rest of your life, don't go to school.'"

Alfredo graduated from college in Mexico at eighteen and became a teacher. But he found he could not earn enough, so on his nineteenth birthday, he clawed his way to the top of a sixteen-foot fence and jumped, illegally, to an uncertain future here in the United States.

"All I wanted to do was come in, make a little bit of money, send it back to my parents."

"You can't pick up a newspaper without reading about illegal immigration," I said. "What would you do about it?"

"Can we build walls?" Quinones asked. "Sure, we can build walls. Can we make 'em taller? Sure, we can make 'em taller. Would that be a solution? As long as there's poverty, and as long as people are dying of hunger in other places, it's human nature. They will try to find another way to come."

The brain surgeon became a U.S. citizen rather than return to Mexico a hero. Dr. Quiñones felt he owed this country for all the opportunity it had given him.

On the evening of the day we met, when other doctors headed home, he went to his lab, looking for clues in the tumors he'd removed in surgery. His lab assistants huddled around him, their faces intense, smart, and listening. They had parents who came to America from many parts of the world. Quiñones had chosen them to test his theory that a diversity of backgrounds could find a cure for cancer more quickly because each scientist would see the problem from a different perspective.

"What if you never find a cure for brain cancer?" I asked.

"It doesn't matter whether you're successful or not," he answered. "What matters is that you give the world the best, and the best will come back to you."

But giving the world your best can take some time.

For fifty years Paul Rokish had watched the trees die, the deer leave, and the grass wither and turn gray near his home in Salt Lake City. His passion, he said, was to return life where it had been taken away. That set him on an odyssey worthy of an epic poem.

"You know, it's hard for people to understand now," Rokish said, sweeping a hand over the vista of dry land. "When I was a boy, the mountains out there were just like this. No green at all."

He grew up in the old American Smelting camp, not far from where we stood. Copper lay beneath the Oquirrh Mountains, and to reach it, workers nearly killed the soil. The Oquirrhs were so polluted that experts told Rokish they could not be saved. One moonlit night he slipped over the copper company's fence, alone in the dark desert with a knapsack and two trees.

Skirting the guards, he climbed to the top of Black Rock Canyon and planted the trees at the foot of a dead willow. Rokish sneaked in again the following night, and the night after that—and all the nights for the next fourteen years, planting and tenderly caring for thousands of trees by carrying in water on his back. Darkness hid what he was doing, but not what he accomplished. The burned-out mountains turned green again. His solitary quest got noticed. When he finally confessed his trespasses to company officials, he figured they'd call the county sheriff. Instead, they hired him. They were amazed that Rokish could have secretly replanted seventy thousand acres.

"I never measure how far I've come," he said, his eyes moving from tree to tree, lingering like a parent watching a roomful of children. "I'd rather measure how much I've done."

From all those nights of trial and error, he found trees that could survive in such a barren land. Rokish couldn't wait on Mother Nature to reclaim the place but plucked some acorns and planted them wherever he could find moisture. He didn't just scatter them. He let the wind do that, sometimes hiking miles to find just the right breeze. The place he took me that day had strong gusts. "From this spot," he said, "five hybrid aspen trees could produce two thousand more."

At first experts were skeptical, but Kennecott, the company that owned the land, made Paul's environmental plan its policy.

He never had much. Before the copper company took him on, he'd worked construction.

"I didn't go ask for things," Rokish said. "I never begged. I'd go earn the money and then buy what I needed. We had to take away from the kids to plant those trees, but they never suffered."

"How did you keep all this secret for fourteen years?" I wondered.

"Nobody'd go up there because it was so barren," he said.

We walked freely through his great success. "My dad worked here. He was sick a lot of the time. I never really had anybody when I was growing up," so he spent his days on those dying hillsides. "Planting that mountain, that was something I always knew I would do." Rokish pulled a branch to him and inhaled its rich scent deeply. "People don't realize what it took to get a tree to grow up here."

They probably never will, because Paul Rokish shied away from fame. Few knew his name.

We stood in the place he had searched his dreams to find. The trees are taller now. The land around them is lovingly tended, and the forest no longer shows scars.

Here's what Paul Rokish achieved with all that midnight wandering: He nourished a movement that connected big business and conservation in a way that was seldom done before. He lived like the seeds he loved. While many lives before his landed and never took root, his did.

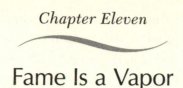

Chapter Eleven

Fame Is a Vapor

In the TV business it's easy to get a big head. After all, we're covering important stories—at least to hear us tell it. People recognize me all the time, but most of them aren't quite sure where we've met before.

"Did you ever run the hardware store in Hershey, Pennsylvania?"

"No."

"Didn't you teach my cousin's Doberman at that obedience school?"

"Well . . . no."

A few figure they might have seen me on a screen somewhere. The backseat of a taxi, perhaps? The post office? I puffed up when Jeff Simpson, a harmonica player in Joplin, Missouri, tagged me as a fellow musician.

"You were in my favorite movie, right?"

"Huh?"

"I was just a kid," he gushed. "Long time ago."

"What movie?"

"Deliverance."

I'm thinking Jon Voight, Burt Reynolds, or Ned Beatty; he's thinking the guy who played the banjo.

I simply have a face that looks like it belongs to someone else. When Boyd Matson, the longtime host of *National Geographic Specials*, worked with me on the *Today Show,* he had a wonderful evening with a woman named Betty Hudson, who kept calling him Bob Dotson. The next day Boyd sent her a headshot of me, but signed his name. They had a big laugh.

Betty told her friends she was fond of a certain NBC correspondent who worked on the morning show. They all tuned in and saw me, not Boyd. A couple of weeks later, one of them stopped me on the street and said, "I hear you're dating my friend Betty."

Linda, my wife, was standing next to me. Fortunately, she stuck around for the explanation. It was harder to explain the letter that arrived a few weeks later from Larry Grossman, president of NBC News at the time, congratulating me on my upcoming marriage to Betty.

"Oh, boy." I wilted.

Linda laughed. "You have to tell him."

"But he'll feel foolish."

"He'll feel worse if you say nothing," she said, "and he learns the truth at Boyd and Betty's wedding."

So I wrote him what I hoped was a funny postcard and considered mailing it from Truth or Consequences, New Mexico. I sent it, and a month went by. No reply. Then a note arrived from NBC, the kind that's written on thick paper and signed in corner offices. I let it sit on my desk all morning. Finally, I pried it open and peeked at the page.

Here is what Larry Grossman wrote:

> Dear Bob,
> I have not been this embarrassed
> since I was a kid and invited a girl
> to watch the Freedom Train pass
> through Brooklyn. I was determined
> to hold her hand. The station platform
> was crowded, but I managed to reach
> behind her back and grab it.
> Except, it wasn't her hand.
> It was a total stranger's.
> I hope you can forgive me.
> My wife says, "Egad, how could he?"

On Boyd and Betty's twenty-fifth wedding anniversary, their friends asked me to write a note explaining my picture in their memory album. I almost signed it "Love, Boyd."

Confusing names is as American as apple pie. I once met a man from New Orleans whose last name was Tony. He said he had no Italian ancestors.

"How could that be?" I asked.

"My great-grandfather couldn't speak any English when his ship arrived at Ellis Island from Lithuania. Naturally, his mother was worried. The boy had sailed to America alone to live with an uncle. So she pinned a note on the lapel of his coat in case he got lost, directing whoever found him to relay him to New York. When the immigration officer asked him his name, my great-grandfather pointed to the note: 'to NY.' The officer wrote down 'Tony' and we never changed it. That's how Lithuanians got that Italian-sounding name."

The same thing happened to some Cheyenne Indians. I met a woman who lived in a neighborhood filled with families named Winchester. None of them were related. When their ancestors stopped chasing buffalo, they went to Fort Reno for an allotment of cattle. If the sergeant checking them off his list couldn't pronounce their Cheyenne name, he called them "Winchester." Those who wanted food answered to that name each time they came back. It stuck.

You'd think all those postcard places I've visited would be foremost in my memory, but looking back, I cherish people and their stories more than landscapes. Places have little meaning apart from people.

Beautiful sunsets are best when shared. "Look around you," Chuck Taylor said, waving at a hawk strafing the wheat field in front of him. "There is beauty everywhere. I just want to express what I am feeling."

He pushed up his feed-company cap and began to sing louder than his farm tractor engine. Chuck's voice boomed over that Colorado field, keeping time to the rhythm of his motor. The tractor turned, revealing a big man, close to three hundred pounds, haloed in the cab. Chuck Taylor was wondering why that sun wasn't a spotlight.

"I wanted to be a rock star," he said, "but Meat Loaf already kind of conquered the chubby, long-haired-guy thing back in the seventies."

So the farmhand from Centennial, Colorado, auditioned for something else: an opera.

"I thought it might be a good way to meet girls," he said with a smile. Elizabeth Elliott, the artistic director of Opera Fort Collins, was stunned when she heard his voice.

"His singing brought tears to my eyes," she recalled. "It's not often that somebody comes in and sings something that just makes your spine straighten. It wasn't just the voice. Chuck had soul."

Just eighteen months after his first opera role in Colorado, he won a national audition to sing—full-time—at the Metropolitan Opera in New York City.

The only Italian he knew was "double latte."

"I'm a college dropout," Taylor confessed. "Before that I was a high school dropout. I can barely read them little notes on the page."

"You're a Metropolitan Opera singer and you can't read music?" I stuttered in disbelief. "How do you get by?"

"I hire somebody," Taylor said, "or have a good enough friend that plays piano to plunk down the notes on a mini-disc recorder for me."

Talent took him to New York. Hard work put him center stage. Six years after leaving the farm, Chuck (now Charles) Taylor had a leading role in the world's largest opera house.

"I still fight the feeling of being a fraud," he said. He felt he'd lived the kind of life they write about in operas. "I should be dead, or at the very least in jail or in a box somewhere, begging change, but here I am living this dream."

Taylor liked hitting high notes but in his youth loved getting high even more. He was kicked out of school for drinking. He started taking drugs and lived in a van. At twenty-four, and after the deaths of several friends, he hit bottom.

"I really thought I was helpless and hopeless," he said softly.

Until he learned to have fun without drugs. He began teaching at Colorado State University, the school from which he did not graduate.

"You're trying to woo this chick," Taylor told a student struggling with an aria. "So woo me!"

Laughter broke the tension.

I smiled at him. "You're one big Cinderella to these students."

"You should see me in a tutu!" he replied.

Chuck even married that girl he went looking for when he left the farm, and managed a storybook ending. His wife, Kelly, admitted, "He is the kind of guy people want to be around just to see what will happen next."

Taylor and I stepped across a creek, watching hawks skim its surface.

"What are you going to do after the fat lady sings on your opera career?"

"I'm going to get back home. Back out here in Colorado." Where the rivers twist and turn, a mirror of his life—the one that could have ended tragically, like the operas he sings.

Doris Travis's talent brought her to Broadway nearly a century before Chuck began his career, but it took her more than twenty-seven million minutes to get back—on her ninety-third birthday.

When Doris was fourteen, she did something no other girl that age had ever done: She danced her way into one of the most popular shows in New York City.

"I had beauty and elegance and loveliness all around me," Doris recalled.

The Ziegfeld Follies was the first Broadway show to feature glamorous chorus girls, style setters for women of that era. Men liked to ogle them, women wanted to imitate them. They were as well known in their day as Lady Gaga is today. Remember Gene Kelly's famous song "Singin' in the Rain?" Doris was the first person to perform it. She was a hot ticket for the rich and powerful. One man asked Doris's mom if he could send a gift.

"She said yes," Doris laughed, "but we didn't expect a mink coat!"

She was Doris Eaton back then, a member of a big theatrical family. Four of them performed in the Follies during the 1920s—a Broadway record.

The glitter did not last, and in 1936 the careers of the Eaton family began to fade. "It was a very sad, painful situation to go through," Doris recalled.

One sister, Mary, drank herself to death, while another, Pearl, was murdered. For Doris, though, there was always dance. It led to her own local TV show in Detroit, where she worked for Arthur Murray, who made dance schools big business. Doris opened his first franchise and soon was running eighteen successful studios. Eventually, one of her dance students asked her out.

"Was it love at first dip?" I asked.

"No."

"How long before he kissed you?"

"About two years," she said. But they kept dancing and dating. One night, after eight years, she refused to go out with him.

"Paul said, 'Why not?' I says, 'Because I have other plans!'—bang! And I hung up the receiver!"

They married three weeks later.

Paul Travis dreamed of owning a horse ranch, so in 1970 they moved to Oklahoma, far away from Doris's dreams. To fill her days in retirement, she enrolled at the University of Oklahoma. The history professor in her American studies class often asked her questions. At eighty-eight, Doris was older than the state.

"It took me eleven years to graduate," she said, "but I finished with a 3.65 average and was invited to join Phi Beta Kappa."

She had more history ahead of her. Six decades after Doris retired from Broadway, workmen restored the old Times Square theater where she once danced. The new owners looked through an address list of long-forgotten names and invited her back. So, with butterflies tap-dancing in her stomach, Doris stepped into the spotlight again. She kept coming back, even after her husband died and all her family passed on.

"When I made the transition from ninety-nine to one hundred," Doris said, "I had a very quiet moment with myself to say, *This is not the end. This is the beginning.* I'm going to keep on dancing as long as I can."

The last time I saw her, she was 105, learning the steps to her next Broadway appearance, spinning across a floor worn smooth by a century of sliding feet. Dance was the only thing Doris could not live without.

.   .   .

Back in the 1930s the Department of Agriculture sent a lot of story-tellers around the country to find folks like Doris Eaton, ordinary people with big dreams. It was make-work, of course, something to put a few dollars in someone's pocket, but it resulted in an extraordinary record of how Americans handle adversity.

For most families who lived in the 1930s Dust Bowl, "depression" was never an abstract economic term. Their farms were buried in burned-out soil; with nowhere to turn, they moved on. They went the way Americans have always gone for new beginnings—westward. In a fifteen-month period, eighty-six thousand desperate people crossed into California, more than twice the number who went looking for gold in 1849. Along the way they liked to imagine little white homes in the orange groves. It was a dream they all carried, but a dream that blew away like the dust they fled. Instead of homes they found migrant camps and two or three hungry families for each job, so they learned to live where there was no work, and then, through hope and daring, they survived. All this may seem like shopworn history, but its lesson is that these people never lost sight of what they could achieve. They followed the dream no matter where it blew them, and some made life better.

I found a trailer camp on the site of the old migrant camp in Modesto, California. During the Depression it was just one of many stops on that endless road. It was still home to Florence Thompson, the Mona Lisa of the 1930s, the migrant woman whose picture haunted the nation. Florence Thompson—no, you probably wouldn't recognize the name, but few can forget her face from Dorothea Lange's iconic 1936 photograph *Migrant Mother*. Florence Thompson was twenty-seven years old when the Depression began. She had five children, was pregnant with another—and her husband had just died.

"I chopped cotton for forty cents an acre in them days," Thompson said. She was sitting with some friends just inside the door of her little blue trailer. Her chair was angled so she could see her carefully tended flower garden from where she sat. There was no copy of her famous picture on the wall. Looking at her that day, it was difficult to find any trace of that younger woman in her deeply lined face.

"I used to fill up those old cotton sacks till I couldn't even lift them," she said. "Worked before daylight till it got so dark I couldn't see. And I didn't even weigh a hundred pounds."

The others in the room—two neighbors and a visiting relative— nodded their heads in understanding. They were about Thompson's age. Outside, a man with a cane stopped to admire her flowers and call out a greeting. She went to the screen door and waved, then turned back to her chair. "I had to drag those hundred-pound sacks of cotton," she continued. "The scales were halfway across the field."

As she looked out at the flowers, the sunlight from the open door fell upon her face. "I'd pick five hundred pounds each day," she said.

The room was quiet. From down the road we could hear a domino game being played, then the neighborhood dogs began to bark, and we heard a knock at the door. Behind the screen were two middle-aged women, Florence Thompson's daughters, Ruby and Catherine. They had come to take their mother to a family reunion. Catherine worked at a turkey factory; Ruby raised pigeons for the gourmet table. They both made more in one hour than their mother once made in a week.

"If she could have gave us all material things, maybe she would have," said Ruby after introductions were made, "but I don't think that would replace what she did give us."

Ruby looked at her mother, who stood before a mirror, fixing her hair. "She gave us a sense of self-worth and the belief that nobody owes us anything."

They did not have much, but they had one another. Florence Thompson remarried and kept that family together. Her ten children and their children still live in the valley, and they gather each year to remember a father some of them never knew.

"Watch the birdie," a photographer called later that afternoon at the reunion. It was a clear, warm fall day, and the family was picnicking in a park. Moments earlier, a dozen kids had scampered to the swings while their mothers begged them to stay clean.

"Move in a little closer," said the photographer. He slipped a black plate into the back of his camera, as relatives ten rows deep wedged themselves between swing sets and seesaws. The smaller children squirmed, and their parents pinched them into place.

Ruby and Catherine squinted into the sun, but Florence was not with them. She had decided at the last minute not to go, but she would not say why. Alone in her kitchen, she looked at a copy of her famous picture.

"I don't think you could take a woman today and put her out and do what I done to make a living," she said. She ran her fingers across the old photo as if to clean dust from the tired face that stared back.

"I worked in hospitals. I tended bar. I cooked. I worked in the fields. I done a little bit of everything to make a living for my kids."

Beyond her screen door the bees and the hummingbirds were at work in the garden. Florence Thompson watched them for a moment, then set the picture aside and stepped outside.

"Did you ever lose hope?" I asked.

"Nope," she said, snapping off a flower to take a sniff. "If I'd'a lost hope, this country never would have made it."

There is really only one genuine measure of success: to be able to live your life in your own way. Many people in Goose Creek, South Carolina, were speechless when Braeden Kershner turned his back on celebrity.

It seemed somehow un-American. Don't we all want to be somebody special? Don't we try to become our dreams? It's not that Kershner didn't try. For months his mom watched him conducting music in front of a mirror with his eyes shut tightly so he could see his dream. The boy from Goose Creek wanted to join John Williams, Arthur Fiedler, and Keith Lockhart, the select few who had conducted the Boston Pops Orchestra.

What did Braeden and conductor Keith Lockhart have in common?

"We're both young and handsome!" Braeden shot back.

Lockhart laughed. "He's more confident than I am."

Never mind that Braeden was just eighteen. To prepare for a career in conducting, he learned to play every instrument in the orchestra.

"If I gave you orders," Braeden explained, "and I hadn't played that instrument, you wouldn't take that order seriously."

The friends he tutored in Goose Creek, South Carolina, knew their pal was serious. While they hung out, doing what teenagers do, he worked eleven jobs. He told his mom he needed ten thousand dollars—fast.

"It was a little shock to me," Diane Kershner said, "because, at that time, I had just lost my job."

The boy with a dream had seen an ad on the Internet, saying fans could conduct the Boston Pops if they donated big bucks to the orchestra.

"It's just money!" Kershner insisted. "If that can buy you the thing you wanted all your life, then it's worth it to me."

He could have had a fund-raiser to get the cash. He did not. Kershner mowed nearly all the yards in the neighborhood. Worked the overnight shift at the Waffle House. Delivered pizzas and newspapers. Six months later, the Pops performed in South Carolina, just down the road from Goose Creek, with a new guest conductor.

"Ladies and gentlemen, in his Boston Pops debut, Braeden Kershner . . ."

The spotlight found Kershner as he strode confidently to the podium and smiled at conductor Keith Lockhart, who offered his baton.

Kershner thanked him, but before turning to the orchestra, he took off his suit jacket and rolled up his sleeves. That got the players' attention. They leaned a little closer, sat a little straighter, waiting for his direction. Keith Lockhart had told me earlier, "If the musicians feel he's not just waving a stick, they'll follow him."

You could see Kershner gain confidence as he realized the orchestra was doing just that. Standing on that stage, he tallied up what his dream had cost.

"All the hundreds of yards I mowed," he said, "the hundreds of cars I washed, all the late-night jobs."

Was the bill a bargain?

"I could have bought a new car," he answered. "It would rust and break down in twenty years. This is something I always will have with me."

In fact, he got more than a memory. The Pops returned Kershner's money to him so that he could pay for college. Some things aren't bought—they're earned.

That night could have made Kershner a star. Instead, he stepped out of the spotlight. After that flash of fame, Kershner joined the marines, just before 9/11.

"The idea was never to be famous," he confided. "It was just to accomplish a dream"—and then help guide others to theirs.

After he left the marines, Kershner took a job teaching band. He spent five weeks one summer getting a commercial driver's license so he could bring players to practice at Stall High School in North Charleston, South Carolina.

"The kids didn't know this, but it was never about the music. It was about keeping them involved in something positive."

Kershner was just as concerned with keeping them in school as teaching them how to carry a tune. The former marine sergeant turned band practice into a happy boot camp. His students learned teamwork—carrying his office couch above their heads, marching in quickstep around the school. On rainy days they put down their instruments and marched in the mud. That convinced drummer Antone Rose that, with practice, anything could be accomplished.

"Mr. Kershner took the word 'can't' outta our vocabulary," he said.

Failure is forgiven in Kershner's band; giving up is not. He taught his students how to craft a note—and then their lives.

"What's the secret of making big dreams come true?" I asked him as we sat in the stands, watching his kids perform.

"Persistence," he said. "The world is full of a lot of talented people. But the ones that seem to be the most successful try after they fail."

They are also the ones who do the unexpected. The man from Goose Creek was about to become a father, but had another dream to finish first. He went on a diet of oranges and popcorn for three weeks in preparation for a shot at a place in the *Guinness Book of World*

Records by wiggling his body through an ordinary tennis racket twenty-two times in one minute. Don't laugh—he won.

Most of the record holders I've met never made it to a hall of fame. Their eyes were on a goal, not glamour. Jim and Betty Sullivan just wanted their eight kids to learn music. It began in an old house, now covered in weeds.

"Oh, look, Jim!" Betty cried. "That's where the boys' front bed-room was."

The couple picked their way past a crumbled wall.

"You and I slept here," Betty recalled, the memory of the tiny space making her laugh. "We slept in the big room!"

Betty was just sixteen when she married Jim. Her mother bribed them with a piano to make sure they would stay in school. Music was the one thing Betty, living on a farm with little money, could give her large family. "Mice ate the two middle octaves," Betty said, "so after the chores, I'd play with my arms spread wide," plunking only very high keys or very low ones.

The kids went to sleep each evening to the sound of that tinkling piano. Mom's music, like wealth, was inherited. Four of Betty's eight kids had successful music careers, each quite different. Son Tim sang coun-try songs. His sister Heather wrote themes for television shows. Stacy had a recording career, and big sister K.T. was a superb cabaret singer.

"She was the trunk of the tree," K.T. said. "We are the branches."

"When you come from a family of eight brothers and sisters," Heather said, "you want to be the exact opposite of the one who came before you."

Betty was no stage mother, however. "I ran from that," she said. "I encouraged them not to live my passion, but to find their own."

Their son Pat became a doctor; three others started successful businesses.

Betty was in her seventies when she finally set aside some time for herself. She started writing songs and went to college to learn how to orchestrate her lyrics. Some of the most beautiful songs were about Jim, her husband of nearly sixty years. Betty sang me a snippet: *"There may be a time when I'll not want you, but not tonight, not tonight . . ."*

On Betty's seventy-fifth birthday her kids got together to sing for their mom. They gathered in New York City, where her great-grandmother had stepped off the boat from Scotland and headed west to herd cattle. The children invited hundreds of their fans to a free concert far from that childhood home with its chewed-up piano. It was held in a place polished with dreams and hard work: Carnegie Hall. Most people came that night to see Betty's famous children, but her words were center stage. She wrote all the music in the concert.

"A song is not for one to own . . ." Betty told them. It is best when shared.

At evening's end the audience rose as one when Betty's eight kids brought her into the spotlight. Her smile matched her shimmering gown. She curtsied to the crowd and then looked each of her children in the eye as the orchestra began playing an encore. Finally she sang them a song with her favorite line.

"You have never left my mind long enough to need remembering . . ."

Dave Densmore has fished for words like that all of his life—upon a sea that took his family.

"My son and my dad were drowned on my son's fourteenth birthday," he explained, when they set out in a small boat for a ten-minute cruise on a beautiful day. They disappeared while a birthday cake for Skeeter was baking in the oven.

"I found my dad floating the next day," Densmore said, "but I never did find my boy."

For twenty years he tried to write a poem about his family's tragedy.

"The anguish of that search, I can't begin to tell," he said.

Alone on the water, he would dial up a quiet channel on his ship's radio and read aloud what he wrote:

"It wasn't the ocean's fault. It was just part of life."

Poetry is seldom written by looking out—it's written looking in. Writing is memory, not moment.

"It's like opening up a wound," Densmore said, "and letting it heal from the inside out."

Some who heard his lonely voice on the boat's radio encouraged him to tell them more. He had plenty of stories. For half a century he had earned his living off the coast of Alaska. One time in the Bering Sea his king crabber fishing boat caught fire. The ocean hissed and wailed, equal parts crushed velvet and jackhammer, pounding his craft into the sea. Waves tossed Densmore's life raft for four days.

"Roaring, hissing breakers, like to stop your heart," he wrote. *"Sometimes they'd go right over and fill the raft with liquid ice."*

One evening an old shipmate, Geno Leech, asked Densmore to read some of his poems at a gathering of poets in Astoria, Oregon. The thought of facing such an audience frightened the shaggy-haired fisherman more than that raft in winter. How could he tell them that writing poetry was a lot like catching fish?

"It's pretty elusive," he reflected. "I lost some good poems 'cause I wasn't fast enough with my pen. The rhyme got away."

Fishermen were poets before there were pens. They told their stories in rhyme, which made them easier to remember. Words may be gossamer on land, but on the water, braving the elements, they become a weighty thing of great value. Language is the fisherman's real estate.

"Paradise isn't really anywhere special," Densmore said as he gazed out at the water that has surrounded him most of his life. "It's in your head and your heart. And if you can find it there, well, then, you're all right."

That revelation was the hook that finally reeled Dave Densmore onto the stage in Astoria. All those who had listened to him cast stories over water held their breath as he struggled with new lines.

"Well, it's been said I'm just a fisherman," he began, *"not really a poet at all. But here's a guarantee to all of you. The highs, the lows, the fear, the love—I've lived! and I'm telling it true . . ."*

Densmore need not have worried about that audience. Just looking at him, it was obvious that he was a poem himself.

His life was fascinating. Mine is not as interesting as the stories I tell. Yes, I go many places and meet wonderful people, but that comes with a tradeoff: I travel too much. My wife, Linda, and I had only one child, Amy, though we joked through the years that we might have had more if I had come home. I missed only one of Amy's birthdays. She was three at the time, and NBC had big news it wanted me to cover. Today I can't remember what it was, but I do recall what Amy said: "Grammy and Grandpa are here. I won't have a lot of time to spend with you, Daddy. Don't worry. When you come home, Mom will bake another cake."

I spent her big day racking up my first million miles on Delta Air Lines, flying in a plane so empty that flight attendants moved me up to first class and brought me a free drink to toast my daughter's big night in the darkness below. Somewhere over Georgia, I decided to steer my own career, forgoing fame for family.

Chapter Twelve

Playing a Bad Hand Well
Over and Over Again

Every memoir I've ever read sets up the author as some sort of guru. I'm reluctant to pose as such an expert. I don't know much—I don't suspect even a whole heck of a lot—but my pilgrimage has given me insights forged over a long life on the road. The people I met can help us learn about ourselves. We discover the best traits in our humanity. These ordinary Americans act with extraordinary personal honor and selflessness and courage. They encourage us to be like them.

I often wonder what I would be doing today had my grandfather Paul Bailey not loved to tell me stories. Growing up, I spent summers with him in a little Kansas town with the lyrical name of Hiawatha. Each evening Grandpa would invite me to glide with him on the front porch swing, where he would whirl me back into his past.

"Did I ever tell you about our honeymoon?"

"No," I answered.

"Your grandma and I went to Salt Lake City."

"On your honeymoon?" I asked, wondering why.

"We had two free train tickets," he said, pausing to let me ponder that. "Anyway, Grandma and I were nuzzling over a meal in the dining car. A conductor swayed up, stopped, and asked, 'Where did you grow up?'

"I answered, 'Ridgeway, Ohio.'

"'How many brothers and sisters do you have?'

"'Eight.'

"'Your name Bailey?'

"'Yes.'

"'Well, I'm your brother Vance.'"

Vance had been missing for twenty years. He went west looking for work. Tried to get a job with the Great Northern Railroad, but when he noticed most of its employees had Norwegian surnames, he changed his name from Bailey to Baileyson to better his chances. The family's letters to Vance Bailey were returned. He never wrote home to tell them he had a new name.

One of Grandpa's most cherished possessions was an old penny postcard with a photograph taken on his honeymoon. Paul and my grandmother, Marguerite, were wearing those old-fashioned spaghetti-strapped swimsuits, floating on their backs in the Great Salt Lake. Grandpa's big brother was there, too. The card, addressed to the boys' mother, read simply: "Ma, we found Vance. More later."

People often ask why I became a storyteller. All my life I've been trying to tell a tale as well as my grandfather.

The first time I did an "American Story" for the *Today Show*, I called Grandma Bailey to see what she thought of it. There was a long pause at the other end of the line, and then finally she said, "Bobby, I think you ought to learn a trade."

"A t-trade!" I stammered.

"Yes, they're not going to keep paying you for four minutes' work a day."

Well, they have, from red hair to gray. I opened NBC's first Dallas news bureau in my home laundry room. The Peacock's PR folks planted a nice blurb in the Texas papers that read: "Please welcome the Lone Star State's newest reporter, Floyd Dobson."

My boss, Arthur Lord, dropped by to make sure we installed a speakerphone near the little bathroom off our laundry room, in case I had to potty-train my daughter while taking a conference call.

Art was thoughtful that way. I soon learned you didn't work for Arthur Lord—you joined his family. Sometimes, literally. During the Vietnam War, Art was NBC's bureau chief in Saigon. At the end he evacuated more than one hundred Vietnamese employees, bribing officials with one-hundred-dollar bills. He and his wife, Susan, took one little girl into their home, and she became their daughter.

Arthur didn't just care for the people; he battled for them. Six months after I moved to Texas, the National Association of Broad-casters held their convention in Dallas. Art took me by the NBC News hospitality suite so I could meet some of the people who signed my paychecks. A former executive I won't name pulled Arthur aside and said, "You know that kid Dotson? He's solid, but dull. He won't last."

Arthur poked him in the chest and announced in a voice that carried to all corners of the room, "People will be watching him on NBC long after you're gone. Remember his name—Floyd Dobson."

The first person to welcome me at NBC was Frank Greene, a whiskery little guy standing on a chilly sidewalk waiting for a crew car to take us on assignment. Greene maintained a two-inch ash on the cigarette that he dangled from the corner of his mouth even when he talked. He greeted me with one eye squinting through smoke.

"I just want youse ta know one t'ing," he said, his voice a low rasp. "I've been here thirty years and I'll be here when you leave!"

Greene was nearing retirement. He must have had underwear older than I was.

Coming up through a small station, I had seldom worked with any-one over thirty and didn't know how to respond. But Greene didn't want an answer—he was simply telling me what to expect.

"When we go out on stories, I sits in the right front seat."

A stiff breeze finally knocked the ash off his cigarette.

"I always sits next to the heater."

He paused to puff.

"The cameraman drives, unless he doesn't want to. Then the elec-trician drives. Otherwise, the electrician—who we call Forty-Watt, 'cuz he's usually a dim bulb—he sits in the backseat on the hump."

Another puff. Greene smoked Camels. Once he lit a cigarette, it stayed in the corner of his mouth until he took it out to light another. He glanced toward the crew's garage, and with no sign yet of our ride, he continued, "The producer always sits in the back left seat, behind the driver, so he can flick 'em on the ear and tell 'em to turn right or left."

A small smile.

"You? Reporters sit in the right rear seat."

He wiggled his index finger.

"Don't crowd Forty-Watt."

The crew car pulled to the curb, and Greene popped into the front seat next to the heater.

"Welcome to Cleveland," he chortled, pointing to my place in back.

This was the first time that I had ever worked with a guy who cared more about heat than stories. At noon I learned he cared about food, too.

"Hey, Dotson," he rasped. "Youse got ten more minutes!"

"Ten minutes until what, Frank?"

"Ten minutes, den I'm pulling my audio plug outta da camera and sittin' in da car until we go to lunch."

We were filming children on a playground. True to his word, ten minutes later Greene yanked his audio line from the back of the camera and left. I looked at cameraman Cliff Adkins, who simply shrugged. "Well," he said. "At least Frank waited until we got a minute's worth of audio in the can. No one can fault him for not doing his job."

I looked around glumly. "Yeah, but what are we going to do?" Was this the end of my big-time career?

"Do you want to drive Frank nuts?" asked Cliff.

I grinned. "Sure."

"He's going to expect one of two things. Either we yell at him when we go back to the car or we give him the silent treatment. If you really want to drive him crazy, let's act like nothing ever happened."

"How will that drive him crazy?"

"You see, he wants to pick a fight so he can file a union grievance," Cliff explained. "That'll take him out of the cold for days while the grievance committee sorts it all out. Meanwhile, he'll be warm and get lunch on time."

"Why doesn't he just talk to the managers who assign the story? It's not our fault he's working through lunch."

"He's afraid," said Cliff. "It's easier and safer to take out his frustrations on us."

"Great," I sighed.

"Well, let's do it," said Cliff. "Let's pretend as if nothing ever happened, but you have to promise me one thing."

"What's that?"

"You've got to talk to Peter Menkes, the assignment editor, and remind him that Frank needs his lunch on time. Food and heat are important when you're over sixty," Cliff said wryly, but he meant it.

We finished our shooting, then walked back to the crew car. Greene was hunkered in the front seat, next to the heater. The motor was running.

"Hi, Frank!" I said. "Hey, where do you want to go eat?"

Two weeks later we worked together again, meeting on that same chilly corner. Greene was pacing back and forth.

"Hello, Frank . . ."

"All right!" he growled. "What's goin' on?"

"Going on? What do you mean, Frank?"

"How come youse never yelled at me?"

"Yell at you, Frank? Why?"

"You know why!"

"Well," I said. "I thought you made a good point about missing lunch, so I talked to the assignment editor when I got back to make sure you didn't miss any more."

"You did?"

"Yeah."

Frank Greene was not our best soundman. He was known for letting the needle ride in the red and he didn't pay much attention to overmodulation, but from that day forward he got better when he worked with me. I always made sure to highlight Greene's audio in my stories. If he climbed down a hill to get sound of a rushing river, I would pause in my narration to let the sound play. Gradually, grudgingly, we became friends.

Linda was eight months pregnant when I became a correspondent for NBC News. The day she flew from Oklahoma to join me in our new home, I met her at the airport with Frank Greene and the crew. We were on our way to Cincinnati, assigned to do a *Today Show* story. Would she care to fly along in the Learjet?

"What's another plane ride?" said Linda.

Off we went.

When we arrived in Cincinnati, Forty-Watt pulled the rental car alongside the plane. Greene hopped out and opened the front passenger door.

"Mrs. Dotson," he said, motioning. "Would youse like to sit next to da heater?"

The next morning, over coffee, Cliff Adkins shook his head.

"I've worked for thirteen years with Frank Greene and I've never seen Frank give up the heater, not even for a pregnant nun!"

Why is it we can talk easily with our friends, but sometimes have trouble communicating clearly with colleagues at work? Perhaps we're too quick to blame others while overlooking our own shortcomings. I say, "My story would be an award winner if the cameraman shot better pictures." The cameraman says, "The editor didn't pick my best shots." Nagging gets us nowhere. The only person we can change is ourselves. We get better by helping others around us get better, too The people who help us thrive in this world are not always the most pleasant. I've learned not to waste life waiting to work with the "best" or cursing fate when faced with a Frank Greene. Life is a rough-and-tumble business, like a football game, in which you have to change your tactics when you see an opening. I remember something my friend Bob Barry once told me when I thought my career wasn't catching fire:

"Try to make yourself one of a kind. That will give you a distinctive voice others will want to hear. You might not get every assignment you want, but someday, someone will say: 'We need a Bob Dotson story.'"

That good counsel sent me searching for the heartbeat of America, a quest inspired not by wealth or fame but by an old man who sparked the curiosity of a small boy on a front porch swing. When I was starting out, CBS television storyteller Charles Kuralt told me, "All the money in the world is sitting on a stool in front of a TV camera in New York City, but all the fun is out there."

So I followed his lead and went looking for the good in people. I lingered with the ones whose values were never preached, just lived.

Wherever I roamed, I asked happy people variations on this question: "How is it possible to stay upbeat in a world full of loss?" The best answers were never spoken. I learned it in their actions, and in the common traits and values they shared.

I learned, for example, that happiness depends on how you handle loss. Even the best lose often. Baseball great Ted Williams failed nearly seven out of ten times when he stepped to the plate, yet today he is remembered as one of the finest hitters of all time because he did not focus on those failures. He saw opportunity.

Loss creeps into all of our lives, but those who manage to live their dreams don't dwell on it, nor do they wait to be dealt a good hand. They play a bad hand well, over and over again.

That lesson I learned from a pair of GIs who could make the faces on Mount Rushmore smile.

Bobby Henline fought on the front lines in Iraq during Desert Storm and went back three more times after 9/11.

"I loved my job," he said, "but that last tour was a real blast."

By then Henline was a staff sergeant in the army and didn't have to go on dangerous missions, but he did anyway, riding in a convoy one morning with the Eighty-second Airborne.

"The last thing I remember is drinking coffee and mumbling a prayer to God," he said. The armored car in which he was riding led the others out of camp. An Iraqi on the terrace of a nearby house watched them go and waited, his finger on a detonator.

"Our Humvee passed over three or four artillery shells buried beneath the road. The bomber set them off. They blasted a hole five feet wide and two feet deep," killing everyone in the car except Sergeant Henline.

Henline stumbled out of the wreck, a human torch.

"The man I had replaced in the Humvee came running with a fire extinguisher and put out the flames, but my skull was burned to the bone."

More than a third of his body was charred. To save him, doctors kept Henline in a medically induced coma for two weeks. It took forty-five surgeries to rebuild his face.

"I didn't lose the chin in the blast," he chuckled. "I just never had one!"

Henline decided humor could defuse what had happened to him. He wanted people to laugh at his appearance, but not at what produced it. So he stood on a stage in a high school auditorium one afternoon and asked the students a question. "Did you guys see the remake of a *Nightmare on Elm Street*?"

A couple of kids nodded their heads. Others at the assembly began to giggle. Beneath his Halloween face, Bobby Henline was no Freddy Krueger. "I went and sat in the front row of the theater. When the lights came on and everybody was getting ready to leave, I jumped up and yelled, 'Sweet dreams, everybody!'"

The crowd blasted Henline with laughter.

"This is who I am," he said. "I earned these scars. They're like tattoos with better stories."

Henline began turning horror into humor at tiny comedy clubs near Brooke Army Medical Center in San Antonio, Texas, speaking for all those disfigured veterans who endure whispers and stares.

"You know about skin grafts?" he asked an audience that seemed reluctant to laugh at his tragedy. "My skin is a patchwork quilt. Doctors took good skin from my stomach to replace the burned skin on my head. Now I have to pick lint out of my ear."

Laughter began to build.

"They put my stomach on top of my head!" Henline shouted. "I eat too much, I get a headache."

Another wave of laughs rippled toward the stage.

"I love the Fourth of July," he announced, pacing back and forth. "I go to a fireworks stand and say, 'Give me that same stuff that you gave me last year. It was great.'"

He paused and then leaned forward, as if whispering in the fireworks seller's ear.

"Have you got a longer fuse?"

Some who undergo such an ordeal have spirits burned beyond repair, but in Henline's view, "There's so much of life I have left to enjoy, and to live! I have to go on."

His wife, Connie, and their three kids found out about his injuries the day before Easter in 2007.

When they heard that army officers had been to their home, "my children thought he was dead," Connie recalled. "I told them their dad was badly injured." But the children were not allowed to see their father for six weeks because of the threat of infection to his exposed skull, when even a child's cold could have killed him. Henline dreaded what they would think when they finally came for a visit, but his daughter Brittany was able to see past the scars.

"You can look in his eyes and tell, that's your dad," she said. "He might look a little different, but he jokes about it, so we're okay with it. It means so much to me that my dad can still laugh."

Laughter masked his pain.

"At first when I looked in the mirror," Henline said, "all I saw was this weird guy," whose care, he thought, was too much of a burden for his wife. But his kids pitched in. Brittany, then fifteen, persuaded the state of Texas to give her a driver's license so she could do the grocery shopping for McKenzie and Skyler, who were eight and nine. Even so, there were days Henline wished he would go to sleep and not wake up. That had to be a wife's worst nightmare.

"No." Connie seemed stunned by that suggestion. "I'd rather do this again."

She knew there was a wonderful man beneath those scars. On the night of his standup routine, his audience did, too.

"I went into a drugstore and filled a basket full of scar removal cream." Henline looked out over a room filled with laughing faces. "Checker said, 'Think you've got enough?'"

They roared. They stomped. They loved him.

Henline's great tragedy became a triumph on a neon-lit evening in Las Vegas. It was a date burned deep in his memory.

"My Humvee got blown up by a roadside bomb," he told the audience, "four years ago today. I was the only one of the five soldiers in the armored car who survived that Iraqi bomber, but I'm now able to go around and help way more people than he'll ever hurt."

The audience at Brad Garrett's Comedy Club gave Henline a

standing ovation, and after the applause faded, they lined up for hand-shakes and hugs.

"I made it," he said, his voice choking with emotion. "Four years to the day. I finally see my dream, what I thought I was here to do, come true."

This from a man who once thought he might as well be dead . . . until he made us laugh.

Matt Keil smiled at his baby daughter, who was teething on the thumb of the one hand he could move. He is paralyzed from the waist down.

"You wake up thinking you're going to have a bad day," Keil said, talking around tiny fingers trying to touch his lips, "and then you come out and you see all those beautiful smiles."

At the moment, the smiles of his babies were bright red from bits of breakfast strawberries spread around their faces. Red was the last vivid image their dad remembers on the day he stopped walking—the day an Iraqi sniper shot him in the neck.

"Felt like somebody kicked me right in the back," Keil recalled. "I fell forward." The bullet ricocheted off his spinal column, collapsed his left lung, and exited through his left shoulder, instantly paralyzing him. He didn't feel a thing.

"Is he coming?" a woman asked, as she strained to see above the crowd of friends who had gathered to welcome Matt Keil home. Every hand waved an American flag; each face wondered what he would look like. They'd been told his wound had left him barely able to move. One face in that crowd was particularly concerned—his wife, Tracy. Army Staff Sergeant Matt Keil had gone to war before their honeymoon. They had been married just six weeks when he was shot on February 24, 2007.

"I almost passed out when I heard," Tracy murmured. "My mom caught me when I got weak in the knees."

Strong arms cradled Keil, too, as he was lifted down from the plane. They placed him on a stretcher and rolled him through the crowd. He was wondering about his new bride.

"I asked her if she still loved me," he said. "She looked me right in the eye and said, 'Of course I love you. You're stuck with me.'"

Tracy and Matt were determined not to let that war wound limit their lives. They longed to have a baby, but were told that might not happen. They tried anyway, implanting embryos in Tracy's uterus, even as Matt battled back to health. Finally, their doctor showed them an ultrasound with three tiny hearts.

"Girl?" Tracy asked, looking closely at the grainy gray image.

"No way," Keil kidded.

"It's a girl!" she smiled.

The doctor nodded.

"I said she was a girl!"

Tracy's smile became a giggle. Keil stared at the screen, mesmerized by what he saw. Doctors had implanted two embryos, and one had split. Tracy was pregnant with triplets.

She slapped her head and shouted, "Oh, my God!"

As she turned to face Matt, their eyes met, sharing the seriousness of the moment, and then they both dissolved with laughter. They were still laughing twenty-nine weeks later when Tracy went into labor. Keil was in the delivery room with her, doing a play-by-play on video for the kids to see one day.

"I'm really excited," he said to the camera. "That's Aunt Chris behind the lens and your mom in the window, back behind me . . ."

The shot wobbled over to find Tracy's face.

"That's me." She waved.

The camera now popped back to Matt, who said, "I already love you kids and I can't wait to see you."

They were born seven weeks early, as the country prepared to remember Veterans Day. Matt Keil would face another fight and suffer a casualty: One boy died. The other weighed just three pounds, and his sister, an ounce less than that. Like their father, they would have to struggle to survive.

Tracy bent over an incubator in the intensive care unit, looking at her babies, who seemed to have disappeared in a tangle of tubes.

"Every scary small detail that you could imagine a tiny person being put through, they were put through," Tracy said, caressing a small foot trying to kick free of a cord.

"Oh, I know," she cooed, quieting a weak cry. "I'm sorry."

Tracy picked up their daughter and placed her on Matt's chest. He stared at the little one for the longest time, then looked up.

"It's hard," he said simply.

That's why they named the girl Faith.

"You making funny faces at your daddy?" he asked.

She was stronger than Matt Jr. Doctors released her from the hospital seven weeks later. As Tracy carried her in a car seat down a darkened hall she paused, leaned against a wall, sighed, and looked back at Matt Jr.'s room.

"I can't believe they won't be together."

Her baby boy would remain hospitalized for two and half months, finally coming home on a cold winter day. In front of their home an American flag snapped in a stiff wind. Veterans built the house on a beautiful acreage in Parker, Colorado, and gave it to the Keils mortgage free. Inside, everything was crafted to help a father in a wheelchair care for his kids.

"Say nighty-night, Dad."

Tracy put Matt Jr. down for a nap. His father nuzzled his sister, who was strapped to her dad's chest, listening to his heart.

The babies were nearing their first birthday, already veterans of a veteran's life. Seven years after that sniper's bullet interrupted their parents' dreams, both children were finally doing well. Keil stroked Faith's hair and said, "Life would be boring if it were perfect and easy."

"Did you ever lose hope?" I asked.

Tracy turned intense.

"Never. No!"

"Did you ever regret?"

"No. No regrets. Not at all."

Life no longer intimidates her. She'd beaten bad times before.

"My house burned down when I was thirteen. My parents divorced."

"Do you ever wonder, 'Why me?'"

"There have been moments when I've thought, *Okay, God, what's going on? What did I do?* But there is no option of not being successful. So I figure it out. Make it work."

Keil's eyes filled with emotion.

"I know without her, I wouldn't be where I'm at. She was there when I came home, when I was injured. I knew I had to be there for her."

"What are you going to tell your children about life?" I asked.

He paused, thoughtful, watching his kids crawling on the floor. "No matter what you're going through, it could be worse. I know that being a quadriplegic in a chair is not the worst thing that could have happened to me."

"But when is enough, enough?"

"We don't dwell on the bad moments. We find ways to tackle them and move on."

Keil rolled toward the front door with both kids strapped in for a ride.

"Wee! Bumpy, bump, bump!" he shouted, as they bounced into the yard, their mother watching them go.

"Matt's here," she said. "That's all that matters. He's part of this family. He's part of our lives. And he's the same guy that he was when he left. He's just got cleaner shoes."

Yes, there are dark shadows on earth, but they make the light seem stronger. That shimmering brilliance draws us to the American Dream—a dream that consists of more than just money and fame. The people whose stories I have told in the pages of this book bank happiness, even when life deals its worst. The simple joy they seek shines on others, showing us how to be joyful, too. That's why I search—every day—for those who will make me smile. They are beacons to a better life. Nothing is more valuable than tracking the course they set. That's where you'll find America's character. It reveals itself not in what people say, but in what they do. These quiet, unassuming people are the engine that runs America. The traits they share are the steel rails that connect this country.

What follows is not my wisdom; it came from folks just like you. If they can find success, so can we all. Here, then, are ten qualities they have in common:

Being willing to explore. They face each day with the same spirit that pulled our ancestors to these shores, a willingness to explore new places and opportunities. It is part of their geography of hope.

Valuing teamwork. Few pioneers dared to face the dangers of the Oregon Trail alone. They knew the value of teamwork. So do their descendants. They are a giving people who work together and find ways to make life around them better.

Seeking and doing good. They open their hearts and minds to the possibilities of life rather than dwell in negativity and pity. "What can I do to help?" doesn't have to be a sacrifice, and simple little things can make a big difference in the world.

Following through on promises. They honor their commitments. You could build a house on their word alone.

Being persistent, yet practical. Their days are filled with a "can-do" pride, but they don't just redouble efforts when something fails. They work smart, looking for different ways to succeed.

Cherishing imagination. They encourage new ideas, no matter who discovers them.

Welcoming change. They live out beyond the limits of their settled lives, making modifications that strengthen communities. There's no limit to what people can do if they don't care who gets the credit.

Embracing our differences. Differences don't divide these success-ful Americans. They know that input from people of diverse circum-stances can help them find solutions more quickly, because each person brings with him or her a variety of life experience. They under-stand that one of our greatest strengths is crafting good ideas out of conflicting viewpoints. They find solutions by working together.

Not dwelling on loss. They find a reason every morning to refute failure and seek new possibilities. They do what needs to be done instead of turning away because they thought the problem was over-whelming.

Being happy. They search each day for what will make them smile. It is a constant in their lives. That's been my goal, too, all these years. I sought the America in which I grew up. It's still there, out beyond the interstate exit ramp, where kids are taught to help one another and make the world better.

Instead of moaning about how bad things are, we need to straighten up, throw our shoulders back, keep our heads high and our chins out, and remember who we are—the people of the United States of America—and live up to our heritage.

We can't understand who we are or where we're headed without looking in the rearview mirror. Some folks we meet along the way pro-foundly influence our lives, even if we don't know it at the time. Too often, we overlook them in our haste to live life.

What's my all-time favorite story? The next one. A storyteller never stops searching. At the core of this lifelong quest lies a simple truth: The shortest distance between two people, no matter how different, is a good story. Once you know a person's story, you begin to see how much we are alike, and that helps you appreciate what each of us brings to the mix of America. That's not always obvious at first. There once was a fellow up in New Hampshire who longed to be a farmer, but he was a terrible at it. He used to milk his cows at midnight so he could sleep late. He lived near a little town called Franconia. Folks figured he'd end up on the welfare rolls because he was forever swinging on birch trees or staring at clouds. Why, he'd even get lost in the forest coming into town. One day they read something he had written:

> The woods are lovely, dark, and deep,
> But I have promises to keep,
> And miles to go before I sleep,
> And miles to go before I sleep.

A neighbor—one who had passed him in the woods many times—finally asked the farmer his name.

He said it was Robert Frost.

I like to reflect on such unassuming people. Perhaps they are put in our path to remind us never to get so caught up in the "big stories" that we overlook a simple poet in the woods. His life mattered. He told us who we are.

Acknowledgments

If you had asked me, when I was a boy, what my dream was, I would not have said, "To write a book." Writing has always been a struggle for me. My mother used to camp outside my room after Christmas and wait days for me to scribble a few thank-you notes to the relatives. She would be proud of me for this page.

A lot of these stories first appeared on the NBC *Today Show*. They were rewritten and expanded for this book during countless evenings after I had covered the news. I want to thank NBC executive producer Jim Bell for his superior managerial wisdom in leaving me alone.

Writing is a solitary profession. Television is not. Many talented people worked on these tales. My special thanks to all those whose names are listed at the end.

I also want to thank Jeff Zucker, former president and CEO of NBC Universal, for allowing me to focus full-time on these stories of ordinary Americans; NBC News president Steve Capus, who graciously let them appear in this book; my agent, Wayne Kabak, for his encouragement and unwavering faith in this project; and Professor Fred Shook, my lifelong pal, who knows my life's work better than I do. He gave this book all the grace it lacked. My editor at Viking, Rick Kot, polished the prose. His insights made this book read a lot better than it had. My thanks to Mary Ann Eckstein, who graciously allowed me to share some of the work I did at WKY-TV (now KFOR-TV), and to historians Bob Utley, Louis Warren, and Bobby Bridger, who added perspective to this oral history.

The lovely Linda Dotson, my partner and my pal, has been with me since the earliest chapters in this book. We've been married—personally and professionally—for forty years. Make that forty *wonderful* years.

We've had a happy life, surrounded from the beginning by people who love us. Linda and our only child, Amy, raised me. That's right—Amy was one of those kids who was born with an old soul. She took me to show-and-tell one day and announced, "My dad loves children. He wishes I had been one." Now Amy is older than I was when she was born, a terrific storyteller and teacher guiding the next generation. She's deputy director of the Independent Filmmaker Project in New York City, home of the Gotham Awards.

Now here are the names of the talented people who will read this page first, the ones who helped shape the stories you've just read. My special thanks to the producers who shared the road with me: Shauna Alami, Stephanie Becker, Kerry Byrnes, Teresa Crawford, Kat Keeney, Amanda Marshall, Bert Medley, Rich Minner, Oliver Murray, Dave Riggs, John O'Rourke, Robin Sindler, Laurie Singer, Jim Thompson, Curtis Vogel, Amy Wasserstrom, Ian Wenger, and George Wesley.

These people supervised story production with a gentle hand: Betsy Alexander, Jim Bell, Bernie Brown, Matt Carluccio, Jack Chestnutt, M. L. Flynn, Cheryl Gould, Phil Griffin, Debbie Kosofsky, Susan LaSalla, Arthur Lord, Antoinette Machiaverna, Andy Montalbano, Javier Morgado, Frieda Morris, Don Nash, Mary Alice O'Rourke, Sara Pines, Matt Saal, Ernie Schultz, Don Snyder, Steve Thode, Dee Dee Thomas, Tom Touchet, Jonathan Wald, Bill Wheatley, and Jeff Zucker.

Finally, my thanks to all the "American Story" video journalists who showed me things I might have missed. Much of what I told you, they saw first: Bob Abrahamsen, Pat Anderson, Ernie Angstadt, Glenn Aust, Bob Bailey, Darrell Barton, Frank Beacham, Roddy Bell, Bruce and Mark Bernstein, John Blackman, Lyle Bogoratt, Bob Brandon, David Brown, Randy Brown, Izzy Cardoza, Jim Caruso, Mike Concepcion, Drew Condell, Helene Darvick, Sara Demarest, Wayne Dennis, Anthony Derosa, John Detarsio, Dave Durham, Dan Edbloom, Tyrone Edwards, David Emanuelle, Steve Entz, Bob Eshbaugh, Mark Evans, Nick Fabilli, Ray Farmer, Joe Friedman, Ned Friedrich, Dennis Fry, Jim Geraghty, Corky Gibbons, Bobby Goldsborough, Bob Gould, Paul Green, Houston Hall, Gabe Hatfield, Bill Heinlein, Lynne Hertzog, Gregg and Joe Hoerdemann, Don Hooper, Sherm Hougeland, Brad Houston, Mike Huntting, John Hyjek, Warren Jones, Rob Kane, Jeff Kleinman, Joe Klimovitz,

Henry Kokojan, Phil Lauter, Bill Locatel, John Long, Stephanie Long-mire, Al Lopez, Jean MacDonald, Harvey Marshall, Perry Meigs, Lupe Mejia, Mark Mostad, Jim Mulligan, Amna Nawaz, Hing Ng, Gilberto Nobrega, Steve Osman, Sara Pecker, Ray Pfeffer, Duane Poquis, Erik Prentnieks, Jorge Pujol, Ira Raider, Rob Rainey, Jeff Riggins, Bob Riggio, Cathy Romine, Daniel Sack, Mike Sadowski, Mark Scoglin, Dwayne Scott, Sam Sewell, Ann Shannon, Johnny Shannon, Mike Simons, Mark Skoglund, Fred Staab, Chuck Stewart, K Su, Paul Thiriot, Joe Torelli, Jim Townley, Kort Waddell, Jim Watt, Russ Westin, Christina Wexler, Craig White, Jim White, Todd Williams, Scott Winters, and Steve Yaconetti.

If I missed a name, chalk it up to Newsheimers.

Bob Dotson
New York City